# The Arcane Veil

As an author her published works are included within *Hecate: Her Sacred Fires* by Avalonia Press and other various popular pagan, folklore and occult publications for over a decade, including *The Cauldron, Pendragon, The White Dragon, The Pentacle, The Hedge Wytch* and *The Wytch's Standard*. The second 2011 edition of *Abraxas Occult Journal* features her most recent contribution on the Mysteries. This, is her second book and she is currently busy on her fourth that continues to explore and explain the deeper aspects and histories of her Craft.

Frontispiece: Insignia of the Clan of Tubal Cain

# The Arcane Veil: Past And Present

(Ten Discourses On The Craft And The History Of Magic)

By Shani Oates

Mandrake of Oxford

Copyright © 2015 Mandrake & Shani Oates

First edition hardback 2012

All rights reserved. No part of this work may be reproduced or utilized in any form by any means, electronic or mechanical, including *xerography, photocopying, microfilm,* and *recording,* or by any information storage system without permission in writing from the publishers.

Published by
Mandrake of Oxford
PO Box 250
OXFORD
OX1 1AP (UK)

Other books by Shani Oates and available from Mandrake:
*Tubelo's Green Fire:*
*Mythos, Ethos, Female, Male and Priestly Mysteries of The Clan of Tubal Cain*
*The Star Crossed Serpent: The Legend of Tubal Cain* (Three volumes)

# Contents

Foreword by Nicolaj de Mattos Frisvold ........................................ 7

**Section One:**

Discourses on the History of Magic. Influence and impact of Christianity upon the Development and Evolution of Magic: 600-1600CE.

1: Survival of Classical, Roman and Teutonic Magical Concepts and Practices under the Early Church. 600 - 1000CE ..... 12
2: The Theological Renaissance 1000CE – 1300CE ..... 40
3: Heresy and Early Witchcraft 1300CE-1600CE ..... 68
4: The Hermetic Renaissance. 1400-1700 ..... 83

**Section Two:**

Discourses on the Craft

5: It's all in a Name: Lucifer, an Ancient Heresy ..... 112
6: The Profane Art of Masking ..... 151
7: Witch-Blood, a Modern Heresy? ..... 177
8: Sin Eating: Its relevance to the Craft ..... 208
9: Traditional Witchcraft in the 21st Century ..... 238
10: Which Craft? ..... 265
Index ..... 293

**Illustrations by Liza Miskievicz**

Baneful Herbs .......................................................................................... 49

Sorceress ................................................................................................... 69

Alchemist ................................................................................................. 84

Mask Diabolique .................................................................................... 153

Sin-Eater ................................................................................................. 211

# Foreword

We make part of a world where its spirit and mover is one of adoration of individuality. The individual often adores its glory by empty self- references rooted in constructs empty of meaning. Man believes progress, a movement towards a given direction, always brings improvement along and sees the modern cornucopia of all possible wisdom being an invitation to uncritical eclectic juggling of this same wisdom. This leads to a situation where Seekers for truth get tangled up in the wealth of possibilities the modern condition opens up for them and they get lost in the manufacturing of their 'own way'. These unique expressions of perceived truth proper for the individual is then established not on doctrine and prophetic inclination, but on taste and passion, much like we choose our material surroundings, entertainments and all else the gods of consume has invited you to redefine as uniquely yours. We might evoke the ghosts of Althusser and Foucault suggesting that often the individual uniqueness is accomplished by interpellation mediated by the ideologies in the culture that offers the discourse we believe to be our own. It is exactly because of this decentralization of the individual Foucault offers the archeological method as a tool for centralizing the individual. This suggests that we look to the past in order to understand the structures and patterns that generated our modern reality. Our modern reality is a fragile construct that we can say is decentralized in itself given the universal positive attitude towards diversity, at least in words, albeit much less in action. This conflict reveals a tendency towards fragmentation and alienation. Fragmentation happens because there is no secure point of reference and alienation is caused by the inconsistency both in dialectic and the discourse itself. This leads to a situation where modern man creates himself from the ideologies of modernity and repeats the past unknowingly and uses repetition as the tool for the establishment of the self and by this dislocated repetition a decentralized uniqueness is born.

Amongst the Yoruba speaking people on the African West Coast, a people that is still adhering to traditional forms of social order there is a proverb telling that "we stand on the shoulders of those that came before us". This tells us that only by remembering our ancestry, be it by blood, history, culture and thought can we realize who we are. And this is exactly what Shani Oates does in her ten discourses on the Craft. The first four discourses present a historical archeology of the roots to what we understand to be traditional witchcraft today. Thus she mends many misconceptions concerning the roots of the Craft. Especially important in these historical discourses of the book is how she orients the roots of the Craft to the tension between folk beliefs and Christianity by referring to the diversity the Church itself tried to be a haven for over time. From this ecclesiastical diversity she points to factors both political and theological that mediated between lawful and unlawful belief and thus shaped heresy. She is not by this saying that the Church defined traditional Craft, but she points out how the tension between the rural practices and the Church doctrine shaped the expression of the Craft. For the Craft must always remain fluid in order to retain truth. When the Craft itself ceases to move it becomes the Lie. This means that in the moment you extract from what now has been said the conclusion that the witches were Christians you define the witch in accordance with a label that the witch itself would escape from – but often accept. This because of the so called dual observance, where the witch sees now conflict between the spirits of the land and God – why should it, is not "the divine light to be found even in the most dark corner of creation?" to paraphrase the

Renaissance mage and priest Marsilio Ficino (1433 – 1499). Interestingly Robert Cochrane referred to himself as a 'pellar', which he saw as a form of 'priest for the people'. Rightly enough this Cornish term of 'pellar' might very well be a corruption of the ecclesiastical order of 'ex-pellar' or the order of the exorcist, the expeller. This speaks both of the intimacy the Craft had with the Church and how at the same time the Craft ignites a need to escape to shape its belief into a doctrine of solidification. The Craft needs to be fluid, like the Moon and open for the ever changing aspects between stars and planets, the waxing and the waning, for this is the mirror of man and his world. As Shani says in her ninth discourse: "The Craft is diverse, encompassing many modes of practice, all of which reflect the variant needs and attainments of its adherents." With this she is nailing the mystery to the cross and lays it down before the reader by asking why there are such varieties in the beliefs and practices of witchcraft today and thus present these discourses in order to learn how we arrived at this juncture.

By both looking at the historical climate that molded and shaped the expressions of the Craft as well as the exegesis on Lucifer, the detailed account of Misrule and masking as well as the Craft itself from various angles she is presenting an important book for the understanding of Traditional Witchcraft. The book is different from most other publications in this genre due to its interest in defining the root and blood of the Craft, leaving the adoration of the uniqueness of self aside in favor of the greater picture, the discourse itself. Instead of using the text as her medium for adoration of a decentralized self she is using it as the field for centralizing herself in the midst of the richness of the Craft. As such this book is a gift from beyond the veil of mystery that will establish a firm understanding of what the Craft is all about. So with this I welcome you to the world where fate is controlled, the hidden realms ridden and explored - and where mastery of your own destiny is brought as a possibility amidst the three hands of mystery.

+Nicholaj de Mattos Frisvold
Extrema, Brazil, 7th of September 2009

# Section One: Influence of Christianity upon the Development and Evolution of Magic: 600-1600CE

Introduction:

This study comprises of four separate though related essays wherein topics raised serve to clarify and confirm how and in what form, many Pagan traditional magical practices survived from classical antiquity to the early modern period, specifically, under an ever increasing Christian influence. Moving through an extensive chronology, it begins with Part One which encompasses: Classical, Teutonic, Celtic and Norse influences upon later 'Anglo-Saxon' magic, (including Christianised forms of Anglo-Saxon magic and Church counter-magic). It then progresses onto Part Two: the input of Jewish, Arabic, Oriental Scholarship and Mediaeval Scholasticism. This leads through to Part Three, covering early Witchcraft before concluding with Part Four: the Hermeticism of the Renaissance including the Early Modern Period. These topics are not mutually exclusive and will be cross-referenced where appropriate, including teleological definitions of terms used. Some chapters will be given cursory attention for the sake of continuity, others, of greater relevance may be studied extensively.

# 1
# Survival Of Classical, Roman And Teutonic Magical Concepts And Practices Under The Early Church. 600 - 1000ce

Christianity began its infancy as an amalgamation of mystery religions and eclectic sources drawn from the Near and Middle East, and not as a product of orthogenic conception, which ultimately facilitated the adoption, absorption and adaptation of many fundamental Pagan practices, beliefs and mythologies. Full of competing factions and conflicting agendas, it was not until the late Middle Ages that the Church presented a united, consistent structure or theology, resulting in continual flux [Bisson, 1999:49]. As the single most influential body upon magic, particularly during the 12$^{th}$ century the Church and its policies will be discussed at some considerable length avoiding devolving into a summary of the history of magic or religious philosophy; though out of necessity, references will be made from within these areas [Wright, 1969:112]. How magic developed in this period and to what extent the Church was able to extend its influence during its own turbulent evolution are questions this study seeks to answer.

First of all, however, it is necessary to establish the essential and intrinsic meaning of magic, both now and throughout the relevant time frames. Magic, according to the famous 20th century occultist Aleister Crowley, a member of the Hermetic Order of the Golden Dawn, is here quoted by Kraig [1990:8]: *"Magick (sic) is the Science & Art of causing change to occur in conformity with Will."* Standard anthropological terms offer alternative though unhelpful definitions regarding religion and magic; Kieckhefer [1989:PX1], places these tenets as distinct from each other believing that: *"religion petitions while magic coerces,"* or *"religion is public and official while magic is private and unofficial."* Cavandish [1990:1] varies this with: *"the religious impulse is to worship, the scientific is to explain, the magical to dominate and command."* Kieckhefer [1989:PX], posits that fundamentally, only the source employed separates one from another, conceding that magic is a crossing point where religion converges with science, further blurring their distinction. Any action using demonic aid or natural powers of nature (*Virtues occultae*) was considered magical, even as those that relied solely upon divine action or manifest powers of nature were not [ibid.]. Such distinctions were invariably subject to legitimacy of use [Cavandish, 1990:8], especially where Popes and Clergy became linked to acts of sorcery and high magic [Russell, 1972:86].

As 'magic' evolved its divergent use distinguished it from the Persian term - 'magia', originally a term of abuse used by the Romans in reference to the objectionable, fraudulent and illusory techniques employed by the Zoroastrian '*Magi*' (former priests, expelled during the reformation of Persian religion). In the 1st century, Tacitus made vigorous attempts to expel these '*Magi*' from Rome. Yet, ironically, it was this early oriental form of magical praxes that was to later underpin the whole 'Western Magical Tradition.' Since ancient times magic has been centred on sacrifice and propitiatory acts: *"I give that you give,"* an issue to prove fundamental between the Church and its later suppression of Paganism. Eliade

[1987:93] explains that positive forms of *'Magia'* found within the *'Greek Papyri'* that were later inherited by the Romans were negatively Latinised into *'magicus'*, *'magus'*; *'maleficium'*, and *'maleficus'*, all meaning acts of malice. Words including *'mirabilia'*, *'miracula'*, and *'mysterium'* have no direct English translation and only vaguely equate to *'magic'* [Flint, 1991:6].

Common to all periods and all major religions was the belief in demons as spirits causing all manner of disease and destruction. Demons evolved from *'daevas'* (Indo-Aryan), the 'shining ones', originally the young gods whose bellicose behaviour rendered them unacceptable to the new and extremely pious concepts of the prophet Zoroaster/Zarathustra. As a later compromise to polytheism, they were re-admitted to support Zoroaster's difficult dualistic monotheism. 'Daeva' is cognate with *'daimon/daemon'* (Greek), meaning *'spirit'* or *'inner genius.'* Both *'daevas'* and *'daemons'*, as intermediates between man and deity, were originally understood to be animistic, amoral, neutral nature spirits, becoming 'demonised' only later under the pervading new Eastern religious philosophy [Zaehner, 1977:201]. Plato (greatly influenced by the works of Zoroaster) and Macrobius believed *'daimons'* to be gifted with divinatory powers. Macrobius in particular, drew attention to this trait within his *'Saturnalia'*, ultimately serving to reinforce the pervading negative view within the growing Church [Flint, 1991:103). It is noteworthy that the Anglo-Saxon words *'deofol'* and *'feond'* are also cognate with spirit or deity as neutral beings and not with any principle of evil [Bonser, 1963: 130]. Unfortunately, *'deofol'* did eventually absorb the negative associations associated with the Christian demon and this is another plausible origin for the word 'devil'.

## Early Classical Influences

Pliny's [c23-79CE] seminal 37 volume entitled 'Natural History' clearly illustrates the intrinsic power of magic at all levels of society, represented in myth, ritual, symbol and language, as practiced in medicine, astrology, astronomy, and divination. Graeco-Roman antiquity avidly postulated the prophylactics of amuletic and talismanic magic incorporating androcentric and zoomorphic imagery, gems, stones and herbs. The Christian symbols, the cross and the fish were later additions. Ironically, the fish (more specifically a dolphin) a symbol of the psychopomp, was the leader of souls across the sea to the Isle of the Blest in ancient Greek, Roman and early Christian myth. Hymns and incantations survive on papyri, commonly inscribed with '*Abraxes*' or '*Abracadabra*' - oriental magical words of power that appealed directly to the gods for aid [Kieckhefer, 2000:20]. A more general form of cursing employed the use of lead tablets - '*defixiones*' from the Latin '*defixio*' meaning: binding spell [Eliade, 1987:94]. After inscription, these were deposited in and around burials; thus consigned to the chthonic realms, their efficacy was assured. This petitioning of the dead formed the origins of necromancy. Curiously, love magic was originally also executed in similar fashion. Kieckhefer [2000:20] offers a striking example:

> "I adjure you, demon of the dead….cause Sarapion to pine away and melt away out of passion for Dioskorous, whom Tikoi bore. Inflame his heart, cause it to melt and suck out his blood out of love, passion and pain over me. . . And let him do all the things in my mind, and let him continue loving me until he arrives in Hades."

Pliny's belief that magic underpins medicine with all its attendant cures found in gems, minerals, animals and plants, in addition to all inherent superstitions and taboos continued comfortably into the Middle Ages. One of the more popular forms of cure used consistently until the early modern period was the 'transfer' cure; Pliny instructs that: "*…the fingernail and toenail clippings be mixed with wax and stuck to a neighbours gate at night, thus transferring* (my emphasis) *the fever to him.*" [Cavandish, 1990:2]. As an alternative, he also recommends the binding of a hangman's noose around the temples [*ibid.*]. Pliny's contempt for general magical practice is clear throughout his work but his greatest polemics against sorcery were inveighed against women. Flint [1991:28-9] provides examples of his horror and fear of the 'evil eye' (*mal occhia*) and his belief in the awesome power of menstruating women to turn mirrors cloudy!

From the 2nd century CE., Christianity also expressed a growing interest in amulets, relics, symbols and signs. Evolving an uneasy symbiosis, such fatalistic Pagan obsessions with astronomy (perceived as deterministic) were at increasing variance with the Church, which, as an optimistic body, promoted hope, free will and divine providence. Ironically, Cavandish [1990:42] reminds us that the Greek gods themselves were unable to interfere with those to whom the *"hand of fate had alighted."* Alexander of Aphrodisias in the 3rd century noted that this did not prevent the Greeks from petitioning against fate's decrees, such was their dilemma, and indeed that of the early Church regarding the dichotomy and alignment of free will and fate. Plato's brilliantly idiosyncratic student Aristotle (384-322BCE.) significantly influenced astrology with frequently flawed but innovative theories, laying foundations for scientific development during the later Middle Ages. Within the *'Tetrabiblos'* of Ptolemy (2nd century CE.), further astrological and cosmological precepts were developed, remaining largely unchallenged until Copernican Heliocentrism re-formulated them.

Magical treatises compiled by Neo-Platonists (particularly Plotinus, Porphyry and Iamblichus) refined and developed *'theurgical'* (divine/angelic) precepts drawn from the Chaldean Oracles, the works of Julian the Theurgist and his son in the 2nd century CE) texts in 3-4th centuries CE. These contrasted markedly with lower forms of *'Goetic'* (demonic) magic or witchcraft. Fictional literature further influenced mediaeval culture, especially in conceptualisations of 'demonic' magic as depicted by Apuleius (d123CE), whose magical deeds within the influential 'Golden Ass' involved gods, initiations, shape shifting, witches, sorcery, storm raising and spell casting. Abhorrent throughout the Classical world, these treasonable offences were justifiably shrouded in secrecy and mystery.

## The Early Church Fathers

Within the Bible, especially non-canonical texts (apocrypha), numerous references to magical practices and beliefs deemed subversive to the Will of God were consequently discouraged by the early Church. Divination and sorcery especially found disfavour within its censure. Origen (c185-254CE.), a devout Christian fundamentalist, postulated the miracles of God as divine while damning all other forms as demonic - an evil delusion, particularly in the cases of the 'Witch of Endor' and 'Simon Magus'. Conversely, Kieckhefer [2000:36] adds that Pagans, for whom magic and religion were indistinguishable, believed their magical aid and instruction to be a divine gift. Augustine, in his *'Civitas Dei'* (City of God), severely condemns all magic as demonic, believing all herbs, simples and gems to be catalysts for the demons that charge them with their demonic energy.

Furthermore, Augustine warns that the agents are instructed by the demons in the *'ars magica'*, especially divination, which he believed to be trickery. Nonetheless, he allowed concessions to weather and movement of animals as acts of 'natural' magic [*ibid.*]. Tertullian was more gender specific, stressing that demons taught their arts of wort-cunning, conjuring and divination to women. [Kieckhefer, 2000:39]. Few references to 'demons' (as being predominantly aerial) are found within the pages of the Old Testament. Yet surprisingly, these 'Earth bound demons' are mentioned in the Apocryphal texts: Jubilees and Enoch, where they are perceived as fallen angels and whose progeny, the *'Nephilim'*, although rejected by the Church, eventually influenced the concepts of *'incubi'* and *'succubae.'* Spirits of the air, however, are mentioned frequently both within the Christian and Jewish codices, and it is to these that the later Church commended all human errors and failings. Subjugation of any poor witless soul to any of the seven deadly sins was considered symptomatic of demonic torment. Classical cosmology grafted upon Christianity, flawed concepts of 'demonology' that later became central to mediaeval condemnatory practices [Flint, 1991:108].

Even within healing, occult agencies though accepted, were viewed with suspicion. Faith in God and the power of his Saints was encouraged as the acceptable alternative. Augustine's rejection of his early Manichean origins prevented him from attributing the 'power of evil' to Satan per se; this dualism was anathema to the early Church that wished to distance itself from rivalling Gnosticism. Moreover, Augustine's unrelenting faith in an omnipotent God caused him to place all evil as subjacent to God's will in order that Man's base nature be controlled, mastered and elevated; his demons are quite literally sent to test us through strife [Flint, 1991:154]. This ultimately positive view meant that Man could still be saved through repentance and baptism in Christ; malefic demons thus take the blame and with it the 'sin' upon themselves, a view that was to change dramatically over the next few centuries.

Incredibly, victims of possession were deemed 'blameless', serving to enforce the need for more powerful forms of Christian-counter magic, increasingly conceptualised as Angels. Augustine believed Angels to be infallible, fiery forms, much superior to the airy forms of the demons, whose divinatory skills were considered flawed and corrupt. Angelology and its complex origins sprang from a synthesis of diverse, patristic, philosophical and scriptorial lineage as magical aids to mankind. Through its interpretive adaptation of the Hebrew mystical system of the 'Kabbalah' during the Renaissance especially, this concept reached its

Zenith. Caesarius of Arles inveighed against people who turned to sorcerers, seers and soothsayers for charms and cures. Especially abhorrent to the Church was blood sacrifice, of augury, traceable back into antiquity and of sacrifices for the dead upon special anniversaries. Both received outright condemnation. Despite official bans, many forms of divination, the use of amulets in apotropaic magic and acts of charming, continued, unabated into the Middle Ages [Cavandish, 1990:41].

## Teutonic, Celtic, Oriental And Later Classical Influences

Origen (ca185-ca254CE) an Egyptian Christian, believed that words were imbued with magical power, which only the correct pronunciation would release. Kieckhefer [2000:39] posits that Origen engendered the caveat that language had to be in its original form; any alteration or translation rendering impotent its power. Coterminous with this is the belief in the written and spoken efficacy of the Koran exclusively in Arabic. Moreover, Sufis describe the composition of the universe as the: *'Breath of the Compassionate'*, producing created beings as it passes through various essences. In the same way, man is said to 'create' words as his breath passes over the vocal chords. Thus man imitates the act of creation upon the human plane through his speech, valorising the power of the 'Word' as an essential pre-requisite to successful magical procedure.

A contemporary layman of Origen, Julius Africanus (ca160-ca240CE) maintained records of the rich social elite in a mainly Pagan Rome, wherein pronounced avocations in magical techniques for healing, love charms, growing of crops and the destruction of ones enemies may be found. Christian (Roman) officials increasingly brought such activities under attack as they rose to prominent and powerful positions, forming decrees against them in Canon Law. Also forbidden under threat of excommunication by the Clergy at the Council of Loadicaea were sorcery, amulatory & talismanic magic [Kieckhefer, 2000:41]. The 4$^{th}$ century, after Constantine's reforms, witnessed an enormous upsurge in the power of the Church, adding to the list of denunciations in love magic, crop blighting, poisoning and storm-raising. Beheadings now awaited all transgressors foolish enough to oppose the new purge against forbidden magical activities where even the consultation of a soothsayer had become a capital offence [*ibid.*].

Later, 5th century England gradually became subject to a whole new deific pantheon and magical structure as it succumbed to Barbarian invasions and settlers following its release from the grip of the Roman Empire. Chaos threatened the infant Church, presenting the dilemma of compromise or confrontation. Outright condemnation was stifled in favour of diplomacy and co-ercian and thus the Church began its slow and systematic process of conversion by adaptation. Pope Gregory the Great's (590-604 CE.) mission explained by Kieckhefer [2000:44], is primarily one of compromise. He advised his missionaries against excessive zeal and instructed them to salvage what they could of buildings (power of place), by re-consecration placing greater emphasis upon the liturgy (power of words), effecting a shift in magical practice to the spoken and written 'Word'. Substitution became Church policy despite internal opposition and is evidenced within later Anglo-Saxon herbals, simples and Leechcraft.

Superficial knowledge of anatomy & herb lore gleaned from the '*Lorica*' of Gilda containing an extensive Hippocratian pharmacopoeia is posited by Bonser [1963:9] as being of shallow efficacy and psychosomatic value only. Moreover, he believes that the Anglo-Saxons were on the whole, ignorantly manufacturing herbals verbatim, lacking in any true comprehension of their classical heritage. Bonser offers the following cure as an example of this naive empiricism - '*For byting of a wodhound, lat hym drynke betayny.*' [*ibid.*: 10]. Native Teutonic sources indicate extensive use of 'nines' in charms and spells, an innate fear of *'elfshot'* (flying venom) and the worm! All feature profusely throughout the Anglo-Saxon period. However, Bonser [1963:214] believes it noteworthy that the Anglo-Saxons possessed excellent magical colour vocabulary, strangely something the Greeks had lacked, linking 'humoural' qualities to colour signatures for cures. This magical reverence for 'divine' objects is believed by Bonser [1963:26] to have ensured the survival of Anglo-Saxon curative magic by an optimistic, hopeful Church eager for positive Pagan attributes to absorb.

Most of England and Gaul were Christianised by the 7-8$^{th}$ centuries as given by the baptismal dates for the ruling monarchs; though in reality, these dates can be stretched forward to the 10$^{th}$-11$^{th}$ centuries. Pagan myths and Sagas were reworked to 'fit' emerging Christian concepts. Complex belief structures became confused and devolved into corruption and ambiguity. Many of them, such as *'Beowulf,'* lost the magical impetus so intrinsically fundamental to Pagan life. Bereft of context, they became sterile, flaccid and even supercilious. The *'Eddas'* retained more of their true flavour, preserving the value and meaning of Runes and amulets among the Northern peoples. Anglo-Saxon charms were meant to be sung, the words *'galdor'* meaning incantation, and charm, are etymologically cognate with the word meaning 'to sing'; *'Valgaldor'*, another derivative, refers to the conjuring of the dead [Bonser, 1963: 146].

Native folklore and mythology is replete with tales of *'elfshot'* - the flying venom, often perceived as a malefic device subject to the control of witches, it is clearly evident within this charm quoted by Bonser [1963:158] from the *'Lacnunga'* (an Anglo-Saxon 'Leechbook' from *'Laecung/Lacnung'* meaning healing), "...*were it Aesir shot, or elves' shot, or hag's shot, now will I help thee*...."Many counter charms/loosing spells existed specifically for cattle, to lift afflictions caused by *'elfshot'* and hexes upon them; Christianised forms involved holy water and masses built around the 'nines'. Extensive use of 'magical' herbs such as St. Johns wort, betony and vervain were frequently offered as curatives for such malevolence [*ibid.*]. Within the Anglo-Saxon herbals can be found many fine examples of magically assisted healing through the harnessing of the intrinsic power of plants and through their signatures and correspondences.

The famous *'Lay of the Nine Herbs'* shows how Woden smote the 'serpent' and how its nine fragments produced nine diseases, which may be neutralised by the nine herbs found within the charm. Native Teutonic peoples possessed an innate sense of *'mana'*, apparent within the words: *'miht,' 'maegen'* and *'craeft,'* all of which awarded beneficent power. *'Elfshot'* is the flying venom, disease and corruption subject to the malefic 'power' of sorcerers. In order that this charm may be fully appreciated, it is reproduced here from Gratten & Singer [1952: 151-157]:

'Have thou in mind, Mugwort, what thou didst reveal,
What thou didst establish at the mighty denunciation.
Una is thy name, oldest of herbs.
Thou art strong against three, and against thirty.
Thou art strong against venom, and against onflight.
Thou art strong against the evil She, that fareth
throughout the land.
And thou Waybroad, Mother of herbs,
From eastwood open, mighty within.
Over thee, chariots have rumbled, over thee Queens have ridden,
Over thee brides cried out, over thee bulls have snorted.
All didst thou then withstand, and dost confound:
So do thou withstand venom and the onflight
And that evil thing that fareth throughout the land.
Stune is this herb named, on stone hath she grown.
She standeth against venom, pain she assaulteth

Stithe is her name, venom she confoundeth,
She driveth forth the evil things, casteth out venom.
This is the herb which hath fought against snake.
This is strong against venom, she is strong against the onflight,
She is strong against those evil things that fare throughout the land.
Rout thou now Attorlothe, the less route the greater,
The greater the less, until to him be remedy from both.
Have thou in mind, Maythe, what thou didst reveal,
What thou didst bring to pass at Allerford,
That never for flying ill did ye yield up his life.
Since for him Maythe was made ready for his eating.
This is the plant that Wergule is named,
This did the seal send forth over the high sea,
As cure for the wrath of another venom.
There did apple and venom bring it about
That she never would turn into the house.
Chervil and fennel, great and mighty two,
These herbs did the wise Lord create,
Holy in the heavens when he hung;
He stablished and sent them into the seven worlds,
For poor and rich, for all a remedy.
This standeth against pain, this assaulteth venom,
This is strong against three and against thirty,
Against bewitchment by little things.
Now these nine herbs avail against nine spirits of evil,
Against nine venoms and against nine onfliers,
Against the red venom, against the foul venom,
Against the white venom, against the purple venom,
Against the yellow venom, against the green venom,

Against the livid venom, against the blue venom,
Against the brown venom, against the crimson venom;
(Pagan lay of the Magic Blasts)
*Against 'worm' blister, against water blister,*
Against thorn blister, against thistle blister,
Against ice blister, against venom blister,
If any venom flying from the east, or from the north assailing come,
Or from the west over the race of man.
*Christ stood above the ancient ones, the malignant ones.*
I alone know the running streams,
And the nine adders now they guard.
All weeds must now give way to herbs;
Seas must disperse, all salt water must disperse,
When I this venom from thee blow.'

## (How to use the Lays)

Mugwort, waybroad facing the morning Sun, lambscress, attorlothe, maythe, nettle, wild crabapple, chervil, fennel and old soap. Work the plants to dust, mingle with soap and the juice of the apple. Make a slime of water and ashes. Take fennel, boil in the slime and foment with the mixture when the salve is applied, both before and after. Sing the charm upon each of the plants thrice before working up, and upon the apple in like manner. And let one sing into the man's mouth and both ears and into the wound that same charm before the salve be applied.

Despite the more obvious later Christian interpolations, this charm retains much of its original virtues and clearly demonstrates the Anglo-Saxon obsession with nines, flying venom and the worm, all neatly extricated within the verse. It is important to note, that many healing activities in 'shamanic' societies such as these, involved 'combat' with the disease, often adjured in the name of a powerful local deity (specific to their clan) to depart; these later became adopted for the rites of exorcism [Kieckhefer, 2000:71]. Flint [1991:270] remarks that in Cockayne's *Leechbook'*, special power is attributed to all herbs that grow in graveyards and burial grounds. An earlier 10th century Leechbook prescribes a salve to prevent the nocturnal wanderings of spirits, and to guard against women with whom the 'Devil' has had intercourse!

Classical sources also advise on plant magic, their gathering and administration, which subject to oriental (Persian, Chaldean, Babylonian and Assyrian via Hellenistic Greece) influences also adopted greater astrological associations. Synthesised within the extant Anglo-Saxon magical superstitions, these potent incantations were eventually banned in the 6th and early 13th centuries. Instructions developed curious rituals in order to safeguard both plant and its gatherer. Some simply involved averting one's gaze, as with sea holly, others required circles to be drawn around the plant, some required use of iron, others eschewed it, almost all were subject to Moon or planetary alignments and phases. Reverence of and taboos surrounding iron are replete within the *'Lacnunga'* with special observance to treatment of wounds dealt with by iron. Iron's magnetic and mystical associations assured a special reverence too for the smiths that worked it, as the following lines within this narrative charm against *'elfshot'* clearly reveal [Gratten & Singer, 1952: 175]:

> "Sat a smith a knife he sledged,
> Small the iron, woeful the wound.
> Out little spear, if herein it be;
> Six smiths sat; battle spears they wrought.
> Out, out spear! not in spear!
> If herein be of iron a fragment,

Hag's work, it shall melt away.
Take then the knife, put into the wet."

Reference is also made within the Anglo-Saxon herbals of 'balsam', not widely available until the 16th century, suggesting that some of these cures may indeed be later copies drawn from oriental sources. Further proof of this is evidenced by the inclusion of obscure Arabic words, unknown to the early Anglo-Saxons. This eclectic legacy provided them with a comprehensive, magical, still basically Pagan system that reflected the higher principles of classical medicine, based upon empiricism, dietetics, pharmacy and observance of the four humours [Bonser, 1963:41].

Since the 5th century, Britain's landscape had become veined with a network of Monasterial enclaves, long established and based around family life with a married Clergy. Although celibacy remained optional until the 12th century, promiscuity, perceived as a distinctly 'Pagan' trait, was denounced in favour of chastity. Ultimately, plagues and pestilence as axiomatic consequence of 'sin' developed as a concept by a Church increasingly oppressive of sexuality. Galen and Isidore saw these vile corruptions of the air, integral to all ancient and classical beliefs, as 'visitations' from God. The Greeks supposed the 'arrows' of Apollo to carry disease and pestilence; the Anglo-Saxon believed the same of 'elfshot'. Within Judaism, the 'arrows' of Satan sorely tormented Job. Integrated by the Church, these 'airborne' pestilences evolved into winged demons, waiting to strike down the sinful. Not until the advent of the Renaissance, when in 1481, Marsilio Ficino began a more scientific study of the causes of Black Death, believing disease to be airborne, was this concept eventually challenged [Bonser, 1963:56].

## Early Church Views On Magic And Religious Practice

Praeternatural phenomena and *'miracula'* underpinned the early Church's inception, yet this did not prevent its denunciation of all non-Christian magic. God's magic was a divine gift to Christians alone; therefore all other forms could not be His work. Conversely the Pagans also believed magic to be an intrinsic gift of the gods. Kieckhefer [2000:10] suggests the issue of the Church's desire to replace all Pagan magic with Christian magic, met opposition both in Augustine of Hippo (354-430CE) and later Isidore of Seville (ca560-630CE), who believed that all magic was sorcery, ergo demonic. The early Church was indeed obsessed with demonolatry and the Devil. Bonser [1963:21] quotes Cassion's oft quoted polemic in 420CE: *"Put on the whole armour of God, that you may be able to stand against the wiles of the Devil…"* Cassion believed that the two ways of dealing with them are either by co-operation (viewed as demonic magic), or by subjugation (magic, still technically in a grey area but authorised by the Church so therefore acceptable) and his views on *'malefici'* were to have tremendous influence upon medieval concepts of demonolatry.

Challenges were presented to the early Church by Pagan cultures, erroneously perceived as illiterate, 'and who also believed in the power of the spoken and written word, employing the use of amulets, many of which were inscribed with Runes' (magical, symbolic symbols/script). Naturally, this iconographical, animistic, healing and amulatory magic was actively discouraged in favour of the use of the cross to effect cures [Kieckhefer, 2000:40]. Generally, *'charming'* continued with Christian words simply substituted for Pagan ones. Invocation, ritual, methodology and principle remained; the magic continued to work and neither Church nor newly converted Pagans questioned this too deeply, not yet. Ironically, Bonser [1963:128] reminds us that the word 'Devil' at this time indicated the outlawed Pagan deity rather than a concept of a 'spirit of evil'; this developed much later.

Held in equal abhorrence were the concepts of 'fate' and 'misfortune', both anathema to the doctrine of free will and divine providence. An adjunct to this was the suspicious practice of Astronomy, also believed subject to demons inhabiting the airy realms between the Earth and the Moon, exerting their unwarranted influences and advises by invocation. This too became another source of growing concern for the Church. Seligman [1997:197] maintains that Isidore of Seville (ca560-636) assumed Zoroaster and Democritus to be the inventors of magic, endowing them with superhuman abilities to confound and distract man from his true work. Despite this, Flint [1991:99] argues Isidore's championing of Astrology in the Fourth Council of Toledo as a Science, concerning the movements of the stars and planets as beneficial knowledge for sailors, farmers and travellers and quite distinct from the condemned Astronomy that concerns itself with superstition.

Even so, Isidore did concede the planetary influence upon nature herself, which came to be perceived as 'natural' magic [*ibid.*]. Isidore's work *'De Universo'* made Astrology distinct as a science in the war against the divinatory and superstitious forms of Astronomy. His 'natural' astrology encouraged Christians to study celestial activity and the laws that govern them, facilitating the survival of many ancient magical beliefs and activities, irrespective of 'official' condemnations. In a poem to King Sisebut (c612CE), Isidore discusses the scientific phenomena of the lunar eclipse, expressing his contempt for the peasantry who believe that the Moon is being drawn into a cave by an old woman with a magic mirror, the achievement of which may be averted by the tremendous clamouring and banging by the peasants, creating the required distraction to free it [Flint, 1991:127].

Fears and superstitions such as these, reflecting a belief that transcends the material order, powerful amongst Pagan and Christian alike, compelled a hesitant Church to respond with the singing of psalms in preference to the former blowing of conch shells, shrieking and wailing. Flint [1991:99] regards this Christian counter-magic to be a prime example of assimilation. Thunderstorms, also viewed as demonic assaults (generally raised by *'malefici'*), engendered the same method of defence, which eventually led to a ruling instructing priests to make haste outside to 'exorcise' these ariel assaults [*ibid.*] The sign of the cross, receiving its power from the death of Christ while elevated in the air, was therefore deemed by Bishop Athanasius to be efficacious in diminishing 'Satan's' power [Flint, 1991:174]. Christian-counter magic thus initiated its prolific building regime; erecting tall stone columnar crosses everywhere, later to be replaced by tall bell towers and Gothic superstructures reaching up into the heavens to neutralize the power of all ariel demons. Modification of ancient myths and legends supported the function of these intimidating edifices. Bonser [1963:120] recounts one such tale between the Devil and the paternoster virtually cognate with the metamorphosis of Gwion Bach and Cerridwen in the Celtic myth of Taliesin. So successful was this early medieval proPaganda that when the Pagan King Aethelbert of Kent received Augustine and his companions, he made sure that it was in the open air *"….lest their magical arts overwhelm him within the confines of his own house…"* [Bonser, 1963:119]. Ultimately though it was the emerging will of the dominant culture that prevailed, which Bonser [*ibid.*] believes was more easily accomplished in England than abroad due to the cultural displacement of the Angles, Saxons, Norse and later Viking peoples.

Central to the beliefs of these Pagan peoples, was the Great Earth Mother, provider of fecundity, fertility and general well-being, whose animistic presence within stones, springs and trees, rendered her veneration impossible to eradicate. This prayer [Bonser, 1963:431] to the Earth (Danish Nerthus) survived Christian editing within a 12th century (English) herbal:

> 'Earth, divine goddess, Mother nature, who generatest all things…
> Thou art duly called Great Mother of the Gods…
> Those who rightly receive these herbs from me, Do thou make them whole.'

A Christianised charm for plough blessing, undertaken around the Vernal Equinox, borrowed from 'Gratten & Singer' [1952:63] also displays clear reference to her alongside the 'Lord':

> 'Erce! Erce! Erce! Mother of Earth,
> May the Almighty grant thee, the eternal Lord,
> Fields growing and burgeoning,
> And the broad crops of barley,
> And the white wheaten crops,
> And all the crops of the earth.
> *"Then let the plough be driven forward, the first furrow cut and say"*
> Hail to thee, Earth, Mother of men, …'

It is noteworthy how this charm ends with a prayer against the 'baleful blastings' and 'removal of crops' by sorcerers and witches [Bonser, 1963:433], for as Cavandish [1990:8] reports, the old Roman law against using magic to 'transfer' crops from one field to another, was inveighed against the later 17th century witch!

Penitentials were instigated to control recourse to these and other Pagan charms, preventing lapses during conversion processes, enforcing earlier Roman prohibitions against magic. Bede's (c673-735CE) Penitential proscribes seven years penance for storm raising [Bonser, 1963:150]. Intriguingly, the Council of Meridia in its decree of 666, ruled against the severe retribution by priests of the death penalty for witches now deemed too harsh for truly 'enlightened' Christians to enforce. Moreover, protection was instigated for *'medici'* and *'herbarii'* who erred in acts of malice, which of course protected them from the capital punishment under secular law [Flint, 1991:82]. Theodore's Penitential (688CE) however, especially attacked many forms of magic, including:

- Idolatry & worship of 'demons' in general.
- Cult of the dead, incorporating necromancy. (*Lic-wigelung*)
- Worship of nature.
- Pagan calendar, customs & festivals. Heathen songs, rites and 'devils' games at New Year were especially forbidden, by the 9th century, most had been assimilated.
- Witchcraft & sorcery.
- Augury & divination.
- Astrology.

Implementation of the above, proved spectacularly problematic as the injunctions occurred in 1282 at Easter against a priest leading a fertility dance around an ithyphallic deity, and again in 1590 in Berwick, against Barbara Napier for dancing at All Hallows Eve.

## Christian & Anglo-Saxon Magic & Healing (Amulets)

Separation and distinction between magic and religion became impossible as their synonymous practice evolved. Prayers were recited over herbs and extracts from the gospels were written on bread prior to inclusion within potions. Kieckhefer [2000:4] believes a serious adjunct to this to be the ritual for exorcism, which, with few minor adjustments also served to summon the unworldly demon. As sympathetic magic developed increasing Christian overtones, the roles of religion and magic become mutually supportive, especially within healing contexts. Aelfric records fantastic feats and supernatural achievements of Saints and martyrs who replace the heroes and ancestors of Pagan myth and fable. Flint [1991:203] notes the use of supernatural angelic power invoked within exorcisms to combat demons, where Michael (whose strength and warrior-like virtues) replaced the Pagan heroes and kings; Woden and Mercury were two deities expressly forbidden.

Christian magic was most powerful in martyrdom, and amazing feats of 'miracula' were attributed to them. Magical intention is grafted upon an act of religious reverence petitioning assistance in sympathetic healing of various afflictions. The adjuration of Saint Peter whom Christ healed of toothache is recalled by Kieckhefer [*ibid.*]. The recitation of the legend asserts a sympathetic link with the patient, before the sentience of the diseases or affliction (in this case toothache) is adjured. The licence to depart is swiftly sanctioned in the name of the Trinity. Further recommendations are given for the names of God (Hebrew or Christian), to be written down upon paper and held up to the afflicted part. Many of these charms adapted by the early Church were of Northern European origin. An example of the popular 'diminishing' magical spell is offered by Kieckhefer [2000:71], *"Fly devil, Christ pursues you…may you be consumed as coal upon the hearth."*

Health and healing, now the domain of a progressive Church that continued to attribute illness and disease to sin, became further subject to cures effected only by God's grace. Vigilant prayer and supplication alone could reverse the natural law to induce a total cure of mind, body and spirit. Despite this, Bede and Aethelbert of Kent bemoaned the popularity of common 'Leechcraft' (derived from Anglo-Saxon word *Laeca - Leche*, for healer), administered at all levels of medical practice. Bonser [1963:18] confirms this in the surviving notebooks of 9th century 'leeches' Oxa, Dun and Bald written in vernacular and dog Latin. Similarly, spells too are spoken narratives, originating in the word 'spilla' (for fable) later cognate with imbued magical qualities. Whispered or muttered charms were 'Runes', hence *'helruna'* - a sorcerer or witch, generally associated with necromancy [Bonser, 1963:147]. Anglo-Saxon diviners were known as a *'hlot'*, whose practices found their highest form in the role of a *'Seidr'* - a prophetess engaged in the casting of a magic circle and the singing of incantations for the invocation of spirits summoned for the purposes of knowledge (usually). Bonser [1963:152] explains this process is the probable forerunner of the later mediaeval Magus as recorded within their idiosyncratic 'grimmoirés'. Divination & Augury guided by a basic knowledge of Astrology were also widely indulged by the Anglo-Saxons; in fact, one Leechbook declares 32 evil days of the year, loaded with misfortune for all who undertake any venture upon them [Kieckhefer, 2000:87].

Pagan ritual practice commonly signified the northern cardinal point as sacred, in contra-distinction with Christians, who faced east. Not lost on the good Bishops, they later utilised this concept within the Christian baptismal rite, where the child brought in through the north door, indicates a rejection of former associations with Paganism. Woden, a God of *'wiccecraeft fyrht'* (closest translation - magic & spell-craft) was believed to be the initiator of power behind all spells and charms, despite his name being removed from many of them [Bonser, 1963:128]. Conversely, witchcraft, termed *'malscrung'*, denoting acts of malice or meanness, was believed similar to the eastern concept of the 'evil eye', an emanation from gifted individuals to afflict grief, harm or suffering. Campbell [1992: 23] compares this to the modern witchcraft practices of the Azande. Of special magical significance was the left hand; deemed to possess greater potency than the right, it was used for all cursing and healing activities. The ring finger known as the 'leech finger' was used (always widdershins) to draw circles around plants before culling them, for tasting potions, and for stirring and their administration [*ibid.* 221].

Recourse to magic for repelling disease caused by *'elfshot'* and other acts of *'malefici,'* was tempered with medicine attributed to Pliny, with many healing plants chosen for their sympathetic signatures. Yellow flowers were given for jaundice and liver disease; red blossoms and berries were administered for haemorrhage etc, a sympathetic system cognate with ancient Vedic methods of treatment [Bonser, 1963:18]. Successful treatment of smallpox utilising this method by a 'Leech' (healer) is again cited by Bonser [1963:219], wherein the son of Edward II receives complete [red] colour saturation around him. Notably, red was the colour believed to repel demons. Furthermore, this method is equivalent with modern scientific Finsen red-light treatment given where blood-disorders occur. Leech-books are replete with the usage of blood, effluvia and spittle, syncretised with Christian liturgy, often prayers or psalms, and of water, salt and oil, for effective cures and charms [Bonser, 1963:225].

Repetition was the key to magical efficacy, hence the need for the paternosters, creeds and Aves to be recited a specific number of times. A whole new synthesis of folk magic evolved involving prayers, amulets, candle magic and conjuration that amazingly survived even the Reformation. Slander and perjury were countered in courts of law through the forced acceptance of Mass and Communion as the 'Ordeal of Poison'. If you balked upon its consumption, you were declared guilty; it is imperative to recall how God-fearing Christians fully believed their souls to be damned if they were so foresworn [Thomas, 1971:41-43].

Amulatory magic (animal, vegetable or mineral) ensured prophylactic success. Amber, efficacious against rheumatism and neuralgia, but most effective against witchcraft (*malefici*), has even been found deposited in graves. Other grave goods, including ceremonial and ritual objects most common to female burials are: spindle whorls, latch-keys, crystal balls and strange perforated spoons. Intrinsic magical power within rare and unusual animals such as toads, goats and llamas rendered them subject to use within various magical practices, especially amulatory and talismanic magic. The 'Toadstone', is frequently but incorrectly confused with the bone taken from the skull of a toad; this stone is in fact the fossilised bone(s) of a specific and very rare and equally sacred fish. One fine example from 14$^{th}$ century Italy, made into a ring is inscribed with *'But Jesus passed through their midst and the word became flesh'* [Kieckhefer, 2000:102].

Charlemagne is reputed to have worn an amulet containing a fragment of the true cross bound together within two crystal hemispheres. The acceptance by the Church of such superstitious reliquary is in marked contrast with the instruction given to Clovis, a Pagan King upon his conversion to Christianity: *"Humble yourself, take off your necklace, Clovis; revere that which you have burned, and burn that which you have revered"* [Flint, 1991:304]. The clergy too made use of amulets often formed from crosses and (paschal) waxed discs, securing their condemnation within the 'Penitentials' difficult to implement [Bonser, 1963:231]. Moreover, knights during the Middle Ages had to swear an oath announcing the lack of such impedimenta worn as a charm or amulet, written or otherwise that could protect them from enchantment.

However, the wearing of a Lady's colours had superseded the Pagan amulet for the Christian knight. Many Pagan practices were thus indulged by a Church that continued extolling the virtue of 'faith' as the only cure for the soul, its primary concern. A Synod of 877 forbade the study of medicine by ecclesiastics, and again in 1131 and 1179, rescinding it to laymen, clerics and leeches. Exorcisms, however, remained within their jurisdiction and received the full weight of Christian counter-magic in the struggle for salvation of the soul, often at the cost of the physical body [Bonser, 1963:4].

## Binding, Ligatures, Bloodletting And Magical Transference

Binding curses *('defixiones')* are a survival into the Middle Ages from Greek antiquity, explains Flint [1991:278]. Usually of clay into which copper pins are stuck, or of inscribed lead tablets, and generally buried. Charms involving *'incanto'*, engaging knots for love and weather magic, especially storm raising, in binding and use of ligatures, were all vociferously condemned by Hincmar and Burchard [Flint, 1991:231]. Campbell [1992:21] also cites the use of binding in love magic, which she believes reveals influence from the works of Apuleius. Epilepsy, a recognised disease of the brain is subject to magical 'transference' within an Anglo-Saxon charm that also involves the use of a ligature in the form of a deerskin strap. During a seizure, it is wrapped securely around the patient's head to effect the transfer and secure the binding of it in the name of the trinity; it is then removed and buried beside a corpse, this incarceration prevents it from returning to the living [Kieckhefer, 2000:6]. Other thinly veiled magical medical cures involving ligatures accompanied by genuflexion or citation of a Saint narrowly avoided penance [Flint, 1991:242].

In response to the increasing use of ligatures and divinatory practices to cure the sick, communion with the Church through the use of 'holy' oil was actively promoted by Caesarius, Bishop of Arles (503-43) as an effective counter-measure, salvaging both body and soul. This ancient Judaic practice was also used to anoint (sanctify) Kings, and in the preparatory rites for the dead or dying [Campbell, 1992:94]. Disease, illness or negativity could be easily 'transferred' to animals, generally a frog or a beetle, using will and intent to transfer the affliction to it before being flung over the shoulders or beyond material boundaries. Toothache could also be transferred by spitting into the open mouth of a grasped frog; again using will and intent [Bonser, 1963:237]. The letting of blood into running water in silence, followed by three spittles, allowed the disease to depart the body, transferred and neutralised by the element of water. Christ's use of spittle was used to justify its inclusion in this particular cure [ibid. 221].

Women as repositories of supernatural power to cure and curse meant their activities were ever under suspicion. Weaving, spinning and dyeing were trance inducing activities and could therefore potentially afford recourse to spell-craft. Suspected magical intent woven into the warp and woof of the thread was severely dealt with, incurring up to five years penance. The *'Homilia de Sacrilegiis'* expresses these fears. A rare archaeological find of a weaving sley of yew wood carved with Runes, confirms its magical purpose, leading Hincmar of Rheims to associate all such female activities as 'witchcraft' in his *'De Divortio Lutharii et Tetbergae'* (basically a treatise on the divorce of Lothar, outlining the malign powers of women as sorcerers and enchantresses) resulting in a total ban on 'measuring with thread'. Curiously, this is also a condemned activity mentioned within St John's 'Revelation'. Eventually, substitution by the virtues of piety and prayer as a working focus ensured an active compromise [Flint, 1991:242]. Penances of seven years were metered to women who placed their children in warm ovens to effect cures. This seemingly bizarre yet common activity does of course make an appeal to the house/hearth guardians, believed to dwell within the 'heart' of the home.

Further rituals, perceived as the 'devils craft', where holed stones, rent trees and niches within the ground, particularly at crossroads, were used for drawing children and cattle through in 'threes' or 'nines' counter-clockwise to 'transfer' their diseases or afflictions [Flint, 1991:251]. This is one of many methods of magical healing cited by Bonser [1963:249] as being in use since ancient times and still popular up until the 19th century. Priests offered alternative blessings by the 'passing' of reliquaries and icons of the Saints and martyrs, further relinquishing the administration of magic to the Church [Flint, 1991:253]. Christian marriage was also considered to be a 'magical binding' before God, thus negating all grounds for divorce except where charges of *'malefici'* (read adultery or necromancy) could be sustained. Again the power of women and their alleged association with promiscuity, divination and magic became legal precedents for their suppression and conformity. Furthermore, Hincmar, seeking to protect women from themselves, encouraged guidance and confession, believing that Christ's blessing in the sanctity of marriage afforded them some immunity from sorcery and *'malefici'* [Flint, 1991:295].

Certain persistent forms of magical practice survive virtually unchanged from Classical antiquity to the early modern period as it moved towards science; these are mainly the use of charms/spells: invocations, often involving the spoken word in chanting or song: ligatures: amulets and talismans to ward off malevolent influences or to attract benign ones and astrology. From its inception, Catholicism was promulgated as a magical religion; acceptance of magic was therefore fundamental to avoid compromise of its own doctrines. Some condemned forms, including Alchemy and Astronomy later acquired favour; Necromancy never did and was afforded the severest of penalties, both in secular and ecclesiastical courts [Flint, 1991:215).

Distinctions were also made between maleficent (demonic) and beneficent (natural) magic. Sanctioned by men in power, Bede, Aelfric and Gregory, magic was ultimately assimilated, generally under the guise of progressive 'science'. Dissension and disagreement engendered friction, percolating down to a confused laity forced to compromise with a Pagan people saturated in superstition, magic and mysticism. Confrontation had never really been an option.

## Bibliography:

Bisson, L. M. 1999 *'Chaucer and the Late Medieval World.'* N.Y. Macmillan Press.

Bonser, W. 1963 *'The Medical Background of Anglo-Saxon England.'* London, Oxford Uni. Press.

Campbell, S. et al 1992 *'Health, Disease And Healing In Medieval Culture.'* New York, Macmillan Press.

Cavandish, R. 1990 *'A History Of Magic.'* England, Arkana.

Eliade, M. [ed.] 1987 *'Encyclopaedia of Religion.'* New York, Macmillan Press, Vol. 6, Pp. 293-302. & Vol. 9, Pp.81-115.

Flint, V. 1991 *The Rise of Magic in Early Medieval Europe*, New Jersey, Princeton Uni. Press.

Gratten, J.H.G. & Singer, C. 1952 *'Anglo-Saxon Magic and Medicine.'* Oxford Uni. Press.

Kieckhefer, R. 1989 *'Magic in the Middle Ages.'* Cambridge Uni. Press.

Kieckhefer, R. 2000 *'Magic in the Middle Ages.'* Cambridge Uni. Press.

Kraig, D. 1999 *'Modern Magic: Eleven Lessons in The High Magickal Arts.'* U.S.A., Llewellyn Pub.

Russell, J.B. 1972 *'Witchcraft in the Middle Ages.'* Cornell Uni. Press.

Seligman, K. 1997 *'Magic in the Middle Ages.'* USA. Pantheon Books.

Thomas, K. 1971 *'Religion and the Decline of Magic.'* G.B., Redwood Press Ltd.

Wright, E. [ed.] 1979 *'The Medieval and Renaissance World.'* England, Hamlyn Pub. Group.

Zaehner, R. C. [ed.] 1977 *'The Concise Encyclopaedia of Living Faiths.'* G.B., Hutchinson & Co (Pub) Ltd.

# 2 The Theological Renaissance 1000CE – 1300CE

### Early Medieval Magic & Monasterial And Lay Practices

Early medieval monasticism is replete with stories of miraculous cures executed by the monks and Bishops by their extreme piety and faith. The attributions of these 'magical' qualities were essential to effect the placebo cure [Kieckhefer, 2000:58]. Within the confines of their cells the monks were free to revise ancient classical texts and herbals ascribed to eminent Greeks such as Discorides, Hippocrates and Galen. Knowledge gleaned from this intense study was utilised and administered to pilgrims and ailing or elderly brethren within the confines of the Monasteries. Magical elements within these cures and simples were cross-pollinated with those of contemporary lay practitioners known as 'leeches', who had received little or no classical training. Semi-literate rural parish priests with scant knowledge of Latin indulged the diverse forms of local folk and Christian forms of magical rites and customs [*ibid*.].

Monastic manuals inculcated the need for prayer; yet so tenuous still was the boundary between magic and religion, that many appear as adjurations. Exquisite illustrations decorate the leaves of these herbals depicting Christ and Mary performing 'blessings' over the herbs to be used for healing [Kieckhefer, 2000:68-69]. Words, considered the catalyst for magical power, once utilised to great effect by druids in blessing the harvests and beating the bounds, were deemed no less so when these activities became replaced by the priests. Roman Robigalia, the supplications for the freeing of the corn, devolved into the 'Rogations' held around the 25th April, involving a chanting Virgin strewing the field with herbs [Flint 1991:186]. Further supplications for beneficial weather involved the frantic waving of the torn garments of the tunics of the Saints around the fields. Tenth century monastic reform continued the battle of assimilation despite opposition by leading Bishops concerning the over-emphasis on *'miracula'* and other related superstitions.

Women were believed to subvert the path of proper love within marriages, and indeed the 'Njal' Saga is replete with spells administered by women for abortificants, aphrodisiacs, impotence, virility, fertility and contraception. Germanic sources freely promoted the power of women in all things magical, creating conflict within the Roman Church whose views were somewhat inclined to misogyny. Queen Gunnhild recommends *"pomegranate peel & rind, giant fennel, rue, myrrh, and black pepper"* as an effective abortificant [Flint, 1991:233]. In the *"Poenitentiale ad Heribaldum"* of Rabanus, the ground testicles of a dead man are offered as a potent aphrodisiac! Menstrual blood and semen were often ingredients within sympathetic magical cures and simples. Where increased ardour is desired, then bread to be eaten by one's intended loved one is first to be kneaded upon the buttocks of she that desires him [*ibid.*]. The following citation from Burchard's 'Corrector' concerning love charms contains some interesting variations upon this theme:

> "Hast thou done what some women are wont to do? They take off their clothes and anoint their whole naked body with honey, and laying down their honey smeared body upon wheat or some linen

upon the earth, roll to and fro, then carefully gather up all the grains of wheat which stick to the moist body, place in a mill, and make the mill go backwards against the Sun and so grind it into flour, and they make bread from that flour and then give it to their husbands to eat, that on eating the bread, they become feeble and pine away. If thou hast (done this) thou shalt do penance for forty days on bread and water" [Flint, 1991:235].

Herbalists retaining astrological guidance for the gathering and administration of herbs, and who merely substituted Pagan names with Christianised forms made Church theologians very nervous, especially when amulatory magic was involved, ultimately reaching crisis point in the later 15th century. Ironically, given the Churches unnatural fear of women, lighter penalties continued for abortive, contraceptive or love magic than those meted by the secular courts. [Flint 1991:327] believes this to indicate a lack of later political concern over such practices.

Seligman [1997:191] reports how the *'Liber Poenitentialis'* of St Leonard (7th century) states that for: *"the dreadful crime of sacrifice to demons was one year's penance if he be of low estate; if he be of higher estate, ten years."* This damning report clearly illustrates the difficulties encountered by the Church during the turbulent conversion period, where even those of higher social status still remained steadfast to their Pagan roots. Reverence for and sacrifices at holy springs, stones and especially crossroads continued over the next few centuries. Remarked upon by Burchard in the 11th century, he bemoans these and other rituals involving the carrying of stones to cairns at crossroads in honour of Hermes/Mercury, God of travellers, thieves and psychopomp of the dead. Curiously, a variant of this archaic ritual is still practised within some branches of Traditional Witchcraft. Kieckhefer [2000:5] emphasises the perception among common folk of certain hereditary skills, with particular regard to the healing and magical arts, and which were accepted as being 'passed' on, in some cases to members of the opposite sex and in others to members of the same sex.

Oratories and shrines were erected at places of power and reverence, often salvaged from the original materials. When the great sacred Geismar Oak was felled, Boniface used the wood for construction of an oratory, ensuring the loyalty of its former Pagan worshippers. Votive offerings were, however, actively discouraged. By way of concession, Runes and grotesques, rings and plaits carved upon stonework engendered familiarity. Incubation at sacred sites and temples, popular in antiquity for the inducement of prophetic dreams, continued as 'vigils' within the churches beside the altars and reliquaries [Flint,1991:255-6]. Dispensation was given to dream divinations only if they contained heavenly imagery and flights, generally of birds, which were deemed to be subservient to the Saints. Acting as guardians of the dead, they replaced Pagan deities, heroes and especially eagles that had formerly held this sacred office [Flint, 1991:214].

Pagan iconography found its greatest sacrifice in the transformation of another great sacred tree hung with the skin of a sacrificed wild beast, along with a golden image of a viper. The 8$^{th}$ century Saint Barbatus convinced Duke Romuald's wife that these Pagan artefacts required Christianisation. Tragically, the tree was eventually felled and the golden viper melted down to become a chalice for the Eucharist [ibid. 268]. In the Anglo-Saxon poem, *'The Dream of the Rood,'* much Pagan symbology is overlaid with Christian imagery. Foliage and blood, birds and beasts all develop into Christ, his Saints and the martyrs. Mary is depicted anointing Christ's foot with oil using her hair, redolent of an ancient tradition associated with a conjuring/divinatory tradition known as 'watching the foot' [Flint, 1991:258].

In the 8$^{th}$ century, Pope Boniface advocated the implementation of the angelic hosts to further advance the growing Christian magical repertoire that now additionally included the control and manipulation of storms. Certainly, thunder prognostics became a serious necessity for the Monks and priests seeking to assert control over the hapless peasants and dispel the threat of all potential heretical or cultic practises. One heresy, condemned by the '1st Council of Braga' in 561CE, is traceable back to the 'Pricillianist' doctrine, in which the Devil caused storms, lightening, thunder or drought. Reported by Orosius, it claims a Gnostic origin:

> "For it says that there is a certain light virgin whom God, when he wants to grant rain to men, shouts her to the Prince of Darkness, who as he desires to grasp her, sweats with excitement and makes rain and when he is deprived of her, causes thunder by his groaning" [Flint, 1991:111].

Despite this condemnation, fear of violent elemental activity prevailed and the Church was forced to address this contentious issue in other ways. In 1289, the Bishop of Chichester ruled that it was the duty of every priest to go outside and pray during storms. Thomas [1971: 30] states that as late as 1543, a storm in Canterbury had its inhabitants flocking into the Church for holy water to sprinkle in their houses to drive away the evil 'spirits of the air'. God's blessing in the benediction of water & salt for health of the body and for the expulsion of evil spirits became expressed in a formula for blessing everything from houses to ships, tools to kilns, and armour to wells, replacing the panoply of Pagan animistic observances. Holy bread, consecrated in lieu of the Eucharist, was regarded as a medicine and a preservative against the plague.

## Wulfshurn & Munich Manuals & Leechbooks

Fascinating manuals revealing the 'magical' practices of mundane tasks, healing and estate & household management, survive in vernacular German. The 'Wulfshurn Manual', most probably written by a layperson, was found within a castle of the same name in Tyrol. Within it, eclectic charms and simples betray the adaptation of existing folk magic, evidenced by the extensive use of 'nines' and 'threes' within Christian liturgy, invoking the Holy Trinity and the blessings of the Lord's Prayer. For successful exorcism in cases of demonic possession, a mixture of 'jumbled Latin, garbled Greek and gibberish is advocated [Kieckhefer, 2000:5]. Advice is also offered for the construction and use of amulets, appealing to ancient authorities for empowerment, which, as a survival of folk and 'natural' magic, contrasts with the later 'Munich Handbook', inferred by Kieckhefer [2000:6] as necromantic in content.

Magic circles, sacrifices of the hoopoe (sacred crested bird, much acclaimed in folklore), together with a crude understanding of astrology commonly gleaned from Arabic sources and Jewish names for God promulgated the manipulation of demons, often through long and protracted formulae. Written in Latin, therefore most probably belonging to a member of the Clergy, are clear instructions that list among its purposes, love magic, social elevation and revelations of the future (divination). Ironically the 'Munich Handbook' contains greater tracts of Christian liturgy in contrast to the scant sentences within the 'Wulfshurn Manual' [*ibid.*]. Medieval 'Grimmoirés', the grand books of arcane magics, were to evolve from this early forerunner of sorcerous and demonic magic.

English Leechcraft as reflected within 'Bald' (10th century), and the later 'Lacnunga' (11th century), written in the vernacular and punctuated with pigeon Latin, contain many similar healing charms and spells to those of the 'Wulfshurn Manual', that collectively reflect the persistent and encompassing belief in sorcery, witchcraft and magic, despite obvious

Christian overlays. Pliny is cited amongst the classical medical references, whose advice, distilled with 'natural' magic, produced such charms as this provided by Kieckhefer [2000:65]. Notice the use of magical 'transference', just for good measure:

> "Take goose fat, and the lower part of elecampane and vipers bugloss, bishops wort and cleavers. Pound the four herbs together well, squeeze them out, add a spoonful of old soap. If you have a little oil, mix it in thoroughly and lather it on at night, (now for the magical part)…scratch the neck after sunset, and silently pour the blood into running water, spit three times after it and say, "take this disease and depart with it". Go back to the house by an open road, and go each way in silence."

Leech-books also contain many cures for 'elfshot', which involve the recitation of Christian liturgy and prayers, albeit usually in Latin. Their efficacy is a combination of observed empiricism and faith in supernatural agencies (Pagan and Christian); ingredients used are herbs, animal body parts and human and animal effluvia. Taboos are listed to maintain the purity and power of gathered ingredients and use of metal, a complex 'magical' ritual often involving a basic knowledge of astrology. Sympathetic magic involving the use of magical signatures, often incorporating arcane language to add a certain mystique, were quite commonplace.

## Church Counter Magic (Post Anglo-Saxon), Talismans And Amulets

Established Church policy that supported magic to counter Pagan magic was met with increasing hostility among its more senior clergy and theologians. Due to the lack of established liturgy, elements of demonic magic began creeping into its practices, particularly within exorcisms composed primarily of elements drawn from folklore and folk-magic. Elves and demons were unequivocally blasted into hellfire through the invocation of God or Christ. Kieckhefer [2000:73] explains that the acquisition and wearing of talismans and amulets imbued with occult virtues, came under increasing attack. Herbs, stones, crystals and animal body parts were popularly bound or suspended from the body. Scraps of Christian liturgy inscribed upon parchment rolls that had been blessed by the Monks and Priests were offered as acceptable alternatives. Rawcliffe [1995:98] advises warily, that even this later practice fell under suspicion; moreover, rituals including the recitation of the office of the holy name and the distribution of water, salt, wax and bread as a defence against illness and epidemics passed into the realms of unorthodox practice.

Improper use of holy objects exposed the practitioner to charges of 'demonic' magic; as distinctions between 'natural' and 'demonic' magic blurred, increasingly, everything fell under suspicion. Isidore of Seville had previously written virulent polemics against these 'execrable remedies' especially those that incorporated the sacred liturgy, written or spoken [Flint, 1991:51-3]. He believed all magic, especially the necromantic and divinatory arts to be a vanity of the human race acquired as a legacy of evil angels. At the beginning of the 11th century, Bishop Burchard of Worms, though much influenced by the work of Isidore, remained sceptical about the alleged power of *'malefici'*, and his 'Penitentials' favour more lenient sanctions than the secular courts. Conversely, in England, Wulfstan, the Archbishop of York considered the Norse to be far worse than the Anglo-Saxons and saw *'malefici'* everywhere, leading to an intensification of the law codes concerning sorcery, conjuring and consumption of psychoactive drugs [Flint, 1991:57-64]. Gregory of Tours confirms these activities in addition to cursing and weather magic as part of their natural life posited by Flint [1991:71] as proof of a complete, functional and intercessional system.

Annual honorary Pagan wakes, funerary rites and other general celebrations of individual deaths of family members, held between the 13th and 21st of February, involving the sharing of a family meal, were held in abhorrence by a Church fearful for the connotations of such activities. Flint [1991:213-16] reveals Burchard's concern for gruesome superstitions that demanded the 'earthing' by stakes through the hearts of victims of unnatural death, instigating a two years hard penance as discouragement. Prohibitions inveighed heavily against other equally primitive acts that necessitated the pouring of water beneath the corpse as it was carried from the house and another for the burning of corn where the body lay. These animistic and purificatory rites were anathema to Christian sensibilities [*ibid.*]. Grave goods were also forbidden, another custom they found difficult to eradicate.

Surviving forms of lot casting and divination using knuckle bones, dice or Runes, occasionally involving sacrifice, around or near to shrines, graves and places of worship (deemed as reservoirs of deep magic), eventually became countered with *'Sortes Biblicae'* or *'Sortes Sanctorum'*. This random reading of the texts within the Bible to gain insights and advice was equally condemned by many leading Churchmen including Augustine, Gregory III, Isidore and Regino. Burchard grudgingly accepted it in recognition of the need by the superstitious peasantry for some form of divine guidance. It was hoped his continued leniency would induce a dependence upon the counter methods of the Church, considered essential for countering fatalism and belief in pre-destination. Unfortunately, over zealous members of the clergy resorted to necromancy; St Martin, believing he had invoked the shade of a martyr, found himself grappling with a demonic brigand [*ibid.*]!

Baneful Herbs

Enormous stress was increasingly placed upon the importance of baptism (the grace of baptism was believed lost through the indulgence of Pagan divinatory rites). Large pools such as the baptistery at Canterbury, however, were later exploited by the Church in another curious practice adapted for trials and ordeals by water. Excused as crowd control, rather than as condemnation by God, the popularity of this 'social service' was short lived. Fortunately, other methods eventually replaced it, although it did resurface during the 16$^{th}$ century for the 'swimming' of alleged witches. Amulatory protection in the form of the Eucharist against the Ordeal was strictly forbidden as Christian magic could not be used against itself [Flint,1991:283]. Parallel to this, was the compelling practice of guilt association relative to murder victims; the accused was required to touch the corpse, which proved them guilty if fresh blood gushed forth from it; if this did not occur, innocence was proclaimed [Thomas,1971:220]. Later, 'natural' scientists such as Reginald Scott and Francis Bacon wholeheartedly advocated comparable activities as a system of sympathy and antipathy.

## Picatrix, Necromancy And Arabic Influences

Philosophy of the Seven Liberal Arts during the Middle Ages was still divided into the ancient classical format of the Quadrivium: Geometry, Arithmetic, Astronomy and Music, and the Trivium: Grammar, Rhetoric and Dialectics/Logic. Yet by the beginning of the 12$^{th}$ century a Jewish Christian convert, Petrus Alfonsi and translator of many Arabic texts, replaced rhetoric and grammar with medicine and necromancy, remarking:

> "…those who admit the possibility of prophecies say that it is necromancy; those who do not, say that it is philosophy….and those who do not study philosophy, say that it is grammar" [Burnett, 1996:1].

This is not so surprising when we learn that Constantine the African working a hundred years earlier, also educated in the seven liberal arts, counted necromancy amongst its number. Burnett [1996:3] believes this may in part be due to Isidore's correct translation from *'nekros'* (dead), and *'mantia'* (divination) becoming corrupted into *'nigromantia'* - black arts used synonymously with talismanic and divinatory forms of magic; ultimately the form by which Albertus Magnus came to understand it. Flint [1991:145] argues against an enormous Arab influence, suggesting instead, that cultural and political factors affecting the education of Bishops in Europe, engendered an increased sophistication of ideology at variance with the simpler symbiosis formerly adopted by the Benedictine Monks. Furthermore, she postulates how the tenacious drive of some of the earlier missionaries and Bishops in retaining many magical aspects within astrology, was as instrumental as the influx of Arabic philosophy in the elevation of a faith in a celestial power outside of man. Nevertheless, Latin scholars, painfully aware of their comparative ignorance amongst their Arabic peers, hungrily sought to redress the balance through their prolific translations of Arabic versions of classical texts.

One of the most infamous of these texts was the 'Picatrix', a work that was to feature prominently during the Magical Renaissance. Full of convoluted instructions for talismanic magic, this magical treatise was, more importantly, richly filled with astrological insights and dualistic philosophy [Kieckhefer, 2000:27]. Thabit ibn Qurra [ca836-901CE], whose work included the highly influential translations of Galen, Euclid, Hippocrates, Aristotle, Apollonius and Archimedes, promoted talismanic magic as the 'noblest part of astronomy' [Merkel & Debus, 1988:6]. This featured significantly in the tide of later *'Hermeticism'*. His illicit use of invocation to the powers of the lower worlds (planets) created many dilemmas for the later Hermetic 'Magi'. Abu Ma'shar (d887) helped to legitimise the correlation between body parts and the Hours of the Zodiac culminating in the doctrine of the twelve signs with its associative astrological consequences for bloodletting and humoural medicine [Rawcliffe, 1995:86].

Astronomy was ever to prove problematic and its cautious acceptance by the Church was reserved and restrained. The terms Astronomy and Astrology were often interchangeable, more specifically and in contra-distinction to modern use, the former defined the nature of influences, the latter the planetary movements [Kieckhefer, 2000:117]. Acceptance of Astrology as a science allowed its official study by reputable clerics. Plato's cosmological concepts, many lifted from *Timaeus*,' became Christianised and absorbed into the greater body of the Church's confused theology. Lunar influences, though accepted were denied a separate sentience from God's divine plan [Flint, 1991:135].

The demands of the Sultans and Caliphs for 'western' knowledge endorsed additional translations of various classical texts, many of which became corrupted and subject to many 'magical' interpolations and annotations. Advances were conceded to Arabic influence within the fields of scientific and medical knowledge, which due to their more liberal, open approach, inculcated the attribution of forms of non-demonic magic to natural causes. According to Seligman, [1997:195] alchemy, though introduced into Europe in the 9th century by 'Geber' and 'Morienus', was in fact based on the earlier work of *Khalid ibn Jazid*' (635-704CE). Avicenna (980-1037CE), 'prince of physicians' wrote exclusively on the powers of the stars and talismans, the virtues of nature, diseases and poisons, all formulated upon the premise that all effects result from 'natural' causes – not miracles, not magic and certainly not demonic.

Compilation of encyclopaedias by Arab scholars was prolific, the basis of which created conflicts of doctrine and theology between later

Humanists and Neo-Platonists. And so the 9th and 10th centuries witnessed the steady translation of numerous Greek texts on medicine and science by many eminent Muslim scholars including 'Costa Nen Luca,' who wrote extensively on the use of talismans and physical ligatures within magic [Seligman, [1997:195]; Alkindi on Aristotle and Ali b Rid on the *'Tetrabiblos'* of Ptolemy, extolling its virtues within the science of medicine for prognostication, for weather forecasting and divination by shoulder blades [Merkel & Debus, 1988:6]. Pre-Muslim history, steeped in magical lore and practice, was enthusiastically absorbed by Islam. Eliade [Vol.9, 1987: 105] emphasises how the Eastern tradition of magic and divinatory arts, as revealed to man via the fallen angels, facilitated the assimilation of this body of knowledge into the Qu'ran.

Many ordinary men accompanying the knights on the Crusades, upon returning home after exposure to these beliefs, could have formulated a magical synthesis within extant medieval magical systems. Folk healing and magic had been sanctioned by the Church throughout the 11th century as it endeavoured to minister Christ's work on Earth, through faith. Hippocrates was conceded as the greatest earthly leech, while Christ was perceived as the 'heavenly' healer. Unfortunately, this afforded scant modes of legitimate magic accessible by newly converted Pagan communities, starved of tales of great deeds and *'mirablia'* [Bonser, 1963:42]. Prior to the 12th century, survival in the West of magical knowledge and the divine mysteries from antiquity had been fragmentary, limited and jealously guarded by those who possessed them. Transmissions were often oral, leading once more to a good deal of corruption and loss of understanding despite the Pagan orators' greater capacity for memory and use of mnemonic devices.

## Aquinas And Aristotle's 'Natural Philosophy'
By the 12th century, Courts and Universities had become cultural centres

of learning wherein the occult sciences of Alchemy and Astrology replaced the stifling 'Concordia', a patristic discourse centred upon the bible. During the 11th and 12th centuries, the advancing tide of Muslim scholarship had presented a problem of magical theology for the Church that now sought to elucidate its definitions of 'demonic' and 'natural' magic. William of Auvergne (ca1180-1249CE) and Albert the Great (1200-1280CE) who had both studied the translations of Adelard of Bath (ca1080-1155CE), cautiously set out their distinctions summarized by Kieckhefer [2000:9] as follows: *"natural magic as a branch of science, not distinct from science; demonic magic as not distinct from religion but a perversion of it."* Thomas [1971:223] further distinguishes these categories as:

- Natural magic – exploitation of occult properties of the elemental world.
- Celestial magic – involving influence of the stars.
- Ceremonial magic – an appeal for aid to spiritual beings.

Defining 'natural' became the subject of many heated debates. Complex issues arose by opposing theologians who perceived all magic to be demonic, therefore to be rejected, claiming that even those elements and knowledge deemed 'natural' were imparted by demons. The occult natures of sympathetic and antipathic magic were similarly rejected for their animistic associations. Extreme mystical piety came to be viewed as 'magical' incantation, invoking Christ's intercession by supplication. Of course, Kieckhefer [2000:16] asserts that the simple peasants made no such distinction, believing all magic to be 'natural'. But the growing awareness of the clerics practising the less credible forms of magic certainly did. Some of these magicians cleverly maintained that coercion of demons was only possible by a prior supplication of God to obtain his divine power over them [*ibid.*].

Cavandish [1977:236] advances the premise that the catalogue of demons drawn up in the Middle Ages were not drawn from Northern and Western Pagan sources but from the East. Derived from Jewish, Greek, Egyptian, Babylonian and Assyrian sources, they surfaced within medieval heretical sects such as: the Bogomils, Kathari, Waldensians and the Luciferians, where they enjoyed mainly 'angelic' status. Pagan forms were adopted by the Christians, evolving into 'decons' or animistic guardians of each planet. Those 'demons' of heretical Biblical lore posed a far greater threat than the 'demons' or supposedly former gods of Paganism. Divination, sorcery and necromancy were obviously demonic; though the use of herbs and poisons within acts of *'malefici'* not yet clearly defined as a sorcerous act, therefore continued to present a dilemma of classification. Ultimately, the criterion became one of method rather than intent. Burnett [1996:6] believes that the difference between licit and illicit practice of talismanic magic also depended upon method of empowerment: formerly by emanation from the celestial planes without recourse to incantation, invocation or exorcism; latterly through the express invocation of demons and devils below the celestial planes.

A complex paradox occurs in a 3rd kind of talisman posited by Albertus from a text involving incantations (therefore illicit), addressed to spirits, not demons or devils (therefore licit). Two versions of this text exist; both are translations of the Arabic text of 'Thabit ibn Qurra' by Adelard of Bath and the 'Magister' John of Seville & Limia, both working in the 12th century. Adelard's includes the invocations/prayers to spirits, John's does not. Burnett [1996:7] further reiterates that Thabit's work did, in general, make much use of invocation. Regrettably, it is not known which of these, is the original text. Thabit was regarded as an expert on the art of talismanic magic, promoting it as the highest form of magic, writing several texts upon their formation and use. 'Magister' John adds that knowledge of astronomy alone is useless without the necessary skills imparted by God for man's use, to employ them [Merkel & Debus 1988: 88].

These skills are inferred to be necromancy and the arts of incantation. Adelard of Bath is known to have taken lessons with an old woman on how to perform magical incantations. He later devised two books on how to construct a successful talisman according to the astrological position of relevant planets and correspondences, with particular regard to the formation of the bases from lead, tin, copper, gold, silver, pitch, & tar. Complex instructions follow on the required fumigations, the relevant personal details, how they are bound and finally, how and where buried at the appropriate time. Most interesting of all are the actual opening lines of an invocation made to decons of the planets: *"O Shining Spirits of the planets, you who descend from the al-alam (macrocosm) effectors of good and evil…"* [Burnett, 1996:8-11]. Clearly this is hermetic, clearly it is heretical and very, very damning.

Thabit ibn Qurra was also a well-known representative of the intellectual branch of the Syriac speaking Sabaeans in 9th century Baghdad, and thought to hail from Harran. Despite the great sophistication of the Sabaeans, they were erroneously perceived as 'star worshippers.' Their religious philosophies had in fact evolved from Aristotle's 'natural science' and hermetic forms of magic. Moreover, Thabit, as a scientist of some renown and who is rumoured to have sourced some of the hermetic texts, believed that the true art of magic was as 'food for the soul' [Merkel & Debus 1988: 88]. Thabit also wrote extensively about the religion of the Sabaeans. He describes seven legendary sacred temples, built, one for each planet imbued with its own associated decon/spirit guardian. The Sabaeans believed that only through propitiatory, sacrificial ritual involving mediation with the planetary decons, could 'God' be reached.

Their two principal prophets were: Hermes and Agathodaimon (Hellenised form of Knum/Kneph, father of TaT/Thoth). Ibn al-Nadim supported the view that their scientific speculation had been based upon the works of Aristotle. Later, during the early 13th century, the historian, Al Makin was aware of the tradition that Aristotle had translated the book of Hermes from Egyptian into Greek, further obfuscating the later medieval understanding of the origins of Hermetism. In fact, within the Corpus of Hermetic works, Hermes speaks through his pupil Asclepius, or in dialogue with Thoth; there is no association with Aristotle or Alexander. By the end of the 13th century, most of the *'Kitab-al-Istamakhis'* ms (Arabic translation) though no longer believed to be the work of Aristotle, was still used extensively by contemporary and later redactors; yet its true author remains a mystery [*ibid.*]. The Church's view upon this obsession with Astrology was often vitriolic. Rawcliffe [1995:85] asserts the extreme pious views that railed contempt upon those 'heretics' who sought instruction from the planets, for only in penitence and prayer could salvation be secured! Intellectual potential, inherent throughout Ptolemy's 'Tetrabiblos' and 'Almagest' tempered such extremism, and scholars were actively encouraged to extract that which the Church could use to its advantage.

Sadly this was short lived, and by the 14th century, things had begun to sour. Warnings that the Devil lay in wait for those who consult the stars, especially in association with geomancy (a method of divination, which, due to its Pythagorean principles, was, by default, related to necromancy and therefore subject to the full weight of the law) effected the slow grinding halt on occult scholarship [Rawcliffe, 1995: 101]. Ceco d'Ascoli, a renowned astrologer and physician went to the stake in 1327 for alleged diabolism, no doubt due to a lack of caution and coherence concerning the unsettled distinctions between 'natural' and 'demonic' magic and astrology [*ibid.* 90].

Thomas Aquinas promoted the Aristotelian view of the unseen (occult) forces as natural and scientific rather than magical in origin, using his analogous if not bizarre explanation of Rhubarb as a (purgative) force and of the repellent and attractive power of magnets to prove it [Kieckhefer, 2000:131]. Conversely, in his 'Occult Work of Nature', Aquinas defines as demonic, the signs and images (decons) of the planets as reservoirs of occult power for magical purposes. Moralists determined that the crucial factor between natural and demonic should be the use of strange or unintelligible words or names [*ibid.*]. Amazingly, Aristotle's *'De Anima'*, found expression through the Arab belief in the power of the individual soul or animating principle of life [Tancred, 1986:12], influencing the deep-rooted Western view of the 'Evil Eye' (mal occhia) as 'malefic', being instrumental in its eventual acceptance as 'natural' magic [Kieckhefer, 2000:182].

During the 12th and 13th centuries, the rise of Aristotelian Scholasticism in Western Europe presented a revolution in intellectual history, fuelled by the logic and faith of the 'Thomist' Scholars, whose fertile debates on issues of exegesis, eschatology, cosmology and entelechism were to profoundly affect consequent Church policy on Theology. Many leading minds of the time, Peter of Abano, Arnold of Villanova and Paracelsus, fearful of charges of 'demonic' magical practices, adopted Christian magico-religious stratagems, effectively assimilating the more objectionable elements denied their less enlightened contemporaries. [Seligman,1997:199]. Philosophy flourished relatively freely under a Church reaching its zenith during this period, allowing many leading Churchmen to investigate it: Magnus, Grossteste, Bacon, Lully and Aquinas; some of whom promoted Aristotelian ethics regarding 'natural' magic, rationalism, and the science of material causes and consequences, rather than 'Platonic' mysticism.

The nature of the soul, of only minor importance to Aristotle, became subject to heated debate through the work of Aquinas, obsessing medieval theology. Plato believed the 'soul' to re-incarnate often, a Pythagorean concept, believing the 'World Soul' to be in harmony with man's individual harmony. Conversely, Aristotle did not believe in an eternal soul or an eternal universe, preferring instead to view it as the animating principle of life within nature, where the Supreme Creatrix was engaged in a perpetual act of self-creating thinking [Tancred, 1986: 46-94]. Avicenna (980-1037CE) adapted many Aristotelian views, incorporating them into his 'Canon of Medicine', presenting the soul as immortal, adding more fuel to the metaphysical dichotomies of Greek philosophy, which even became part of the syllabus at the University of Paris. Naturally, the Church supported Avicenna [*ibid.*]. Medieval scholasticism revealed a universe separate from God's, through which the rationalism of Aristotle could be explored. In fact, Avicenna had studied the Neo-Platonic works of Proclus: *'Liber de Causis'* and *'Theology of Aristotle'*, unwittingly believing them to be Aristotle's; an error not realised until the 13th century. Quickly it was realised that not all the works of Aristotle could be trusted and strict censure of his work was advocated by Pope Gregory IX, leaving Aquinas to ponder on how to combine logic (reason) and faith; within three years of his death, much of Aristotle's work became condemned.

Philosophical enquiry was severed; faith alone sustained all enquiry, which further increased the dilemma of categorisation for 'natural' and 'demonic' magic. Early science struggled vainly under the yoke of such prejudice. Ironically, Thorndike [1934:36] maintains that rumours concerning Pope Innocent VI (Pope between -1352-1362CE), his clergy at Rodez and the Monks of Bonnecombe publicly implicated them in acts of sorcery, magic and the invocation of demons. Eager for scapegoats, the Church turned on Peter of Abano (1250-1318CE) for heresy. His extensive studies included geomancy, prophecy and physiognomancy, additionally translating many works of Aristotle into Latin. Inevitably, as an associate of Marco Polo, from whom he was able to enrich his knowledge of the Orient, his wisdom and wealth brought him many enemies. He escaped death, but was burned posthumously by the Inquisition. Later, Agrippa was to publish Abano's work alongside his own [Seligman, 1997:199].

Arnold of Villanova (1240-1313), an alchemist, erudite scholar and renowned physician also fell foul of the Inquisition for his heretical literary work concerning fatalistic Gnostic eschatological prophecies. Only the Popes intercedence saved him, he instructed Villanova thus: *"Occupy thyself with medicine, and leave theology alone, and we will honour thee"* [*ibid.*]. Paradoxically, Villanova penned many virulent polemics against witchcraft and magic, deeming them contrary to science. Contemporary alchemist, Franciscan friar and avid Aristotelian philosopher, Roger Bacon (1214-1294CE) postulated magic as a marvel of nature, relating alchemy to physics, insisting that only those understanding the meanings of the deer, the serpent and the eagle were suitable to study it. Occult powers, inherent within nature obsessed the medieval alchemist seeking power through knowledge. Another learned scholar and cleric, Albertus Magnus (1193-1280CE) championed alchemy as the only true art advising that the 'divine mysteries must remain so' [Kieckhefer, 2000:140]. Profligate legends reiterate the immense power of these fringe scientist/magicians; one attributed to both Albert the Great and Roger Bacon, concerns the animation of a bronze bust that so infuriated its pupil by its incessant ramblings that it was smashed to pieces.

Roger Bacon believed that demonic magic lay within the intention of the sender but the later Oresme in the 14th century believed the power to reside within the actual words uttered [*ibid.*183]. Reification of 'natural' in acceptable terms, continued to task the mediaeval mindset as Oresme too strived for more scientific explanations of this ambiguous form of 'magic'. De-emphasising demonic intervention, he insisted that magic was an illusion induced by mind altering drugs, fumigations, fasting, even fermentation of a sensitive humour, opposing utterly the views of Alkindi and Algazel who regarded all magic to be explainable by 'natural' means. Oresme believed that some things remained inexplicable and unprovable by scientific means, therefore attributable to 'demons'. Interestingly, he conceded that sound was a natural power able to effect changes within the mind and body [Thorndike, 1934:410], an idea given greater credence in the 15th century by Ficino. Doctrines of animism, rationalism, the sentience of nature and 'natural magic' laid foundations for later occultists such as Bruno and Duns Scotas, all of whom held favourable views on astrology, in their promotion of science as 'natural philosophy' [Thorndike, 1934:7].

Both Astrology and Alchemy had featured extensively within the works of 12th & 13th century eminent Churchmen, heirs after all to the Hippocratian concept of the four 'Humours,' resulting in an enormous influence upon weather forecasting, agriculture and medical practice, especially concerning the most auspicious time to employ blood-letting [Flint, 1991:13]. The Church recognised two major benefits within these philosophies; firstly, that scientific knowledge, understanding and reasoning could stifle Pagan superstition, and secondly; the freeing of the spirit from earthly matters, which very much appealed to medieval Church doctrinal premises [Flint, 1991:8-].

Of course Isidore of Seville had long supported the study of

Astrology to better understand the working of the human body, believing in the Greek and later Hermetic maxim of the micro-macrocosmic relationship between Man and his universe. In reality, Rawcliffe [1995:99] postulates that the increasing hostility of the medieval world forced people to extort all available knowledge in their struggle to impose order and reason over the prevailing chaos, harnessing the vast reservoirs of occult qualities that had always been man's natural recourse and resource. Celestial activity developed primary importance as fears concerning war, disease, pestilence and power struggles increased. Adjunct to this, Cavandish [1977:80] reveals the fateful juxtaposition of Jupiter, Mars and Saturn in 1345 which was heralded as the harbinger of the plague. Rawcliffe [1995:82] believes faith in pre-destination led the Church to campaign more urgently its ministry of suffering for 'sin' and the divine providence of God for elevation above it.

At the level of lay practitioner, Rawcliffe [1995:94] argues that despite the influx of Greek philosophy, medicine was still a quasi-magical activity merely bolstered by an increased knowledge of astrology. Eclectic influences were eagerly absorbed without question including necromancy, its practitioners concerned only that it worked, not how or why. From the notebooks of Leonardo da Vinci, Thomas [1971:212], concludes a scathing comment: *"Undoubtedly, if this necromancy did exist, as is believed by shallow minds, there is nothing on Earth that would have so much power, either to harm or benefit."*

## Midwifery, Surgeons, Saints And Old Relics

Remembering that everything in mediaeval life was linked intrinsically to astronomy/astrology, magic and religion, books bursting with medical knowledge and methods of divination began circulation within the centres of excellence at Toledo and Salerno. Translated from manuscripts, many of these were available in the vernacular. Town doctors slowly replaced the magico-religious practices of the Monks and Clerics. Chaucer lampoons both activities so eloquently here offered first by Bisson [1999:111]: *"Thou woldest make me kisse thyn olde breech! And swere it were a relyk of a seint;"* and secondly by Bonser [1963:37]: *"He knew the cause of everich maladye were it of hoot or cold, or moiste, or drye,"* confirming the questionable value of humoural knowledge and Galenic medical practical. The following chart [Rawcliffe, 1995:33] displaying the humoural qualities, reveals many similarities to magical correspondences still given validation today:

| | | | | |
|---|---|---|---|---|
| Summer | Fire | Hot & dry | Choleric | Yellowbile |
| Autumn | Water | Cold & wet | Phlegmatic | Phlegm/mucus |
| Winter | Earth | Cold & dry | Melancholic | Black bile |
| Spring | Air | Hot & dry | Sanguine | Blood |

In contrast to this, Hildegard of Bingen, a highly influential Abbess and visionary mystic, following on from the 11$^{th}$ century magical advice of the legendary dame 'Trotula', advocated the administration of birthing amulets, girdles, pregnancy and fertility testing alongside her medicines [Rowland, 1981:32]. Remedies comprising of: herbs, trees, fruit, minerals, and animals, were made up into lotions, potions, unguents and suppositories. Within the country however, these things remained the domain of the 'Cunning-folk' or the Lady of the Manor who often owned notebooks similar to the 'Wulfshurn Manual', containing charms, spells and simples. These were supplemented by the continuing and damning use, as charged by the Bishop of Salisbury in 1538 during childbirth, of 'ligatures, girdles and measures' [ibid.]. Believed latent with cumulative supernatural potencies, girdles were often passed down within families for centuries. Edward the confessor is known to have presented Westminster Cathedral a girdle, summoned for use by a later Queen during her birthing in 1242. Many of these were later made from the relics and clothes of Saints and from long rolls of parchment (again, assimilation and displacement). Trotula recommends snakeskin as the finest; accompanied by the 'eaglestone' it was held to prevent abortion and to ensure safe delivery, a superstition to which even the Talmud concedes. Hildegard of Bingen suggests Jasper for use in birthing amulatory impedimenta [Rowland, 1981:3].

Women, many of whom were illiterate, were able to obtain licences to practice medicine from the 14th century, receiving much opposition in France and England [Rowland, 1981:9-27]. By 1567, midwives could be licensed, though their oath taken forbade the use of sorcery and magic. Faced with the imminent death of an infant, midwives were empowered to baptise it. A popular birthing charm is believed by Rowland [1981:32] to reveal the Christianisation of even this profession: *"O infant, whether living or dead, come forth because Christ calls you unto the light,"* repeated, as ever, three times. Women wishing to refrain from sexual intercourse, that is to decrease ardour within a spouse, during their pregnancy, are advised by 'Dame Trotula' to apply crushed camphor or lettuce to the male's kidneys and vervain upon the flesh; the most efficacious precaution was brimstone, carried (always) in the left hand [Rowland, 1981:157].

Numerous Pagan rites of passage were subsumed by the Church, often displacing their former emphasis. Baptism in particular, became regarded as an exorcism rather than a blessing by 'God' into the faith. Moreover, seven became the recommended age for confirmation, effectively separating these two formerly con-joined activities. Thomas [1971:35] here draws attention to the irony of a baptism involving the tying of a linen band around the head, effectively a chrisom, to be worn for three days, lest bad luck befall the child, asserting its clear Pagan ritual elements. After birth, the Church seriously but unsuccessfully opposed the growing tradition of 'churching' women, surprisingly a Pagan superstitious taboo surrounding the new mother. Within the 'Dives and Pauper', it states that: *"they that call them heathen women for the time that they lie in, be fools, and sin...full grievously"* [Thomas, 1971:38]. Their early return was avidly encouraged by the Church who chose to view the ritual as one of thanks for a safe delivery rather than one of cleansing. Even more difficult to eradicate were the superstitious fears and prejudices surrounding women and children who died during childbirth, whose spirits could be called forth by the cunning necromancer.

Many of the 'magical' customs formerly associated with marriage (despite its sanitation), including the dress, the ring, flowers etc, became preserved within the new sacrament of the Church. Death and burial were similarly strictly censured, bodies now faced East instead of North or West. Extreme unction, quite literally the 'death sentence' (a spell to bring forth spirit), was only sanctioned upon point of death [*ibid.*]. However, Thomas [1971:34] reveals that many priests perverted the death mass, using it on living persons to hasten their demise. Blood was deemed sacred and taboos delegated its shedding to the barber surgeons who also made use of astrological knowledge. Sex and death, ever-close companions in magic led the surgeons to eventually legitimise their own profession in line with physicians [Pouchelle, 1990:72].

Great pilgrimages during 13th-14th centuries to the tombs of major Saints induced the adoption by guildsmen and tradesmen of some of the more popular Saints as patrons of good luck & prosperity becoming much satirised by Reginald Scott in his 'Discoverie' written after the Reformation. An example is quoted here by Thomas [1971:27]:

> "Our painters had Luke, our weavers had Steven, our millers had Arnold, our tailors had Goodman…was there a better horseleech than St Loy? Or a better sow elder than St Anthony, Or a better tooth drawer than St Apollonia?"

Invocation of the names of Saints was deemed to bestow their relevant powers and strengths upon the summoner. Even after the decline of the 'Cult of the Saints', tales of *'miracula'* and *'mirabilia'* continued among a people starved of the supernatural. The Church had created a paradox from which it was increasingly difficult to extricate itself.

The 'Reformation' had extracted much of the 'magic' from religion leaving a vacuum the Cunning-folk and Witches were eager to exploit. Yet as magic and science advanced together, the natural elements of the former became subsumed within the latter. Supernatural elements once ejected, tentatively survived as 'folk magical' practices. Mediaeval peasants made no distinction between science and magic, or between magic and medicine, nor indeed were they encouraged too [Thomas, 1971:668]. For them, terms such as 'demonic' (supernatural), and 'natural' (elemental laws/forces or nature), were synonymous; both were occult whether by Saint or demon, therefore ripe with attendant superstitions. Intellectual theorising and Neo-platonic philosophies were the province of the scholars and clerics, for whom such distinctions had meaning. Despite Aristotelian logic, reason and ethics, these learned men continued to combine acts of will with complex techniques and incantations to influence matter in an invisible platonic world seething with spirits, demons and occult forces - *'sympatheia'* from within the 'Great Chain of Being', ironically, the 'supra-nature' of an all-encompassing God.

# Bibliography:

Aristotle. 1986 *'De Anima'* (Trans.) Lawson-Tancred, Hugh. G.B. The Chaucer Press. (Penguin Classics)

Bisson, L. M. 1999 *'Chaucer and the Late Medieval World'* N.Y. Macmillan Press.

Bonser, W. 1963 *'The Medical Background of Anglo-Saxon England'* London,

Oxford Uni. Press.

Burnett, C. 1996 *Magic and Divination in the Middle Ages: Texts and Techniques in The Islamic and Christian Worlds'* G.B., Ashgate Pub. Ltd.

Cavandish, R. 1977 *'The Powers of Evil'* London, Routledge & Keegan Paul Ltd.

Copenhaver, B. 1988 *'Hermes Trismegistus; Proclus and the Question of a Philosophy of Magic in the Renaissance'*, in Merkel, I. and Debus, A.G. (ed.) *'Hermeticism and the Renaissance'* London, Ass. Uni. Press, pp. 79-105.

Eliade, M. (ed.) 1987 *'Encyclopoedia of Religion'* New York, Macmillan Press, Vol. 6, Pp. 293-302. & Vol. 9, Pp.81-115.

Flint, V. 1991 *'The Rise of Magic in Early Medieval Europe'* New Jersey, Princeton Uni. Press.

Kieckhefer, R. 2000 *'Magic in the Middle Ages'*, Cambridge Uni. Press.

Pouchelle, M. C. 1990 *'The Body and Surgery In The Middle Ages'* England, Polity Press.

Rawcliffe, C. 1995 *'Medicine and Society in Later Medieval England'* England, Sutton Publishing.

Rowland, B. 1981 *'Medieval Woman's Guide to Health'* G.B., Kent State Uni. Press.

Seligman, K. 1997 *'Magic in the Middle Ages'* USA. Pantheon Books.

Thomas, K. 1971 *'Religion and the Decline of Magic'* G.B., Redwood Press Ltd.

Thorndike, L. 1934 *'History of Magic and Experimental Science'* Vol. Iii. N.Y., Columbia Uni. Press.

# 3
# Heresy and Early Witchcraft 1300CE-1600CE

### Early Trials Against Heresy And Witchcraft

Church theology of the 12th century was seriously influenced by Thomas Aquinas' belief that demonic magic was a pact between a demon and the magician. Moreover, the clerical underworld manipulated this notion to deflect attention away from their own nefarious practises, vociferously condemning the often-similar associations of the Cunning-folk engaging in geomancy, divination and astrology [Kieckhefer, 2000:201]. Emerging Scholasticism and its increasing grip on the medical world exerted little influence upon the peasantry and the rural folk whose only recourse reverted to those persons renowned as Cunning-folk. One such was the notorious Matteuccia Francisci of Todi, whose bold and unsavoury magical services in 1428, in particular her ability to 'transfer' illnesses, and her knowledge and use of love magic, brought her to trial for witchcraft [Kieckhefer, 2000:59]. Her acquittal is a keen indication of the lack of later hysteria regarding these same issues. Moreover, many trials within the 14th century were directed at clerics performing necromancy; others were to stem the rise in charges against sorcery during a social disaster that pitted neighbours against each other when illness or misfortune befell them. Ultimately, the victims were the hapless souls who, oblivious of external politics, continued with their magical arts, which of course

The Sorceress

included the forbidden use of divination, ligatures & binding spells, love magic, exorcism and invocation.

In 1396, Alice Perrers, mistress to the ailing King Edward III, fell foul of court politics; charged with necromancy she had to swear to leave the King alone in order to avoid prosecution. Governments recognising a foolproof method of eliminating enemies increasingly began associating witchcraft with treasonable acts. Margaret Beufort and Henry Duke of Buckingham in the 1483 rebellion against Richard III, were both accused of necromancy to secure their treason [Rawcliffe, 1995:92]. A later case involving conspiracy and alleged necromancy encompassed Eleanor Cobham and Roger Bolingbrook who sought to cast the young King's horoscope with a view to determining his death. Such sensitive issues were ripe for Machiavellian politics and charges of witchcraft [*ibid.*]. The traditions of 'Courtly Love,' to some extent revived for women their power as teachers, psychopomps, and initiators. For a brief time the 'feminine' once more attained status verging on the divine. Evidence that educated people sought 'divine' guidance and instruction reminiscent of ancient mystery religions can be found in Renaut de Beaujeu's 'Nekyia', written early in the 13$^{th}$ century. It is an account of a knight's journey towards a new life via a series of encounters and trials with death and the Devil. His transformation is painful; salvation is granted only upon full submission to the abyss, within the enchanted castle surrounded by the city of the dead – the serpent's kiss, affecting his completion.

This Gnostic theme, particularly among the Ophites of late antiquity, is the culmination of sacred liturgy [Heer, 1993:147]. Russell [1972:69] confirms that by the 12$^{th}$ century, heretical Gnostic theology incorporating 'demonic forms' derived from Judaic sources relating to 'fallen angels', posed a far greater threat to the Church than Pagan demons. An earlier 8$^{th}$ century prayer to 'Angels' by a heretic preacher in France named Adelbert, invokes: Adinus, Saboac, Simiel (Samael/Satan), Uriel, Raguel, Tubuel, Tubuas, and Michael. With the exception of Michael, none of these are 'orthodox'; Uriel, Raguel and Tubuel are from Jewish apocalyptic texts, Adinus, Saboac etc are all Gnostic forms. Though perplexing, Russell [*ibid.*] believes it unlikely that Adelbert believed himself to be invoking 'demons', despite the accusation as such levied against him. Curiously, an 8th century missive of Charlemagne condemning the use of non-scriptorial angelic names also warns against sacrificial practices. This was really a separate issue, running parallel with the condemnation of Pagan worship of trees, stones and sacred springs [Russel, 1972:66].

In Orleans, in 1022, the first heretics were burned for claiming to have been filled with the 'Holy Spirit' from an 'Angel of Light' that appeared before them, instigating the revival of Roman Law (secular death penalty) in Europe for heresy and sorcery [Russell, 1972:87]. As dualistic heresies developed into a serious threat to accepted theology, a vindictive and greedy Church purged various sects in some of the most horrific pogroms within history. The Inquisition was set up in 1233 by Gregory IX to eradicate all opposition to accepted theology. Thousands of Bogomils, Kathari, Albigensians and all other associated sects including the Knights Templar were subsequently slaughtered or burned. A 13th century 'Papal Bull' relating to a proposed section of the Waldensians, the Luciferians (first heard of in 1310 in Austria) who were allegedly worshipping the principle of evil, reveals this genocide was not totally successful. Furthermore, the 'Bishop' that headed them, known as 'Neumaister' (New Master) claimed that the 'Luciferians' had been in existence for a very long time and to have 80,000 followers despite only around 30 of them being captured and burned by the Inquisition [Russell, 1972:178].

Influenced by Jewish Apocalyptic ideas and doctrines derived from apocryphal books Elias and Enoch; their aim was to restore Lucifer, whom they believed to be the true God of the Old Testament and the other fallen Angels to 'Heaven', accompanied by all his faithful followers. Russell [1972:141] points out that in a perverse act of heresy against the asceticism of the Kathari,[1] the 'Luciferians' ate meat every day and rejected the mass. Their alleged free sexual license, believed similar to the alleged orgies of the Waldensians, was expressed as a "blasphemous communion" - *"vir in virum, foemina in foeminam."* Experienced in the dark, deep within underground caves, such activities were considered exempt from the 'above ground' rules of sin and morality [*ibid.*178].

More imperative than this however, was their heretical belief that the 'Devil' (Lucifer) transported them over large distances to these orgiastic celebrations. This belief in 'nocturnal flight', long perceived as 'demonic' by the Church, now clearly associated with heresy, is further advanced by Russell [1972:94] as engendering diabolism within witchcraft. In support of this view he stresses that charges of alleged diabolical witchcraft repeatedly and co-incidentally arose in the same areas as these heresies [*ibid.*]. The Church, anxious to obliterate all traces of the growing heresies, turned from one sect to another, ignoring in their desperation how the 'Kathari' still viewed Christ as the true Saviour, despite believing the 'Devil' to be the 'demi-urge' and 'God of this world [*ibid.*124]. Demonic flight and the nocturnal wanderings of women, once dismissed by Burchard as fanciful, thus came under increasing scrutiny of a nervous Church [Flint, 1991:125]. Patristic, misogynistic bishops influenced ecclesiastical law, developing the later stereotype of the 'sorceress', wholly devolving her image with diabolic associations and acts of heresy.

Later, during the 14th century, additional Papal edicts against witchcraft and further heresies were published. Ritual copulation with the 'Devil' as a goat or a black man first appears on record. Diana, Herodus, Holda and sometimes Hekate, as leaders and mistresses of the Sabbat and the 'Wild Nocturnal Rade', begin to take a back seat as the emphasis transposed from Pagan to heretical elements, and from female deific leadership to male deific leadership. Russell [1972:77] contrasts this view with Regino's 9th century quote that: *"the Devil incited women to follow and obey their mistress on their nocturnal wanderings,"* thus exposing a considerable paradigm shift. Russell [1972:183-6] further argues that most of the 14th century witch trials were early attempts by the Inquisition to combine sorcery with heresy.

Based on the Penitentials of Burchard [Russel, 1972:77-81], the four main constituents of Witchcraft derived from Pagan folklore establishing the pattern for medieval prosecutions were:

- 'Strigae' – night vampires who drink human blood.
- Daughters of Hekate or airborne Valkyries.
- Fear of Ghosts abroad at night.
- The Wilde Rade/Hunt.

Foundations for the damning of later witchcraft may be found in the Barbarian Law Codes that refer to the cannibalistic practices of the 'strix' or flying creatures as strictly 'demonic', implying satanic influence [Flint, 1991:12]. Existing Church tolerance, subject to increasing political pressure began its rapid disintegration. Geddes and Grossett [1997:230], cite the first witch-hunt in Switzerland in 1427, the production of the *'Malleus Maleficarum'* in 1486 following a Papal Bull in 1484 and the *'Sammis Desiderantes'* authorizing death for witches. Yet it is important not to forget that for many 'witches' of that time, unlike the beliefs of pre-Christian Pagans, their 'craft' was not a religion, remaining for the most part outside it, not aligned to any particular faith or creed. It was therefore not accountable by the laws surrounding heresy, though generally exercised within the ruling belief of its time; it remained a liminal practise of dubious moral and ethical beliefs. Maleficium (a secular crime) gradually became associated with heresy and diabolism (pacts with Satan), during the late 15th and early 16th centuries, culminating in the re-enforcement of the

Ethelstan order for the execution in England for *'wiccecraeftum'* where such acts resulted in death [Russell, 1972:73]. These indictments assert that although Paganism, to a large extent, had become absorbed into the body of the Church; witchcraft and heresy never were.

## Legislation And The Reformation

By the late 14$^{th}$ century, the growing shift in spirituality within a Church that had become the repository for all supernatural power, dispersed at will to the faithful, employing Saints, relics and martyrs, slowly moved towards Calvinism and reform [Thomas, 1971:32]. Plagues and schisms had ravaged faith in an impotent Church whose insecurities became vented upon the subversive activities of its people (still entrenched in magic) throughout the next three centuries as battles raged between the Catholics and the Protestants, each seeing the 'Devil and all his works' within the practices and beliefs of the other [Thomas, 1971:49]. Protestants denied the magic of 'holy' water, the sign of the cross, the use of Latin, shrines and relics. Of the seven sacraments: Baptism, Confirmation, Marriage, Mass, Ordination, Penance and Extreme Unction, only Baptism and the Eucharist retained some of their former character, the others were devalued and modified, viz., altars, church & grounds were no longer subject to 'hallowing'; some practices were however, re-introduced at the end of the 16$^{th}$ century.

Calvin denied the miracle of transubstantiation within the mass, an act not affirmed until the Fourth Lateran Council of 1215, replacing it with a simpler rite centred upon the doctrine of consubstantiation [Thomas, 1971:52-58]. Most fascinating of these is the 'mystery' of the mass, which, since the 13$^{th}$ century, had been withheld from the populace by the erection of screened inner sanctuaries within the churches. The 'magic' purportedly lay in the *spoken* formulae, the ritual that facilitated 'transformation' within the cup; Protestants naturally denied this, believing the change to take place within the individual after consumption. Eucharistic ecstasy, the empowering passion of many mystics, generated through repeated fasting and feasting upon the perceived 'body' of their God, facilitated healings and miracles in His name. The Church, ever anxious to negate fanaticism, actively discouraged female hysteria induced from this excessive practice. Even so, Bynum [1987:138-9] discovers Collette Corbie in the 15th century noted as allegedly eating nothing but the 'body of Christ'. Adherents of this bizarre practice believed great power, grace and inspiration was imparted from this extreme abstinence; Aquinas himself was a strong advocate declaiming: *"abstain to be ready"* [Bynum, 1987:113]. One espousal led to another and eventually many old Pagan, albeit Christianised rites were banned, including Plough Monday, Rush rites and Misrule. They were forbidden, lost and distorted during the Protestant purge on all 'magical' elements from within the Catholic religion as it sought to establish a faith independent of 'supernatural power'. May Games, Morris dancing and Maypoles were gradually re-introduced in moderation after the Restoration in the 17th century [*ibid.*].

In times of crisis however, Thomas [1971:495] asserts that both Protestant and Catholic alike resorted to folk magic practices - in 1596 a 12-year-old girl protected herself against the apparition of a big black dog by uttering the 'Holy' name. Cunning-folk continued to make extensive use of the old formulas. Even John Dee anointed a maidservant whom he believed to be possessed, with 'Holy' oil in 1590 to effect a cure [*ibid.*]. Curiously, the seductive powers and magic of the 'white witch' were deemed more damning than the diabolism of the 'black witch', the Devil was seen everywhere as a tempter and agent of divine retribution [Thomas, 1971:470].

The 'Reformation' engendered dramatic change that necessitated the divergence of magic into two parallel courses: those of high and low magic; the latter was diametrically opposed to the Church, therefore doomed; the former was to develop a metaphysical and theosophical guise among Rosicrucians and Freemasons during the professed age of 'reason and enlightenment' wherein 'magic' simply became un-fashionable. Definitions between secular and ecclesiastical laws in England became extremely tenuous after the 'Reformation;' guidelines for prosecution developed despite the fact that the actual laws changed very little. Campaigns began in earnest on the Continent; this resulted in the Council of Malines in 1607. Outlawing all forms of demonic magic, witchcraft and sorcery, it ruled that,effects other than those from natural causes were the work of the Devil, which of course allowed the Church to continue its own indulgence of 'natural magic'. In response to this, Reginald Scott wrote sardonically: *"He canonizes the rich for a saints and banneth the poor for witches"* [Thomas, 1971:49]. A vicious polemic against the Pope named him the 'Witch of the World' [ibid.] and his administration of the Eucharist as positively demonic [Walker, 2000:153].

Sickness deemed as a visitation from God for personal sin was emphasised in the new Elizabethan prayer book. And Thomas [1971:30] quotes a curious Protestant railing against Catholic 'popish' magic: *"About these Catholics necks and hands are always hanging charms, that serve against all miseries and all unhappy harms."* Thus, effectively deprived of legitimate magical support and resources, Thomas [1971:257] believes the (new) Church to have turned back the populace to Pagan and folk magical devices of Cunning-folk. This can also be seen as the point of divergence of magical practice, one outlawed as performed by the general populace, and the other accepted within the body of the Church, ultimately to be termed low and high magic respectively. Alchemy and love magic remained a capital offence until 1689. Within England, any form of magic had always been an offence liable to prosecution before Church courts. Cases of *'Maleficium'* were occasionally dealt with in this way before and after 1563 act against sorcery and conjuring. Variations within many local assizes expressed uncertainties about statutes, despite secular statutes extant from Cnut and Anglo-Saxon laws in place for indictment of witchcraft [*ibid.*].

## Later Witchcraft

> 'Sorcerers are too common, Cunning-men, wizards and white witches, as they call them, in every village, which if they be sought unto, will help almost all infirmities of body and mind."
> - Robert Burton, 1621, *Anatomy of Melancholy*. [Thomas 1971:176].

Girdle measuring, a superstitious procedure of fabled faerie origin, for detecting supernatural causes for illness, generally by faerie malice, was still in force at the end of the 16$^{th}$ century despite its official ban, carrying a charge of sorcery. Divination and the use of talismanic magic and birthing amulets also continued albeit discreetly. Elizabeth Mortlake, a popular wise woman is recorded in 1566 as "measuring with a 'girdle' the sick for signs of 'faerie'", paralleling the case a hundred years earlier of Agnes Hancock who also inspected her patients with a girdle for signs of 'feyrey' (sic) [Thomas, 1971:184]. Even more amazing is the case of the London Empiric Robert Booker, who in 1622 informed a patient of his bewitchment, stating that three biters bit him: *"heart, tongue & eye; three better shall help him presently - God the father, God the son, and God the Holy Spirit."* Thomas [1971:185] maintains this to be a standard formula representing the three sources of witchcraft: concealed malevolence (heart), bitter-words (tongue) and ocular fascination (eye); while serving to emphasise the power of religious faith to overcome them all. Classification of these Cunning-folk activities as 'natural' or 'demonic' was further obfuscated by the parallel activities of their intellectual rivals, the Renaissance Magi. Ironically, throughout the 17th century, love philtres, spells, natural magic and incantations were all studied at Oxford by 'Jacobean' students, whose necromantic activities are explained by Thomas [1971:220] as comparable to the drug/drink indulgences of the modern student.

By the late Middle Ages, *'Maleficium'* (acts of malice or crime) in Europe came to denote witchcraft, generally with diabolical overtures, though not so commonly in England where acts of malevolence continued to be prosecuted by the state [Russell, 1972:65]. In 1552, Bishop Latimer observed: *"we be in trouble or sickness, or lose anything, we run hither and thither to witches, sorcerers we call wise men....seeking aid and comfort at their hands"* [Thomas, 1971:176]. Cautious use of ritual charms and spells continued to beguile the illiterate and superstitious. One of these from the 17th century displays clear Anglo-Saxon heritage [Thomas, 1971:80]: *"Two angels came from the West, The one brought Fire, the other brought Frost. Out Fire, out Frost. In the name of the Father, the Son and the Holy Ghost."* Devil worship however, was rarely alleged in England, though the trial of Dame Alice Kyteler in 1324, was the exception rather than the rule. As a means of resolving controversies, sorcery had, since 785 been banned, leading to its development with anti-social offences and witchcraft (maleficium). Sorcery thus continued to develop increasingly diabolical overtones. [Russell, 1972:242].

Reginald Scott wrote that every parish had its own 'miracle' worker whose low profiles were due to outlawed magical practices, mainly in the use of ligatures and amulets. Some Cunning-men and Wise-women even advocated fasting to enhance the efficacy of their charms; generally this also included astrological consultations [Thomas, 1971:186]. Relative to this, Russell [1972:272] presents the bizarre request by a churchwarden to a Cunning-woman in the 16th century to discover who had stolen the local communion cloth from within the church. A popular divinatory rite, of some relevance to historians of traditional witchcraft, is *'tourner le sas'* (turning the sieve). Coscinomancy, was a very popular divinatory method used by Cunning-folk during the Middle Ages for determining the identity of a thief involving both sieve and shears in a complex balancing act. Agrippa[2] was convinced the sieve turned at the behest of demons. Certainly, an invocation exists that accompanies such an act known as the *'Bagabi'* Rune. A Basque charm, it is presented by Seligman [1997:219] for use in the summoning of Satan. Crowley [1996:109], however, presents it as a mediaeval Rune, gleaned from a 13th century ms of the Troubadour Rutebeuf as a possible invocation of witch God names. It is now commonly used within some modern neo-Pagan/witchcraft 'All Hallows' Eve rituals, where divination does form part of these rites. Crowley [*ibid.*] offers the following form of it, conceding that slight variations are extant:

> "Bagahi laca bachahe
> Lamec cahi achabahe
> Karrelyos
> Lamec lamec bachalyos
> Cabahagi sabalyos
> Baryolas
> Lagozatha cabyolas
> Samahac et famyolas
> Harrahya!"

Rutebeuf, a 'jongleur' of some renown, satirised 13th century French court life providing pungent commentaries on the orders of society and ribald adventure tales, many of which, are now happily translated. Michael Harrison [3] after translating the Basque Rune, concludes his belief that this 'Rune' may (allegedly) accompany the 'tourner le sas' as a medieval divinatory rite. Naturally, this does not preclude the invocation of 'God' (demonic) forms within the full version of the text for other purposes. Catholic and Protestant condemned sorcery equally. Tudor law statutes prescribed heavy penalties for magical activities due to the now alleged affiliation with the Devil, whom the Protestant Church saw everywhere as a soul stealer and tempter. Acts of *'maleficium'* continued to be prosecuted by the state relatively unchanged since the Middle Ages, but now the Church began to tighten its grip on heresy. Increasingly, from the early 17th century the continental view of witchcraft became reflected within England, though the secular emphasis shifted rather more towards sorcery than heresy. Anne Bodenham, a Cunning-woman in Salisbury was executed for witchcraft in 1653 for calling upon the power of Jupiter *"...the most fortunate of planets"* to cure a little girl of convulsive fits [Thomas, 1971:438]. Trials peaked during the reign of Elizabeth I, whose 1563 statute ordered the death penalty under civil law for witches and sorcerers, dwindled during the reign of James I, despite his personal obsession that had increased the hysteria of people falling prey to scrutiny by the Witch-finder General, an office commonly of self-appointment.

Trials for witchcraft, sorcery, enchantment and conjuration almost disappeared after the Restoration, ceasing to be statutory offences in 1736 and are recorded as remaining in English rural life well into the 19th century. Prosecution prevailed for those pretending to possess magical powers that this new law denied the reality of [Russell, 1980:122]. Thomas [1971:468] argues that prior to the 1563 witchcraft act, it had not been an offence to conjure spirits or to engage in natural 'magical' activities; however, if fraud, malice, injury or treason were alleged, the offence was indictable under secular law. He further argues that the union between diabolical witchcraft and sorcery (invented during the Middle Ages), had been a deliberate and temporary artifice engineered for political motives, having no basis or association with folk-magic. Moreover, he sees sorcery as a distinct practice from witchcraft, generally employing the use of fetishes, magical implements and materials, being extant before, during and after the 'witchcraft' trials. Blaming the Church's elevation of a personal and immanent 'Devil' for fuelling the 'diabolical' compacts, Thomas [*ibid.*] also believes the deprivation of ecclesiastical counter measures for magic by the Protestants, which had been indulged to keep sorcery under control, created the dissension and fear at the level of the populace, allowing it to escalate to its ultimate and tragic conclusion.

## Bibliography

Bonser, W. 1963 The Medical Background of Anglo-Saxon England. Oxford Uni. Press.
Bynum, C.W. 1987 *'Holy Fast and Holy Feast'* London, Uni. California Press.
Crowley, V. 1996 *'Wicca: The Old Religion in the New Millennium'* G.B. Thorsons.
Flint, V. 1991 *'The Rise of Magic in Early Medieval Europe'* New Jersey, Princeton Uni. Press.
Heer, F. 1993 *'The Medieval World: Europe 1100-1350'* G.B. Orion Publishing.
Kieckhefer, R. 1989 *'Magic in the Middle Ages'* Cambridge Uni. Press.
Rawcliffe, C. 1995 *'Medicine and Society in Later Medieval England'* GB, Sutton Publishing.
Russell, J.B. 1972 *'Witchcraft in the Middle Ages'* Cornell Uni. Press.
Seligman, K. 1997 *'Magic in the Middle Ages'* USA Pantheon Books.
Thomas, K. 1971 *'Religion and the Decline of Magic'* G.B., Redwood Press Ltd.
Walker, C. 1995 *'The Encyclopoedia of Secret Knowledge'* London, Rider.
Walker, D.P. 2000 *'Spiritual and Demonic Magic'* Sutton Publishing.

# References

1. Cathars - whose extreme dualism elevated the 'Devil' to share equal status with God, an eternal cosmic principle, which led to their belief that all things are God, including the 'Devil'.

2. Provides a plausible illustration depicted in Walker's *Encyclopaedia of Magic* 1995, p208

3. In his excellent book, *The Origins of Witchcraft* (which I have unfortunately been unable to re-trace for full refs)

# 4
# The Hermetic Renaissance 1400-1700

## Renaissance And Hermeticism

During the European Renaissance, the Catholic Church, running parallel to the Reformation in England, eagerly explored the legendary writings of 'Hermes Trismegistus.' Its high Neo-Platonic ideals ripped open hoary convention and orthodoxy. Humanism reached its apogee within the 'classical man of power'; whence the old Pagan ideal of the 'universal man' seeking to control and master his environment, was resurrected [Cavandish, 1990:84]. Hermeticists believe that true wisdom may be inspired by nature and imagination (divine thought). This quest for *'Prisca Sapientia'* (ancient wisdom) led them to the magic of Zoroaster, Moses, Orpheus and Pythagoras, all sourced from within the legendary *'Picatrix'* and the *'Sefer-ha-razim'* [Eliade, Vol.9, 1987:98]. Origins for the *'Hermetic Corpus'* remain speculative at best, though much evidence points confidently towards the East, where the 'thrice great' sage, priest and philosopher was generally synonymous with the Egyptian God Thoth (Tehute), to whom authorship of the 'Book of Thoth', concerning traditional Egyptian wisdom lore from the archaic world is attributed.

Somewhat appropriately, three major works are acknowledged as carrying the Hermetic principle. These are:

❖ The *'Corpus Hermeticum'*, a tractate compiled by several translators during the Renaissance of approximately 17-19 dialogues between Hermes and various others, including the divine 'Poimandres'(God), who instructs Hermes in the ways of philosophy and religious belief through a series of discourses, which are delivered in turn by Hermes to Asclepius and his son Tat. The first of these is where Poimandres/Pimander is concerned with the creation of the world and the fall

Alchemist

of man; the others are an eclectic collection of inconsistent musings and magical instruction, which are now thought to have been compiled by several authors over 2-3 hundred years and much influenced by both Neo-Platonism and Gnosticism. The hermetic maxim, *'Know Thyself'*, derived from: *"He who knows himself - knows the all,"* is in fact Gnostic in origin (confirmed among writings found at Nag Hammadi in 1945).

- ❖ The *'Tabula Smaragdina'* or Emerald Tablet, said to express the three wisdoms of the universe - alchemy, astrology and theurgy, were all mastered by Hermes, hence his title of thrice greatest. For a long time it was believed the earliest known fragments were preserved upon the Leyden Papyrus, found in the tomb of an unknown Egyptian priest in 1828. Alchemy, concerned with the 'Great Work' or purification of the soul, is aptly named, the 'Operation of the Sun'. Astrology, as the 'Operation of the Moon' is concerned with the understanding and manipulation of specific influences caused by heavenly bodies upon the Earth. Theurgy is the 'Operation of the Stars', or the beneficent and malefic forms of magic which are either divine (angelic) or demonic (evil spirits). It is the science of divine works which when mastered, accedes to union with the One. Even so, the Emerald Tablet is a short, euphemistic allegory, a poetically philosophical draft, rich in enigmatic metaphor, from which the oft quoted maxim, 'as above, so below' is derived. Though a full and better rendition reads as *That which is Below corresponds to that which is Above, and that which is Above corresponds to that which is Below, to accomplish the miracle of the One thing.'*

- ❖ The 'Kybalion', a book of more recent provenance, published in

1912, by three mysterious initiates seeking to condense and refine the philosophical corpus of the great Mage. Underlined within its tenets is the hermetic maxim of the: *"all within the one"* - expressing a panentheism that insightfully denies a distinct and transcendent God as separate from creation and one that includes other deities, elementals, angelic spirits, avatars, mankind, and all manner of flora and fauna etc. All 'things' exist along the great chain of being, a vibratory thread connecting every organic thing to the next stage of its evolution towards the eventual realisation of its divinity, within that of the Mind of the One. Causation is expressed simply as an undiscovered law of 'Chaos'; chance must consist within the parameters of being in accord with universal law. Nothing is outside the equilibrating harmony of the One who is All. It does however, pronounce a morality towards the 'right' action, choice or thought, as determined by intrinsic tenets of Hermeticism. This (Gnostic) choice instinctively errs towards evil, which must be overcome through continued gnosis.

With the exception of the Kybalion, earlier Hermetic fragment were analysed by Issac Casaubon, a Swiss philologist in 1614, who having discovered linguistic anomalies and discrepancies, placed their written form to no earlier than the first century CE. Importantly, many Neo-Platonists were familiar with and certainly influenced by these profound yet pragmatic examples of Egyptian wisdom literature. Arabic translators of these works imbued another dimension, causing some confusion for those encountering such syntheses during the Middle Ages. Composed in Spain, the most famous of these works (falsely attributed to Maslama Al-Majriti), is the 11th century Arab compendium *'Ghayat Al-Hakim.'* Best known to us as the *'Picatrix,'* it was translated into Spanish and then two centuries later (back) into Latin for Alphonso, King of Castille. It was the most commonly accepted source of Hermetic science particularly during the Middle Ages, whence the greater and purer sources had not yet been discovered. Found in a Benedictine Abbey in the Bavarian Alps, Burnett's [1996:84] study of a manuscript copied in the 13th century, begins:

> "… Aristotle full of good sense said: when the Moon enters its first mansion, which is called *Sartan*, make a talisman for love…when it alights in its second mansion, *Albotain*, make a talisman for the favour of princes … animate statues, call angels unto you!"

This curious use of Arab names for the mansions of the Moon suggests a non-Greek origin for this passage. Moreover, it is very similar in form to a 15th century ms found in Baghdad written in Arabic. Some scholars believe both pieces to derive from the *'Kitab-al-Ustuwwatas,'* where all 28 mansions of the Moon are supplemented with detailed instructions on how to formulate talismans, and summon angels by their secret names. Advancing this text as Hermes' book of causes of spiritual forces, Hunain ibn Ishaq (c809-873CE) believed the work to be an Arabic translation of a Greek work by Aristotle written for Alexander, his pupil. It is commonly held to be the sequel to the *'Kitab-al-Istamakhis'* [*ibid.*].

Yet, curiously, texts attributable to Aristotle had been in circulation for some time before the *Picatrix*. One of these, translated by Hermann of Corinthia in 1143, in his own work, *'De Essentiis'*, corresponds closely enough to derive from the same source as the *'Kitab-al-Istamakhis'* (ms now in the Bodleian library). In it, Hermann discusses the nature of incorporeal beings, sacrifice (of a ram) and manifestation of deity. Burnett believes that work to be the source of the *Picatrix* [1996:86]. Though there is no earlier extant version, Hermann could have accessed a more complete source than that found within the *Picatrix*, now lost to us; thus posing the possibility of other works carrying 'Hermetic' ideas and magic into the Middle Ages.

Many scholars though now deny Greek translations of earlier Egyptian texts attributed to Hermes, or the correspondence between Aristotle and his pupil Alexander concerning the Hermetic texts, despite the numerous claims by Arabic historians of the 11th -13th centuries. Their popularity and origin appears to be a largely eclectic syncretism for use among a non-elite minor sect or community of the Middle Eastern world during the first two centuries of the new millennium; copies were written in Greek, Syriac, Coptic Arabic and Armenian.

In response, Burnett [1996:86] discusses Persian influence evident within doctrinal instructions and Reitzenstein's support for the greater similarities between Arabic and Pahlavi texts, especially regarding the creation story, where certain key words within the Arabic texts are not Greek but Pahlavi. Furthermore, the 28 mansions of the Moon, derived from classical Indian astrology, became known to the Arabs only through mediation of the Pahlavi texts. Reitzenstein's [Yamauchi, 1973:21] studies of Hellenistic mysticism encouraged him to conclude that early hermetic literature could have originated from within a pre-Christian infant Gnosticism or radical ontological dualism, largely drawn largely from Iranian and 'Mandaean' (derivative of 'manda', meaning knowledge) sources, which in turn are based upon ancient Babylonian and Persian traditions. General academic study has concluded that due largely to the nine names of Jupiter used for invocation, they can establish the manuscript's cultural origin from within the Sabaean community, whose two principal prophets, Agathodaimon and Hermes are also quoted within the works of Hermann of Corinthia, who places the latter as a pupil of the former [Burnett, 1996:87]. Within an astrological treatise of 'Abu Mas'har,' the legend of the three Hermes, or Hermes Trismegistus, appears and is explained as:

"first all wise Hermes lived in Egypt before the flood, and is identical with Enoch (named as an angel in a Latin prologue in a later work); the second Hermes lived in Babylon and revived the Sciences after the Flood; the third and final Hermes is once again found in Egypt, and it was he who taught the alchemy and wisdom to Asclepius; this third Hermes corresponds to the Hermes of the *'Corpus Hermeticum'* [*ibid*.231]."

After originating with the peoples of India, Hermann shares Abu Mas'har's belief that astrology influenced the West through the syncretised traditions of the Persians, Arabs and Sabaeans, extant only within his own work, *'De Essentiis'* [*ibid*.]. Other traditions attribute the origins of the *'Picatrix'* to Thabit ibn Qurra [c826-901CE], master of magic and science. Technically, the Church viewed the practice of astrology as equal to necromancy, an ignominy to be abjured. Prevailing Church policy upon necromancy stated that while blessed souls resided in heaven out of reach of spirits, any thus recalled were demons, whose domain was below the firmament. This definition was to prove problematic for Renaissance 'Magi', where inconsistency prevailed regarding 'demonic' and 'natural' magic practices.

Ficino (1433-1499CE) steered clear of these muddy waters, elevating theurgical (Orphic) music and harmony as a way to God while advocating the vital belief in will and intent [Yates, 1964:74]. From within his 'natural spiritus' (absorption of energy from the Sun), Ficino identifies the generating current as (divine) love through which 'Magus Man', in honour of the 'divine Pimander', is created; from such communion, develops true magic [Yates, 1964:121-6]. Ficino had translated the *'Hermetic Corpus'* for his Florentine patron, Cosimo de Medici. These texts, largely concerned with alchemy, astrology, necromancy, divination and talismanic magic, were condemned outside the bounds of the Church. Sidestepping these, he expounded the astral body's subjection to planetary influences.

More infatuated with Plotinian metaphysics and cosmology than crude forms of talismanic magic, Ficino shunned the 'Hermetica' believing the work of Egyptian priests to be corrupt and a gross deception, preferring instead the purer theurgy of the Chaldean Oracles. Even so, he did attempt to justify talismanic magic, utilising the works of Plotinus to add credence to their manufacture as 'divine reflections' of nature's powers.

> "when any piece of matter is exposed to superior things, immediately it suffers a supernatural influence through that most powerful agent of marvellous force and life…which is everywhere present…as a mirror reflects a face" [Yates,1964:66]

Frustrated by obscure and often contradictory texts within the 'Hermetica', he sought answers relating to his own 'philosophies'- those sciences of Cosmology, Cosmogony and Eschatology. gnosis was always a means to perfection and the way to God. [Merkel & Debus, 1988:80]. Believing the true source of Renaissance magic and philosophy to be culled from Neo-Platonism and not from the eclectic pieties of Hermes Trismegistus, Copenhaver [Merkel & Debus, 1988:84-87] asserts that Ficino's work reveals other (more Neo-Platonic) influences, in particular the centrality and importance of 'solar' currents, those too of love and all the erotic forces intrinsic to nature. Binding them together in the warp of the universe, Ficino fully established the 'Cult of the Sun'. Cautiously, Ficino advised fasting, lustration, fumigation (generally by solar incense) and incantation to release the astral self; food and wine were consumed to complete the Eucharist.

Blatant Pagan theurgy was anathema to the Church and presentation had to be couched in Christian overtones to render it palatable. Hymns and incantations were made to the 'higher self' to facilitate a raised consciousness, emphasising power raised from within, thus avoiding the implicit charge of evocationary, therefore 'demonic' magic [Walker,

2000:31]. He worked effortlessly, translating the much prized Hymns of Orpheus, and Plato's theology of the immortality of the Soul, and for whose lofty ideals he was cautioned to study the more sober works of Aristotle, exampled by the renowned Thomas Aquinas. Nevertheless, this vital concept, the philosophy of the Soul, became central to medieval theology and scientific enquiry into the nature of being, inspiring generations of philosophers after him.

Though the name 'Hermes Trismegistus' is given only cursory attention within two chapters of Ficino's *'De vita coelitus comparanda'*, one of these does relate the infamous 'God making' passages of Asclepius (animation via magical correspondences). Of paramount importance to Renaissance occultism was the work *'De Sacrificio'* by Proclus, a treatise based on the Chaldean Oracles on Theurgic magic, translated by Ficino from the Greek original in 1484. Based primarily on the principle of correspondences, manipulated by will through knowledge and understanding of the nature of the 'Great Chain of Being'; the ultimate maxim of the Neo-Platonists: *'as above, so below'* is also reflected within the Hermetic Texts [Merkel & Debus, 1988:84].

Another later work, *'De vita libre tres'* in 1489 saw Ficino charged with heresy, from which he narrowly escaped. This tentative work explored the possibilities of astrology (astronomy) as comprehensive to the divine plan, intrinsic to vigour of mind and body. In particular, it considers the matter of causation and personal culpability. Evidently, The Holy See was not yet ready for such a revelation, preferring temptation and salvation to rest firmly within the dogma and histrionics of its own Church. In 1492, Ficino announced his joy in the valorisation of the seven glorious liberal arts (rhetoric, grammar, logic, music, geometry, astronomy and arithmetic), the embodiment of the Renaissance man and the means by which mankind may achieve egress towards gnosis. Great works of art particularly, were understood by Ficino as talismanic templates for contemplation and induction into the higher mysteries. For Ficino, man must reflect the truth and beauty of God's great universe; through excelling in the arts and achieving greatness, the dignity and duty of mankind is fulfilled.

He had been a precocious child, born to gifted parents; his mother was rumoured to have been blessed with the 'second sight' and whose own advanced years pre-deceased Ficino by only a couple of years. His life was one of abstinence and chastity; unusually, like Leonardo da Vinci, he was a vegetarian. A strict disciplinarian, he rose with the Sun, to greet the manifest light of God. Humble, hunchbacked, and prone to severe bouts of melancholia, due, Ficino claimed, to the overbearing yet paradoxically beneficent influence of Saturn in his house of Aquarius, this quiet but charismatic man beguiled many who heard not his lisp, only his heartfelt passion for the truth. This profound gift of perception and comprehension is awarded all who fall under the sway of that dark and hoary master, Saturn. Temperaments and humours of mind and body were given studious precedence during this advancing period in our scientific historicity. The theory of balance and harmony between the four elementals (later determined as humours) as key to individual pathology, again finds instruction in the work of Plato.

Ficino nonetheless recognised his own genius and high intelligence as being subject to influence through his saturnine humour, going so far as to state that divine madness alights only upon those whose countenance *is* predisposed by Saturn. He adds that Plato and Aristotle were both confirmed melancholics, both of whom were fine examples of the once marvellous Golden Age of Saturn [Toohey, 2005]. This astute acceptance of a negative influence having positive results relays the heart of Neo-Platonism, that even the basest influence is closer to the divine than all manifest form. Should anyone become touched by this complex force, their misery is a blessed madness, leading to tormented genius and poetic insightfulness. Curiously, certain modern occultists have professed such attributes under the ambivalent auspices of Saturn. And like them, Ficino realised that to overcome the potentialities of fate, they must be confronted and sublimated - transposed via alchemical means to a higher force, entirely through free and active will. In this, he finally recognised the merit of the non-determinative hermetic sciences. He dedicated the remainder of his life to the translation and dissemination of these virtuous and humanitarian works for the reification of all mankind.

Ficino's pupil, Pico della Mirandola (1463-94CE), under the burgeoning influence of Savonarola, the Dominican priest (and anti-Humanist) who had caused Ficino to vacillate briefly against the new sciences, refuted utterly the principles and causations of astrology (astronomy). Mirandola chose instead to concentrate upon and to synthesise the traditions of Aristotle and Plato within the Kabbalah, most specifically those based upon Abulafia's mystical system of knowing God [Cavandish, 1990:58]. It is suggested that Mirandola, like many of his peers, invoked angelic forms from within the Kabbalah, where the 'Word' is God, and through which he shall be known, and where *communion* with the divine contrasts sharply with the hermetic *union* with the divine [Seligman 1997: 332]. Yet another prodigy, at the age of 23 he announced his intention to defend no less than 900 theses on religion, philosophy and natural magic from polemical attack.

His finest piece was the *'Oration of the Dignity of Man,'* also known as the 'Manifesto of the Renaissance.' A section of this inspired work relative to the contentious matter of re-incarnation (which expounds the immutability of the eternal soul) and metempsychosis (or transmigration that conversely upholds the mutability of the eternal soul) is worthy of our attention in the pursuit of the development of innovative and challenging thought during this period.

> "The Pythagoreans abuse villainous men by having them reborn as animals and, according to Empedocles, even plants. Mohammed also said frequently, "Those who deviate from the heavenly law become animals." Bark does not make a plant a plant, rather its senseless and mindless nature does. The hide does not make an animal an animal, but rather its irrational but sensitive soul. The spherical form does not make the heavens the heavens, rather their unchanging order. It is not a lack of body that makes an angel an angel, rather it is his spiritual intelligence. If you see a person totally subject to his appetites, crawling miserably on the ground, you are looking at a plant, not a man. If you see a person blinded by empty illusions and images, and made soft by their tender beguilements, completely subject to his senses, you are looking at an animal, not a man. If you see a philosopher judging things through his reason, admire and follow him: he is from heaven, not the Earth. If you see a person living in deep contemplation, unaware of his body and dwelling in the inmost reaches of his mind, he is neither from heaven or earth, he is divinity clothed in flesh." [Hooker, 1994]

This stresses emphatically the choice (free will) given to mankind by the Creator to evolve, progressively over successive incarnations, as humans, even if disposed to debased or bestial natures. Principally, this single work exponentially advanced 'Humanism,' the belief in the worth and dignity of all mankind as rationalised by exhibition and expression of determinative factors of qualities that are natural rather than supernatural or divine. Truth was to be ordained by rational means, by logic, not revelation. It promotes observation and empiricism, the exposure of superstition and free-thinking where science is the key to understanding the universe. Truth and beauty, expressed through the Seven Liberal Arts were the means by which these could be achieved.

Unlike his esteemed tutor, Pico was a wild and passionate youth, whose many love affairs constantly found him under duress from various officials. These affairs hardly distracted him though from his real passion, which was to unite the opposing pedagogic tenets of Aristotle with those of Plato; those too of Humanism with Christianity. He believed the key to this lay within both the magical system of the Kabbalah and the philosophy of Hermetics. He was a reactionary against extremism and always sought the way of *'concordia'* or harmony. Nevertheless, his progressive views were met with some scepticisms and condemnations, especially those that skirted around 'natural magic'. He was forced to retract some passages and submit apologies in order to avoid prosecution.

Fortunately for Pico, the infamous Borgia Pope Alexander VI, replaced his less than sympathetic predecessor. Possessing favourable views on magic and astrology, this Pope heartily endorsed Pico's work such that in 1492, Alexander VI decorated his private apartments with hermetically inspired iconography and art, fanning the flames of disapproval among religious fundamentalists [Yates, 1964:114-16]. Sadly, Pico's singular devotion to Savonarola, whose vociferous attack on the excesses and corruptions of the Medici family, was to instigate his downfall along with that of Savonarola. In 2007, when his body was exhumed, traces of arsenic poisoning were found, probably from the hands of the troubled and vengeful Medici family.

His enduring legacy to modern Hermeticists, philosophers and would be Magi, is his profound insight into the cosmology of mankind, alone of all species to have the capacity to ascend the 'great chain of being', exempt from its ranked hierarchy, rigid ordering and influence from external forces. We change (and advance) in accord with our own will and our wits. Should we decline either, then we 'vegetate', that is, we become *as* beasts or plants, not *the* beasts or plants. He said that:

> "Human vocation is a mystical vocation that has to be realised following a three stage way, which comprehends necessarily moral transformation, intellectual research and final perfection in the identity with the absolute reality. This paradigm is universal because it can be retraced in every tradition." [*ibid.*]

Pico had bravely attempted to reveal the inconsistencies of variant cosmologies, as non contradictory, but simply as alternate perspectives. Everything therefore becomes a symbol of the divine, a key to its perception, all leading to the One truth. Therefore, it mattered not whether we view everything as created by or within God, or whether the divine force was expressed as self-creating and perpetuating emanations; all that matters is that they are divine, they are all 'God' and may be communed with and experienced. The truth therefore, lies in our capacity for change, for growth, for transformative evolution, of mind and spirit. He had dared to reject eternal damnation. This 'freedom' was considered highly heretical; most especially, it denounced the concept of 'original sin' and it rejected determinism. It did invite scientific enquiry.

Not all his contemporaries were so enlightened. Other Renaissance Magi, like Paracelsus and Agrippa reverted to the condemned medieval magic of Avicenna, boldly espousing the use of talismans and astrology to manipulate and compel planetary angels to their will [Walker, 2000:92]. In England, John Dee, seeking progression into the higher spheres, conversed with angels to discover the true nature of God [Seligman, 1997:318]. Even so, there was no real contradiction during the Renaissance between magic, astrology and science. Furthermore, as their practises came under increasing attack, various 'apologies' promoted their work as subject only to 'natural' magic. Saturated with Christian piety and theology, their work continued throughout the theological furore between Catholic and Protestant, desperate to establish an unchallenged harmonic [Knight, 1978:19].

In opposition to Yates, Copenhaver [Merkel & Debus, 1988:80] posits the value of Hermeticism to be much overstated, adding that the work of Agrippa more closely resembles the direct work of Proclus than that of Ficino with whom it is traditionally linked. Agrippa (1486-1535CE), a man of great erudition, cut to the quick promoting the more 'demonic' aspects of the *Picatrix* in addition to asserting the power of will as crucial to any magical success. Agrippa [1974:4] challenged Church doctrine of 'creation from nothing' with his theory that matter (substance) was eternal. Sharing the view of his contemporaries, Agrippa [*ibid*.47] believed the 'Sun' to be the demi-urge, explaining that:

> I am the Light of the World", - which is true fire, the Father of Lights, from whom every good thing that is given, comes, sending forth the light of his fire, and communicating it first to the Sun and the rest of the celestial bodies, and by these, as by mediating instruments, conveying that light into our fire. As, therefore, the spirits of darkness are stronger in the dark, so good spirits; which are Angels of Light, are augmented, not only by that light, which is Divine, of the Sun, and Celestial, but also by the Light of our Common fire."

Recommending that fire is the most sacred of all elements, he advises all worship and sacrifice be accompanied by it; though conceding that water, as the element of creation is the most powerful. Elemental comparisons are drawn between the Four Archangels and the Four Infernal Rivers: Fiery Phlegethon, Airy Cocytus, Watery Styx and Earthly Acheron/Ocheron [Agrippa, 1974:59]. Espousing the merits of the Kabbalah, especially the power of the 'Mirific word of God', Agrippa appears convinced that its source was ultimately Adam, Abraham or Moses, received from the 'Watcher' Angel Raziel. Later, he developed Neo-Platonic ideals, expressing Adamic philosophy synthesised with later 11th century Jewish derived Geomatria, remaining subject to further Angelic guidance in which God becomes both omnipresent and transcendent. Intriguingly, Agrippa [1974:236-242] posits the curiously unorthodox view that the material realm of Assiah is inhabited by spirits/fallen angels, fighting under their chiefs Zamiel and Lillith against the armies of Metatron and Sandalphon [Agrippa, 1974:236-242]. Naturally, the Church detected a dualist heresy within his work and he was hounded from one country to another until he eventually recanted all his works in later life [Seligman, 1997: 314].

Paracelsus (1493-1541CE) totally rejected the Galenic form of medicine as practised by Villanova, seeking more experimental forms that led him to develop a primitive homeopathy, ultimately fundamental to modern chemistry. His obsession with alchemy condemned him to wander Europe seeking empirical cures and the philosophers' stone, where his associations with Cunning-men, gypsies, wise-women, barbers, witches and vagabonds became legendary [Seligman, 1997:199].

Medieval obsession for the redemption of man's soul, angelology, eschatology and theology is beautifully reflected within the exoteric work of Dante's 'Divine Comedy', reminiscent of the ancient mysteries where salvation is achieved through the intervention of a psychopomp. Only when love replaces knowledge is he awarded his final transcendence, clearly demonstrating within this spiritual exegesis, that love is once more the key, in complete accordance with Ficino's view [Knight, 1978:87]. Combined with the search for the magical 'City of the Sun' or Utopia, where love as a 'divine' concept predominates, eminent men such as Thomas Moore, Campanella, Bruno and Dante were driven to seek it further, obfuscating the distinction between prayer and magic as formulae for activation of process of assimilation [Knight, 1978:108]. These men dared to seek the 'Truth'; casting off the 'rock of ages', they reached out to grasp the 'fire' of gnosis, changing forever the way we explore and express our relationship with the divine.

Pompanazzi (1462-1525) also stressed will and intent as determinatives for success, opposing them only on the precepts of Aristotelian limitations of effects over distance. His whole treatise attempts to justify Aristotle's disbelief in demons and angels, seeking natural causes for everything [Walker, 2000:110]. Many Protestants, including Erastus and Wier, in denying the existence of angels, ironically placed superstition at the hands of demons. Wier postulated the illusory effects of magic to be subjective, existing only in the imagination of the magician, whether for healing or exorcism. Del Rio went further still, declaring the scriptorial words used in charms and spells carry no inherent power, being chosen by Adam, not God. [Walker, 2000: 154-156]. With everything deemed delusional, and contemptuous of magic as an easy option, Francis Bacon advocated this piece of advice within his *'Historia vitae et Mortis'* in 1623, that one should:

> "…take opium, breathe cold air, smell fresh earth, eat garlic, avoid violent emotions, in order to promote excellent health, not only in body, but more importantly in spirit…" [Walker, 2000:199]

Curiously it was the alchemical obsession with spirit and its relation to the soul that held the vital key to the avoidance of any form of 'demonic' magic, for religious doctrine required the transcendence of the mind, the perceived seat of the soul in order to remain free of astral/demonic influences.

Of course astrology and heliocentricity were immensely significant to the Renaissance Mage, and most especially to Giordano Bruno (1548-

1600) who travelled Europe to proselytise his religious synthesis. The animistic elements of these beliefs were to eventually cost him his life for non repentant heresies and blasphemies. Primarily, the eventual charges against him specify a belief in metempsychosis, multiple worlds and for dealing in magics, which were really forbidden sciences. Always he was driven by the reference to the Sun as Demi-urge. From within a text of Asclepius, Hermes advises:

> "The Sun illuminates the other stars, not so much by the power of its light, as by its divinity and holiness and you should hold him, O Asclepius to be the second God - governing all things and spreading his light on all living beings of the world, both those which have souls and those which have not..."

Bruno advocated Copernican heliocentricity (erroneously) believing it to reveal the divine mysteries, therefore championing his own intensely religious calling [Yates, 1964:152-55]. This 'dualism' is also clearly reflected in the earlier passage of Agrippa regarding the Demi-urge. Moreover, Seligman [1997:126] speculates that the allegorical writings of Hermes Trismegistus, within the *'Tabula Smaragdina'*, are profoundly Gnostic. Certain sects of Gnostics worshipped the serpent of paradise that planted within man's heart the yearning for *'Prisca Sapientia.'* Thus the Ouroborous became an important alchemical emblem. It is also believed that this serpent is divided into light and dark, bound in matter together – pronouncing the axiomatic statement: *"One is all, by him is all, and for him is all. The serpent is one: he has two symbols (for) good and (for) bad..."* [Seligman, 1997:134].

A Dominican priest and master of mnemonics, Bruno freely promoted the texts of Asclepius, blending elements from his own Solar religion, Egyptian Hermetism and Judeo-Christianity. Some academics believe that the controversial 'God making' passages of 'Asclepius' are a later interpolation by its Latin translator, Apuleius (of the 'Golden Ass') [Yates, 1964:183-7]. If true, then this would leave the bulk of the *'Hermetic Corpus'* to be a religious, philosophical work. Ironically, the Nag Hammadi Coptic scrolls have authenticated 'the Asclepius' as ancient Egyptian in origin [Yates, 1964:431]. Certainly, the lack of coherent evidence utterly confused the Church during the 16th century, inducing cautious and closely monitored study.

Bruno moved across Europe, teaching where he could the works of Aristotle; but he was too often outspoken and opinionated. His freethinking views in support of the Arian heresy and the nature of the divine essence particularly that of the Holy Ghost, which he perceived as the World Soul, began his long courtship with the stake that would eventually seal his doom. His views concerning an immanent God, and a redeemable Devil, merely added insult to injury. Within England, sophisticated Humanists, focused on rhetoric and literary precision, gleaned from their study of original pre-annotated Greek texts, and uncorrupted by Arabic interpolations. An enraged and frustrated Bruno, on his (sub-rosa) mission to England in 1583 was forced into a battle of words with such Humanists; Bruno called them 'grammarian pedants' and 'blind, ignorant fools'; an attitude that did not endear him to the forces of the Counter- Reformation [Yates, 1964:160-8]. His support for Copernicus opened him to considerable ridicule. He managed to offend Calvinists, Lutherans, Catholics and the Humanists with equal aplomb. He was even excommunicated.

Nevertheless, Bruno believed in an infinite non-hierarchical universe, one that could be traversed via astral ascent and that exhibited experiential ubiquity. Everything in it was composed of the four elements suspended in aethyr or spirit. He balked at the ignorance of a belief in a system of fixed spheres within the heavens, even metaphorically. For him, magic and religion were indistinct. Central to Bruno's magic was archaic symbology. Favouring the Tau cross as the true cross, he believed that the Church had sanitized it, robbing it of its real power and potential as a talisman and a magical aid to achieving ecstasy. Surprisingly, he ignored the statutory but acceptable angelic forms offered within the Kabbalah, in favour of controversial Egyptian forms deemed 'demonic'. Supported by occult, animistic sympathies in a multitudinous free flowing universe, Bruno expressed ecstasy, his personal and highly experiential ascent to 'The One' [Yates, 1964:273].

He was burned in Rome and his ashes strewn into the Tiber in 1600; an act for which the Papacy recently expressed regret. Intriguingly, Bruno, like others before him, had sought to establish a Solar City or Temple, faced towards the setting Sun, where he believed the ancient Egyptian God forms could be restored [Yates, 1964:233]. In particular, his ideal model closely parallels Sir Thomas Moore's vision of 'Utopia', of dark brooding Gothic churches, lit only by tapers through which priests enter, gloriously bedecked in multi-hued bird feathers, reminiscent of peacocks, to teach and assist in the revelation of the divine mysteries. From descriptions it is clear that these priestly garments resemble the conjuring garments worn by ancient 'Magi'. Although Moore is known to have been a scrupulously pious and stalwart Christian, this 'vision' nevertheless evokes the temple rites of both ancient Egypt and Babylon.

Campanella (1568-1639CE), another to be condemned as a heretic, narrowly escaped death by feigning insanity. An advocate of astrological forms of magic, he is recorded as having performed acts of alleged 'necromancy' with Pope Urban VIII. In reality, these were attempts to avert disaster portended within a malign conjunction of Mars with Saturn [Walker, 2000:206]. Campanella's attempt to establish his 'City of the Sun' eventually became partially realised in the glorious court of the 'Sun

King' Louis XIV, whose birth he had forecast [Walker, 2000:236]. His model, gleaned from the heart of the *'Picatrix'* consisted of a city of rainbow hue, with a castle at its core containing the fruit of all generation, with four gates each facing the compass points, in honour of *'Adocentyn,'* God's lost city, built in myth by Hermes Trismegistus himself [Yates, 1964:370]. Campanella, like Bruno, had believed in a sentient world, and Asclepian theurgy. His death heralded the decline of Hermeticism. Casaubon's re-dating of the Hermetic Corpus to 1-2$^{nd}$ century CE and the advances in scientific research based on Aristotelian empiricism, led to a tremendous paradigm shift where 'magic' was no longer credible. Science followed seamlessly in its wake.

Less well known for his extra curricular activities is Isaac Newton, who studied alchemy throughout his life, producing a rather unique document, a commentary upon the *'Tabula Smaragdina,'* in which he explores the relevance of Hermes Trismegistus to it, especially with regard to the pairing of material opposites. Dobbs' [Merkal & Debus, 1988:182] argument rests on the cryptic text of the virtually incomprehensible 'Emerald Tablet', included in Newton's 17$^{th}$ century English here for elucidation:

> "Tis true without lying, certain & most true.
> That wch is below is like that wch is above & that wch is above is like yt wch is below to do ye miracles of one only thing.
> And as all things have been & arose from one by ye mediation of one: so all things have their birth from this one thing by adaptation, The Sun is its father, the Moon its mother, the wind hath carried the seed in its belly, the earth is its nourse.
> The father of all perfection in ye whole world is here.
> Its force or power is entire if it be converted into earth.

Separate thou ye earth from ye fire, ye subtile from the gross sweetly wth great indoustry.

It ascends from ye earth to ye heaven & again it descends to ye earth & receives ye

force of all things superior & inferior.

By this means you shall have ye glory of ye whole world & thereby all obscurity shall fly from you.

Its force is above all force, ffor it vanquishes every subtile thing & penetrates every solid thing.

So was ye world created.

From this are & do come admirable adaptations whereof ye means (Or process) is here in this.

Hence I am called Hermes Trismegist, having the three parts of ye philosophy of ye whole world.

That wch I have said of ye operation of ye Sun is accomplished and ended."

This activating spirit, symbolised by Hermes, he called 'a fermental virtue', which revealed to him the generating (Neo-Platonic) principle as divine and all the secrets of creation, viz., that matter arose from the primeval depths of chaos. Moreover, motivated by accusations of atheism inherent within the mechanical Cartesian universe, he strove to prove the animating principle and presence of the divine - of spirit within matter [*ibid.*]. This is clearly evidenced within Newton's work where he refers to the animistic principle 'having dominion' within the animal, vegetable and mineral kingdoms. Thorndike [1934:37] finds support for this controversy in another commentary, possibly written by Ortolanus in the 11th century who also compares the alchemical process with the creation of the world. Dobbs [Merkal & Debus, 1988:187] interprets this to confirm Newton's (Arian) heretical belief in Christ and God entering a 'unity of Dominion' (consubstantial with God), placing Christ as the demi-urge. Not surprisingly, the Church advocated only those forms that included the spiritual aspirations of Neo-Platonism combined with the Aristotelian belief in natural causes for 'magical' activity. At the heart of Hermetic study was the search for redemption, lost at the 'fall', a truly alchemical path of transformation, and one subject to severe restrictions. Alchemists claimed that knowledge direct from the angels was the only truth.

Russell [1972:143] argues that the shift towards 'Neo-Platonic' based magical ideology, stressing the relationship between sympathy and antipathy, contrasting with the previous Aristotelian system of contact-action (cause and effect), promoted its perception as 'demonic'. Fludd (1574-1637), an alleged Rosicrucian philosopher, if not an actual member chose to ignore the dating of the Hermetic texts by Casaubon and continued to study them; he naturally defended the system of sympathy and antipathy with his famous 'weapon salve' treatment to effect cures. Fludd, obsessed with the Neo-Platonic 'World Soul' and 'Hermeticism,' hungrily absorbed the broader medieval ensemble, including a synthesis of Christian and Jewish ideology that remained distinct from 'Hermetism' (the original Alexandrian Corpus of writings attributed to Hermes Trismegistus, somewhat Gnostic in its ideologies), promoting his angelic Kabbalah as a way of elevating man through the 'Great Chain of Being' [Godwin, 1979:10-12].

Such a heady mix generated earnest enquiry into both empiricism and mysticism. Henry [1997: 42] supports the view that the Renaissance Magi, inspired by the Neo-Platonism inherent within the Hermetic Corpus promoted 'natural magic,' leading to the scientific revolution in which answers to occult phenomena led to absorption of core elements within its praxes. Mathematical philosophy or 'natural magic' influenced Kepler in his study of astronomy, and whose conclusions were in opposition to Fludd's metaphysical view of the universe. Ironically both views are based within platonic ideology. Gradually, 'natural magic' and alchemy developed into physics and chemistry, ultimately combining Aristotelian 'evident cause' with Neo-Platonic 'manifest qualities,' seen and unseen forces at work within, around and through the grand design of the divine Creatrix [*ibid.* 52-53]. Thomas [1971:223] postulates three types of magic extant during the Renaissance:

- Natural – exploitation of occult properties of the elemental world.
- Celestial – involving the influence of the Stars.
- Ceremonial – an appeal for aid to spiritual beings, aided by symbols, incantations and the power of will and intent of the individual.

Not surprisingly, as all three were subject to 'demonic' classification, the Church advocated only those forms that included the spiritual aspirations of Neo-Platonism combined with the Aristotelian belief in natural causes for 'magical' activity.

During the Interregnum (Commonwealth) many translations into the vernacular, of Hermetic and alchemical texts saturated with pious devotion, evinced their study, but more importantly, their survival. Astrologer/Magicians also had to be mindful of astral determinism, ever incompatible with the Church's view of free will and divine providence. This was accomplished with the compromise that though the stars influenced the body, the soul, will and intellect remained free. Furthermore, all misfortune was God's will for sin, not fate. Flint [1991:40] believes that Pythagorean principles, revealed in the harmony of the spheres, promoted the huge response of psalm singing to please God, and though their music be drawn closer to the divine.

The inclusion of this vast and wide ranging subject (much of it beyond the remit of this modest study) facilitates an awareness of an acceptance by the Church of specialised forms of 'high' magic, which in reality differed very little from those of 'low' magic; technically the difference was often one of religious ideals, cleverly constructed within the praxes of the Renaissance Magus to ensure his own security. Yates [1964:81] adds that pneumatics, incantation and astrological observance, were central to both forms of magic. Although texts concerning the cosmological treatise of Asclepius, regarding the soul, the divine and the formation of the worlds were banned during the Renaissance; the acceptance by the Church of Neo-Platonism, particularly the pious references to 'Our Father' and of Hermeticism, is seen by Yates in her seminal work, as the culmination of the history of religion [1964:83].

## Conclusion

Bonser [1963:117] believes that despite weak and missing links, magic remains traceable from the earliest Indo-European forms, surviving into modern times, clearly visible within the body of Catholicism. Some of the oldest classical forms employing the use of signatures and correspondences vital to rituals of Renaissance Magi, were held in mutual esteem by 'Witches', 'Leeches' and 'Cunning-folk,' all or none of whom may have been in ignorance of their 'Platonic' overtones. Activities of Cunning-men and women parallel the pursuits and methodology of the Magus, separated only by the philosophy of the latter and his desire driven by scientific curiosity to understand how magic worked. As empirics, the Cunning-folk were satisfied that it did, they did not need anything more from their magic or their cures instinctively understanding that "all is one." Morally, there is little difference between them. All employed equal use of sympathetic and antipathic magic, charms, herbs, talismans, amulets, astrological correspondences, rhymes and conjurations through varying degrees of sophistication. Intellectual concepts prevalent within the activities of the Magi were generally absent from those of the Cunning-folk, whose concerns were normally more physical and immediate. Though all claimed to be practicing 'natural' magic, in truth, elements of 'demonic' magic can be discerned within all practices.

Seventeenth century rationalism had utterly rejected occult variables and dogma seeking scientific empiricism. As science evolved from the freedom to study the plethora of intellectual information instigated by the Christianisation of the Hermetic Texts by Ficino, this catalyst of stimulation fed the enquiring mind to its full fruition. John Henry [1997:43] sees this understanding of nature as the crux of the Scientific Revolution, the magical elements (modus operandi) of which became absorbed into natural philosophy as a legacy to 18$^{th}$ century science. Groundbreaking works of many spirited Renaissance men led to advances in pharmacy, chemistry, optics, mathematics, mechanics and physics, whose emerging concepts were actively encouraged by the Church anxious to stem the tide of superstition and ignorance. Ironically, it was the belief in the natural power and magic within the forces of nature that instigated this search for 'truth.' This search for God, for *'gnosis'*, for *'Prisci Theologi'* and *'Prisca Sapientia,'* ultimately led to Descartes' (1597-1650) view of a mechanistic universe, though Newton's (1642-1727) 'Occultism' smoothed its edges, revealing the forces of nature yet again to triumph in the laws of the emergent 'Natural Sciences'. And thus the occult virtues of Plato's 'World soul' survived Cartesian rationalism fundamental to modern magical practices including the manufacture of talismans, absent healings, exorcisms, bindings and banishings.

Fludd's metaphysical ideas transcended the boundaries of science surviving as remnants of less tangible forms of demonic magic subjugated within a religious philosophy known as the Rosicrucian System. Grant [1996:203] asserts that Renaissance magic freed 'natural' philosophy from the shackles of Aristotelian Scholasticism, leaving empiricists free to explore endless possibilities and wonders of a now limitless universe. In the final analysis, all magic was absorbed into science as it unified opposing views held alternately by Aristotelian, 'causal' scientists and Neo-Platonic 'effectual' scientists, as they sought illumination of manifest qualities of Nature's (God's) laws. Cavandish [1990:96] postulates that in reality, little difference existed between high magic, deemed to be philosophical and cerebral, also pretentious and theatrical, and low magic, the 'simpler' magic of the Cunning-folk; the religious aspect involved in the former was generally absent in the latter [Yates,1964:81]. Ultimately though, man's (God-given) free will, his driving force as a reflection of the Will of God- known magically as 'True Will', merged with his intention giving him a causation of purpose, ensuring the triumph of magic into and through the 'age of reason,' surviving the Scientific Revolution in his continuing search for unity and order (most prevalent within Aleister Crowley's 'Thelema').

Religion had been the prime mover in this search to know and experience the divine 'Truth' and one's ultimate identity within it, to understand the mechanics of a created universe and man's own place within it; truly the micro-cosm within the macro-cosm. Science had been servant to its old enemy in spite of itself. Allowing Knight [1978:105] to make this succinct closing statement, the historiographical parameters through which all ideas eventually synthesised are given unparalleled clarity:

- Religion - knowledge of divinity.
- Science - knowledge of the mechanics of creation.
- Magic - synthesis/confusion between the two.

## Bibliography:

Agrippa, H.C. 1974 (1531) *'Philosophy of Natural Magic.'* New Jersey, Uni. Books Inc.

Burnett, C. 1996 *'Magic and Divination in the Middle Ages: Texts and Techniques in the Islamic and Christian Worlds.'* G.B., Ashgate Pub. Ltd.

Cavandish, R. 1990 *'A History of Magic.'* England, Arkana.

Copenhaver, B. 1988 *'Hermes Trismegistus; Proclus and the Question of a Philosophy of Magic in The Renaissance'*, in Merkel, I. And Debus, A.G. (ed.) *'Hermeticism and the Renaissance.'* London, Ass. Uni. Press, Pp. 79-105.

Dobbs, B.J.T. 1988 *'Newton's Commentary on The Emerald Tablet of Hermes Trismegistus: Its Scientific and Theological Significance'*, in Merkel, I And Debus, A.G. (Ed) *'Hermeticism And the Renaissance.'* London, Ass. Uni. Press, Pp. 182-191.

Eliade, M. (Ed.) 1987 *'Encyclopoedia of Religion.'* New York, Macmillan Press, Vol. 6, Pp. 293-302. & Vol. 9, Pp.81-115.

Flint, V. 1991 *'The Rise of Magic in Early Medieval Europe.'* New Jersey, Princeton Uni. Press.

Godwin, J. 1979 *'Robert Fludd.'* Boulder, Shambhala Press.

Grant, E. 1996 *'Foundations of Modern Science in the Middle Ages.'* Cambridge Uni. Press.

Henry, J. 1997 *'The Scientific Revolution and the Origins of Early Modern Science.'* New York, Macmillan Press.

Knight, G. 1978 *'A History of White Magic.'* Oxford, Mowbray & Co. Ltd.

Russell, J.B. 1972 *'Witchcraft in the Middle Ages.'* Cornell Uni. Press.

Seligman, K. 1997 *'Magic in the Middle Ages.'* USA. Pantheon Books.

Thomas, K. 1971 *'Religion and the Decline of Magic.'* G.B., Redwood Press Ltd.

Thorndike, L. 1934 *History of Magic and Experimental Science.'* Vol. Iii. N.Y., Columbia Uni. Press.

Walker, D.P. 2000 *'Spiritual and Demonic Magic.'* Glous. Sutton Publishing.

Yamauchi, E. 1973 *'Pre-Christian Gnosticism.'* Suffolk. Chaucer Press.

Yates, F.G. 1964 *'Giordano Bruno and the Hermetic Tradition.'* London, Routledge and Keegan Paul Ltd.

Toohey, Sue. 2005 *'The Influence of Marsilio Ficino'* www.skyscript.co.uk

Hooker, Richard. (trans) 1994 *'Oration on The Dignity of Man'* www.wsu.edu:8080/~dee/REN/PICO.HTM

# Section Two

# 5

# It's all in a Name: An Ancient Heresy

"How art thou fallen from heaven, 'Hel-el ben Shahar'…"
Isaiah, 14:12

Nomenclature can be a minefield for the unwary, especially when connected to the perennially thorny realms of biblical exegesis. The modern perception of 'Lucifer' sprang enigmatically from the above passage in Isaiah, 14:12 and has ever since presented a not easily resolvable and hotly disputed theological debate. Millennia of agenda filled obfuscation compounded by mis-translation and unsubstantiated interpretations have rendered considerable quantities of research virtually worthless. Variant spellings of the name i.e. Heylel, Helal, Helil, Sahar, Shachar, et cetera have been imaginatively constructed to support tenuous etymological associations that underpin one theory after another reliant upon mythological, astronomical or historical modalities. However, no such agenda is herein expressed; my purpose is simply to present a historiography from which others may then at least formulate an informed opinion.

Many of these theories are not wrong, per se, just misleading, being very much dependant upon the views of the researcher and the parameters of their enquiries. Academia is too often subjective, though it has to be stated, there is no definitive translation upon which to even begin an exploratory interpretation, either literally or metaphorically; so oblique were the enigmatic rantings of our biblical poet and prophet Isaiah. However, the primary task of any researcher should always be – context; an exacting premise proposed within this summative and detailed analysis of the world surrounding this biblical priest, known astronomy, then and since, and myths pertinent to them. My analyses will naturally be open to further scrutiny, though this challenge to perceived opinion will hopefully affirm that myths are eclectic, superlative, multi-complex and whose all encompassing applications confirm how their planetary associations do not preclude other possibilities.

In the Myths of the Cedars of Lebanon,[1] the writer asserts how 'Shahar' as the Canaanite God of the Rising Sun is resurrected each morning from the Cedar Gate/Vagina of the Great Mother, who is of course the 'Whore' of Babylon, Ishtar, represented and symbolised by the planet, Venus. The 'Gate' refers to the magnificent Ishtar Gate, the Royal Lion gate re-built in her honour by the Babylonians in the 7th century BCE with a dedication by King Nebuchadnezzar. Venus is however, more popularly linked with the epithet, 'Evening Star', and this is where further complication opens up the playing field. She shares connections to the 'Morning Star' along with Mercury, the Moon, Jupiter and Mars. [2] Mercury waxes as a *'Matutine'* (morning/day) 'star' and wanes as a *'Vespertine'* (evening/night) 'star'. The Moon waxes as an evening star, waning as a morning star, which apparently infers Mercury as solar in Matutine mode, holding the *'Promethean'* qualities of vigour and evolution; and lunar in Vespertine mode, maintaining the less progressive qualities of a deliberate and conservative *'Epimethius'* (sic), his 'brother' and co-creator of the human race.[3]

Initially, the Babylonians believed the Morning and Evening stars were two separate celestial objects, so did the Greeks, naming one for

Hermes, the other for Apollo. Moreover, Mercury even glows red as the evening star, resembling Mars (naturally its barren surface actually more easily resembles that of the Moon, but ancient astronomers could not have known this). Hermes was a Greek deity adopted by the Romans as Mercury and after whom the planet associated with him was later named. According to Pliny (23-79CE), Mercury (the planet) was also referred to as Apollo who normally though not exclusively represented the Sun. [4] Speculative writers [*ibid.*] assert that 'Her'- stems from Hor-us (also 'Sun' God), and 'mes'- is from the Egyptian 'to draw forth'; so the name Hermes could mean son/offspring of Horus. Hermes, an early pastoral God in Arcadia, embodied the qualities of fertility, offering protection to cattle and sheep. An epithet 'Ram-bearer' suggests a close affiliation with Pan and Dionysus. He later developed other qualities, appropriate to the needs of an evolving populace, including chthonic guide of souls, psychopomp, conductor of dreams and messenger of the gods; libations were customarily offered to him before retiring. A popular patron of travellers, he also acquired guardianship of treasure (hence the favoured God of merchants and thieves). Ultimately, his alliance with Thoth, the Egyptian God of wisdom resulted in the dedication of Greek pseudo-gnostic texts (c 150BCE-215BC) as 'Hermetic.'

Having briefly explained planetary aspects and their relevancies to certain deific forms, we need to retreat further into the 8th century BCE in order to explore the context of Isaiah's world. Here we discover a fractured, disparate loosely affiliated group of tribal city-states, separated into the Northern and Southern kingdoms of Israel and Judah, still bereft of an established unifying religion. Many 'Jews' (not a name they yet referred to themselves by, being 'of the tribe of' Levi, Israel, Benjamin, Dan et cetera) continued to worship Pagan, tribal gods, all variations of the Baals and Asherahs of the Canaanites; having only the Law to bind them. It is important to remember that 'The Covenant,' is a Law document, a legal agreement between a tribal God and His (my emphasis) 'chosen' people. This stricture is rigorously imposed via the directives of the Prophets, who as the 'mouthpiece' of God acted as the conscience of the King and his people.

The role of the prophet in the ancient world was to deal with the philosophical issue of *Destiny*. Prophecy, in biblical times, was not about prediction as we understand it today. It expressed Karma, true karma, in the sense of immediate retribution for any and all transgressions against this 'Law.' God's Law was the *'axis mundi'* around which these disparate Tribes ran their lives. Punishment was swift and (perceived as) just. Good Kings adhered to the wisdom of their 'prophets' expounded as the literal 'word' of God, a divine check on ambitious monarchs. But the power-politic was strictly based on terra-firma. The priest's role was to undermine the King, to keep him humble before God's Word and the Law, should they ever seek to rise above it; only God was deemed perfect. It is no coincidence that these prophets were all priests of the religious sect that eventually complied and redacted the Torah - The 'Book of the Law' upon which was based all subsequent biblical codices.

Assyria, eager to extend its imperial power had moved into Israel in the north, absorbing forever the fabled 10 'lost tribes'; in truth, a great many of these migrated south, others re-settled and merged with the peoples of Samaria. Squeezed between Phoenicia (Canaan) to the west and Babylon to the east, the southern Kingdom of Judah had much to fear. Babylon, under Nebuchadnezzar finally conquered Palestine, moving into Judah, extricating elite, wealthy citizens to Babylon c 597BCE. These were to return from their exile barely 60 years later c539BCE (all dates are approximate) as the Medes (Persians) pushed into Babylon (fallen temporarily to Assyria), freeing all former evacuees. In their despair, the people of Babylon had called for help to Cyrus of Persia, who promised to restore their Cult of Marduk, the Supreme God at that time. [5] Cyrus, in order to retain political control over his empire, practised religious tolerance, encouraging homogenous expression. In reality, however, Judah remained a Persian satrap until the conquest of Alexander the Great in 333BCE.

Exilic priests/prophets, influenced by power, by wealth and the prestige of their Babylonian counterparts, began moves to extend control of both secular and religious activities. In fact the whole religious schemata, including legends of the flood, creation, manticism, mythology et cetera, were all extrapolated by this elite faction during this period of exile. Pre-exilic 'Jews', served by the Levite priesthood ('shamanic' in nature), believed in an anthropomorphic, capricious, tribal God who demanded nothing short of absolute obedience. This contrasted considerably with post-exilic migrants tainted by perceived 'corruptions' of a more formalised, influential priesthood now headed by a developing Sadducee sect. These latter priests usurped the former controlling status of their predecessors, dissolving forever their vice-like grip on the 'chosen people'. It was here that their God acquired his nebulous omniscience.

Temple theocracy developed in line with the Babylonian and Persian ideals, providing a lucrative trade in offerings, sacrifices, tithes, social control and the means and method of worship; effectively enforcing the inevitable elevation of Yahweh as sole God. It forever banished the role and purpose of the prophet. Most scholars believe 'The Torah' to have been compiled at this time from fragments of oral traditions and various writings composed in the main part within the previous 200 years; speculation still abounds how much older even the primary sections of the Bible really are, but few would push it past these dates. The recording of History and Law now fell to Sadducee descendants of the Zadokite priesthood of the House of David, a separate tradition entirely from the Levite priesthood of the Exodus traditions of Moses. Ironically, it was under their direction that the splendidly impressive Ishtar Gate and Ziggurats of Babylon provided an inspirational ground-plan for re-building the second Temple (tired of endless rebellions; Babylonians had destroyed the 1st Temple of Solomon c587 BCE).[6]

The Book of Isaiah offers revealing insights into his world; he rails against the corruption of his race, he berates all who obsess after material wealth and power, against magics and treasure seekers of the East. He calls to his people for a return to the way of God as prescribed by 'The Covenant.' Most of all, his interdictions are against valueless gods (2:18) and of El's superiority over them (Isaiah's style is specifically identified by scholars as Elohist rather than Yahwistic, although elements of Yahwist worship are evident in Judah from the brief unification of northern and southern tribes under David in the 10th century BCE). God's wrath will manifest in tyranny of mind, body and soul. Confusion and anarchy will ensue in the wake of karma. Again and again, Isaiah condemns the Kings of Syria and Assyria for their attacks upon Israel and Judah. *"I shall make an accounting for the fruitage of the insolence of the heart of the King of Assyria and for the self-importance of his loftiness of eyes"* (10:12 NWT). The Assyrian King is posed as the oppressor in the mold of Egypt [chp. 10:24], whom God (El) will overcome (in chp. 10:26), *"...and the high ones themselves become low"* (10:37 NWT). However, he goes on to exclaim how God will yet extend his hand for a second time to his people, his wayward flock, he will not abandon them, if only they surrender once more to Him, with faith, trust and belief. Only then will he restore all remnants, all the lost tribes from all four corners of the Earth. This love will abate his anger and hostilities will cease.

In chapter 13:2, Isaiah finally turns his attention to Babylon, and verse 13:10 expresses the power of 'El' over the light emanating from the heavens, the Sun, the Moon and all the starry constellations. Yet these clear references to celestial objects are described unambiguously, using terms reflecting precisely the author's poetic imagery; 'kockab,' 'aster,' 'stellar,' in Hebrew, Greek and Latin Bibles respectively. This absolutely negates argument for any association of 'Hel-el ben Shahar' in 14:12 founded in astronomy. His intention here is *something else* entirely. In speaking of the desolation of Babylon by the Medes in chp. 13:22, he refers to it distinctly as she; *"And the season for Her is near, to come, and Her days themselves will not be postponed."* All pre-exilic books in the Bible have post-exilic editing. Additions, interpolations and annotations update and renovate data as later revisionists deemed appropriate; the clear reference to Cyrus as King of the Medes and 'Cyrus the Great' typifies this. Isaiah *could not* have known these details in his own time. In chp.14:3-11, Isaiah directs his people to taunt their former captives with the might of God (El), in bringing down those who would test His strength and Will, upholding His ability to render all things to His desire. No earthly King is equal to His power. Their pride is humbled before such a display; how easily He banishes them from the heights of power to the depths of disgrace.

Another epithet for *'Elyon'* is *'El Shaddai'* - Shining God of the Mountain. Zaphon means north in Hebrew and refers to the location of the Holy mountain of God and is mentioned, not in a geographic sense, but as a mythopoetical allusion to a sacred place of worship, a 'high place' (term refers to Jerusalem four times in Old Testament.). Heaven and Sheol are poetic terms to artfully expose the extremes of this pronouncement. There was no afterlife or heavenly existence; 'Heaven' was reserved for God alone. God's messianic kingdom was on Earth. Sheol, not a hell but a melancholic shadowy existence of the dead was seen as the end of His grace. It must be remembered that Hebraic peoples believed God punished the wicked in life, (passing judgement even onto future generations), *not* in death; both the righteous and unrighteous resided together in Sheol.

Not until the later apocalyptical texts of Enoch does Sheol become a place of punishment and judgement. Powerful poetic metaphors speak widely of a material realm; no usurping God is implied. Rather, the King of Babylon is contemptuously portrayed as dazzling heir to a corrupt and glamorous Kingdom, ruled in the name of the Great Whore – Ishtar, Bride and Mother of God. He, the Bright Light of Dawn, is 'son', 'born of' the Morning Star – Venus, the despised symbol of Babylon itself. She is not named, but the inference is clear from the context, not only of this chapter within Isaiah as a Book, but from the Book within the whole Codex. Chapter 14:16 subsequently clarifies this association with a mortal King rather than a God: *"Is this the man that was agitating the earth, that was making the Kingdoms rock?'. . . 'that opened not the house of his prisoners"* (14:17). The remainder of Isaiah 14, reiterates the wrath of God upon Babylon for its hubris.

A King ruling through aegis of a goddess is the worst slight possible against Isaiah's God (El), thus he would be perceived as setting himself higher than El. In fact, all 'Kings' who sought to take His land in conquest were accused of great pride and in chp. 15-17 Isaiah makes it perfectly clear how Moab, Phillistia and Damascus will all suffer the fate of Babylon, the Glory of the East and precious Jewel in the Pagan crown. Each chapter is a pronouncement against abjurers, sinners and oppressors of the 'chosen' people; Egypt, Ethiopia et cetera, will all be laid waste. Each must succumb to the Will of God, or perish. The message is clear and uncompromising. It is also prudent to understand how the entire construction of the Bible rests upon destruction of hostile nations under the lineage of David and restoration of a holy state according to God's original plan as agreed under the Law. No more, no less.

Contemporary exegesis[7] believes that although the Bible reflects less than 5% (an intellectual elite in fact) of the social and ideological beliefs of the Hebraic peoples, it does reflect their struggle to control, maintain and impose their subjective religious and political reforms upon them. It therefore offers a more earthly cause, (14:12) concurrent with all the above, these not being mutually exclusive. Israel (northern kingdoms) and Judah (southern kingdoms) were not united and fought each other as readily as other invaders. The northern confederates sought religious freedom from the Jerusalem faction of the Temple and the line of David (Israel was founded on the Yahwist/Moses legacy of the Exodus). Such interior political strife exposed them to their enemies. Isaiah urged them to unite under One God to defeat them, and win again His Grace. This exposes the rivalry of two tribal gods, Yahweh, the Storm God and El Elyon God Most High of the heavens that eventually became glossed over to preserve a deception of Monotheism.

Kings of Israel occasionally sought coalitions with Syria against Assyria despite the period of conflict between the priests of 'Baal' and those of Yahweh. Baal is however, a generic title, a prefix for Lord and there were several 'Baal's overall, one of whom could easily have been Yahweh himself. He certainly shares many attributes of Hadad in particular as a son of El (also generic, therefore quite problematic). However, a curious strand of folklore may link both Baal Hadad (Canaanite) and Yahweh (Hebraic) together; both are known to be storm gods. The coastal Phoenicians (Canaanites) were known masters of the purple/blue dye extracted from the shell of a sea mollusc, which as merchants they exported all over the Mediterranean. Only this single colour, by stringent law may legitimately be employed to create the strands of the Prayer shawls worn by the priests and Rabbis even today. It is said to represent the colour of the sky, especially during a storm, as a symbol of their High God.

During the reign of the Assyrian King, Tigleth-Pilesar, the Israelite King Pekah joined forces with King Rezon of Syria against King Ahaz of Judah (Isaiah, 7:1-14) in 734BCE, in an attempt to force him into a coalition against Assyria. But, in doing so he ignored the warnings of Isaiah, who advocated caution, trusting to the Will of God. Ahaz appealed instead to Tigleth-Pilesar for assistance, paying him tribute to stem an invasion. In this Isaiah saw a direct conflict with God's plan; this eventually led to the annexation of Israel by Tigleth-Pilesar, and it became a client Kingdom when it later fell in 722/1. Some scholars therefore suggest the curious passage 14:12 refers to a rant against the hubris of his own King, while others insist the rant is directed against King Pekah of Israel. Fleeing Levitical prophets and priests migrated into the south which had an enormous impact upon the growth of Yahwistic traditions.

During this fractious period, a boy King Josiah of Judah implemented the newly 'discovered' section of the law book (later compiled within Deuteronomy) in 622 BCE. From this a directive was implemented against 'High' places, the local shrines, altars and sanctuaries, instigating an iconoclastic purge within the Temple itself. This book represents a fusing of polarised religious practices of both northern and southern kingdoms, establishing a single sanctioned place of worship to a single God – The Jerusalem Temple. In spite of this, Yahweh was not recognised as sole God until well into the 3rd century BCE, immediately prior to the apocalyptical writings in which the siblings of Yahweh become demoted to the mere status of angels, and where Anath and Asherah, spouse and Mother disappear (though remain within the Kabbalah as Shekinah and Matronit). Yahweh finally absorbed all the qualities and titles and associations of his Father, El Elyon/El Shaddai. Of course, Assyrian power eventually waned as Babylon's star rose again to defeat Assyria, Egypt and Syria before moving on Judah, decimating the Kingdom of David. For this heinous act was reserved the bitterest of tirades by later biblical redactors, embellishing the original 'prophecies' of Isaiah.

Certainly, 2nd Isaiah (40-55) denounces the heathen hedonism of Babylon, its profligate gods and immoral religion. Hostile negative psalms record their anguish in exile and the origins of a rhetorical history, coloured by retrospective hindsight. Many revisions transform the message of each book into that of the whole Bible not fully collated until sometime between 2nd century BCE and 1st century BCE. Its proscriptions are against the near future for acts of the present or past. The entire theology is one of guidance for man in order to live in harmony with his God. Many books are pseudo-graphical, over-layered and compiled to emphasise and clarify specific issues. Isaiah spans a period of 250 years, encompassing the conquests of three empires; chapters 1-12 concern Judgement and Hope for Zion; 13-23 (1-23 = 1st Isaiah) are Oracles against foreign nations. Salvation occurs only via obedience to the Word!

Academic study of the Bible allows us to correct bias presentation in order that we may achieve a realistic perspective of the life and times of its original exponents. This lengthy though essential excursion into the biblical world asserts a relevance for the book of Isaiah, who having witnessed the fall of Israel to Assyria (c722/1) penned his infamous polemic (chapters 13-15), beguiling many with its ambiguity ever since. In conclusion, it seems scholarship remains divided: some believe that he refers to the toppling of a mortal King, others to the fall of a God. Within the context of history, politics and religion, all of these options must be considered credible.

Due to a perceived association of the reference in Isaiah to Lucifer (and therefore the 'Devil' by common default), this passage has since been erroneously expressed ad finitum by many who are by no means all fundamentalists. Examination of influences prevailing upon various scholars, theologians and historians throughout the ancient world may assist us to discover the origin of this misappropriation, where such external factors may even contribute to the true apprehension of this title. Written in Hebrew, the phrase *'Hel-el ben Shahar'* translates rather awkwardly as: 'Bright One, son of Dawn's Light', but more succinctly as 'Light of the Rising Sun'. It must be stressed however, there is no mention in the original (Masoretic) text of the Hebrew word - *'Kochab,'* meaning 'star' within this phrase. Hel-el is also problematic, we simply cannot be certain what it means, even a Hebrew dictionary tentatively expresses it as a derivative of the stem - Helal, meaning: to clear, to shine, to make a show, to boast, to rave, to be foolish, to celebrate, to mislead and to stultify; AV translators add: to rage, madness, to sing praises and even vapid logic (a mystery). [8] Therefore, it could literally mean 'Light of the Rising Sun', coterminous with Ra-Horakte/Khephre; it could also read metaphorically as 'Powerful son of Glory/Magnitude.'

G.D. Bouw, in his paper on Biblical Astronomy [9] postulates that the Greek word Helios becomes transposed into German as 'Hellen', from which 'helder' derives, meaning 'clear' or 'shiny'. Though he adds, there is a sense of blinding, in the sense of a covered 'hell', a place of darkness, a place far from God. Furthermore, he asserts that 'helel' entered the English Bible as 'hell' - a covered place [*ibid.*]. Interestingly, we find Hades/Hawides/Aides, as the eldest son of Kronos and ruler of Greek Underworld of the Dead, means 'blind' or half seeing. This mystery of the 'Lord of Light' as the 'Lord of Darkness,' has served to fuel fires of an association with a fictional Satan, providing several imaginative speculations relating to the more obscure interpretations for 'Helel'. 'Helel' can therefore mean anything from a Shining 'God' in a positive sense to a God of Hell in a negative sense. Bouw [*ibid.*] discusses H.T Gaster's claim that Shachar (sic) and Helel are one and the same due to their relationships with the (assumed) 'Morning Star'. Yet one is not synonymous with the other, one is 'drawn' from the other, an extension, rather than a form of; son of, or light of the dawn - not the dawn! They may both have associations with the 'Morning', but in entirely different ways. Furthermore, Bouw quotes Hislop [*ibid.*] who concludes that the name (believing it to be a proper noun) 'Helel' is cognate with 'Elelus,' one of the epithets for Bacchus, meaning to bring light, to irradiate, supporting the association with Lucifer as 'Lightbearer'.

This extremely interesting correlation is valid in spite of the writer's intentional pejorative sense. In the same article, Hislop notes how in the myth of 'Phaeton', son of the Sun and Klymene, a mortal woman, also known as a Titan, is referred to metaphorically as Aurora (dawn) viz: woman 'birthing' the Light. Herein is suggested a true comprehension of Lucifer as the Son of the Morning, the 'Enlightener' of mortal souls. According to the '*Pancarpium Marianum*' (chpt. 41 pp171-172), the Virgin of Rome is also given the title - Aurora, meaning pregnant with Light, the Enlightener of the World. [10] This interpretation is clearly the one implied by Jerome in the Vulgate Bible when he substituted 'Lucifer', inferring fallen or false light, as compared to the risen/true light of the Christ. Bearing this in mind, it becomes clear how carefully we must use original Hebrew sources.

Hislop continues to elucidate the role of 'saviour/son' and his 'bride/mother/consort' within mystery religions, discovering how Horace (65-8 BCE) equates '*Phaeton*' with '*Janus*' as the '*Pater Matutinus*' (Father of the Morning). '*Matutinus*' as correlate of '*Matuta*,' goddess of the Morning, makes Janus his own son! (of the morning). Pliny in his '*Natural History*'

(50CE) also refers to the (wandering) star of Venus rising in the east, named *'Lucifer'* as a second Sun hastening the day. When setting in the west, she (Venus) is named *'Vesper'* [*ibid*.]. This knowledge, attributed to Pythagoras is only realised almost three hundred years after the historical period of Isaiah. In fact it must be understood that the Romans of Pliny's time, although aware of 'Venus' the Planet, appearing in the morning and evening as a celestial object, were prone to make free associations of titles and epithets, shared by many gods and goddesses. Venus was likened to Juno and Isis in Her aspect of 'Mother of the Gods' and bestower of fertility and generation. Ino (often confused with Juno) is similarly identified as *'Matuta'* after she and her son changed into sea divinities.

Ovid (43BCE-18CE) records how *'Matuta'* became a common name for *'Leukothea,'* meaning firstly, to set on fire or 'to light', and secondly to 'glean'. This quality links her to the star *'Spica'* (Virgo and Ishtar), fertility goddesses of grain and generation. So again, a virgin gives birth to a son, Lucifer, who assumes the title of the Sun - 'Like the Sun' - 'Likened to God' - or 'He who is as God' [*ibid*.], all ambiguous epithets for a 4th century Church Father seeking to present the truth of Lucifer as the false and deceiving light. However, Leland connects *'Leukothea'* (the pale-one) to Venus as 'Morning Star,' and as Mother of the 'Light of the Day'. Moreover, he shares this belief with that of the Etruscans who understood Mater Matuta, the Mother of the Dawn (light) to be none other than Venus as the Morning Star. Tertullian also records a possible early form of this name found in the Etruscan Venus - *'Murtia'*. [11] In fact, all fertility gods are sons/lovers of the all mother - Alma Mater. His lightening seed falls to earth to penetrate and fertilize her; he rises from his mother the seed and progeny of himself, the Shining One of the Morning Star. In relating the Cedar Myths [12] it is revealed how the Moon goddess, named *'Lebannah'* (Levanah) has an epithet - 'She that is White' (the Pale-faced-One) linking her again to the *'Shekinah,'* the bride of God.

Throughout the biblical world, both Sun and Moon are cosmologically represented by the union of divine couples: Anath & Baal, Artemis and Apollo, Ishtar and Tammuz, Solomon and the Shekinah, even El and Asherah. Cedar poles dedicated to Asherah were erected within the oak groves of El. Asherah/ Ishtar/Anath were all Queens of Heaven, the stars, the Earth and the Seas, encompassing all earthly and celestial phenomena except the Sun, which was reserved wholly for the son of El. She was awarded many epithets relating to her roles as *'Stella Matutina'*, *'Stella Maris'* et cetera, all symbolising the power of manifest light, His light expressed through Her. Origen, when composing the Greek Septuagint, records the phrase referring to the lineage of Jesus within Revelation 22:16 as: *'ho aster, ho lampros, ho prwinos'*; this became written up as *'Stella Splendida et Matutina'* in the Latin Vulgate Bible of St Jerome.

In both cases they distinguish themselves by their specific reference to the Daystar, or Star of the Morning, not present in Isaiah in either codex. [13] So to whom then was Isaiah referring in his rant, Tigleth-Pilesar, King of Assyria; A future King of Babylon; the end of the Reign of Babylon; his own King of Judah, or a foreign God/goddess? If the latter, then which one? Further problems arise as we learn how no earthly/ mortal King literally 'fell' from Heaven, nor did any God known to Isaiah attempt to usurp the 'Throne of Heaven.' No extant myth including those of Baal and Marduk, who remain beloved of their fathers, has been found that convincingly links a known 'fallen' or displaced deity in Isaiah's time with the assumed (mis) reading of the text. Ah, but, 'lack of evidence is not evidence of lack'; this is true, but gradually, as we progress, I hope clarification will render this axiom superlative.

A partially restored Ugaritic myth refers to the twin 'sons' of El,

Dawn and Dusk, *'Shahar'* and *'Shalim'* respectively; again consistently translated incorrectly as the Morning and Evening stars. Again, no star is mentioned or implied, they are simply aspects or qualities of Light. Moreover, the cuneiform tablet from which this myth is transcribed makes no mention of any son of Shahar; an oversight for all those who wish to link this myth with the passage from Isaiah. Neither is Shahar etymologically linked with Helel, Mercury, Hermes, Vesper etc; Helel as a morning star is simply too circumstantial and unconvincing, as mentioned earlier, this would require the suffix *'Kochab'*. Many scholars now believe Shahar simply means 'light of dawn.' Even the mention of Mount Zaphon as the seat of Baal finds only scant mention in the myth of *'Athtar'* (originally a sky God) attempting to succeed (though not overthrow) Baal, but whose diminutive stature prevents this. Baal of course is later resurrected and returns to his Throne atop Mount Zaphon. Conflict is absent within this myth and later an explanation serves to clarify a clearer context for this Holy Place within the text of Isaiah. Bouw's agenda is to irrefutably link 'Helel' as a displaced God with Lucifer.

By default, this affirms his position within occult religions; a schema clear from the onset. Even so, his argument conversely exposes other, more plausible alternatives. He correctly asserts that Lucifer has much in common with Hel-el, sharing the following qualities: they have both been named 'Son of the Morning;' they are both 'bearers of light'; both have associations with the Sun in mythology and with mystery religions. Yet, he insists, these remain distinct from *Eosphorus*. Here however, he has overlooked the obvious: *'Eos'* (Dawn) *'phorus'* (light). Thus, he postulates, the English translation of Lucifer as the Morning Star as Venus is quite erroneous. Though he does suggest Mercury could possibly be the 'false' or 'second' Morning Star [*ibid.*].

The author of the Greek Septuagint in choosing *'Phosphoros'* (sic) for the passage in 2Peter:1:19, rather than *'Eosphorus'* (light of dawn or daylight) as it appears Isaiah, clearly infers the 'Son of Righteousness.' metaphorically the (Sun) light rising in men's hearts. This distinction further reduces the credulity of Lucifer as the 'Morning Star', at least in the enlightened view of Origen. Angelis however, asserts that *'Eosphorus'* is used indiscriminately within both Old and New Testaments! [14]

Within the Old Testament, in the Book of Job 38:7, renowned for its associations with Satan (the dutiful angel sent to test the fortitude of Job in adversity), plural 'Mornings Stars' are mentioned as 'singing together'; but which planets, stars or celestial phenomena are suggested here? Bouw, true to his purpose assigns both Venus and Mercury teleologically to support the myth of the fall from grace of Lucifer as an angel to God. Importantly, it must be remembered that at this time Babylonian astronomers/astrologers also referred to the Moon and Mars as 'Morning Stars.' Biblical exegesis accepts that the actual term 'stars of the morning' in Job correlates to angelic beings of the divine assembly, even to sons of God. It is a generic reference to these beings and is not meant to infer celestial objects at all. Revelation too makes controversial mention of Jesus *'as the root and offspring of David,'* and the bright Star of the Morning. Again, for many the implication 'reads' - Venus. This cumulative supposition is therefore probably also incorrect. Bouw makes another point that in the Occident we now refer to Venus as the Morning Star, adding how throughout the Orient, Hebrews, Greeks and Romans never consistently held this belief.

We must always be mindful of the diverse views of people writing these texts to each other and to our selves. Furthermore, within mythology, all sons of the 'Morning Star' have names that translate to many celestial objects other than Venus, compounded further by the profligate ambiguity of many ancient texts [*ibid.*]. Classic authors such as Plato (427-347BCE) and Socrates (469-399BCE) whose knowledge of astrology/astronomy was vague and lacked specific entitling of deities, ambiguously refer to *'Eosphorus'* with characteristic qualities now associated with a Morning Star, and which at that time could mean anything from the Moon to Venus, or even just the light of dawn. Authors have over subsequent centuries massaged these terms to fulfil the needs and purposes of variant agendas, some deliberate, some in ignorance, but all in error.

English literature records its earliest references to Lucifer as Satan c1000 CE and as the Morning Star as late as c1050 CE. Bouw links these to beliefs of 20th century 'Luciferians', falsely assuming conceptual commonalities, conceding as different only the modern view of Lucifer as a saviour and redeemer, notwithstanding his satanic legacy! Lucifer, however, is not Satan, He never was. Neither was 'Satan' ever the Devil. Such blind prejudice jeopardises the value of truth in face of the perpetual Lie. The Christian Devil is a fictional construct, a symbol formed as a theological necessity for an insecure Church during a time of socio-religious turmoil. This personage provided a rod with which to subdue unruly Pagans ripe with superstitions and correlate mythologies. Fear made the populace gullible, so much so that even now in the wake of 'rationalism', many blithely adhere to illusion and falsehoods.

Several revisionist Bibles indiscriminately use the term 'Lucifer', daystar and morning star, except the NWT, which substitutes a more enlightened and accurate translation of the Masoretic phrase into 'Shining One.' Bouw concludes his discourse with his desire to expunge the use of 'Daystar' or 'Morning Star' from Isaiah, maintaining its use only in reference to Jesus, asserting the implication of Venus for Lucifer is ill-defined, ambiguous and religiously heretical. Modern parlance and word comprehension suffers many perversions from original meanings and use. To those contexts we should apply our analyses as scholars [*ibid.*].

Some researchers have made the correlation between Hel-el and Helios, indicative of a solar root for the phrase. This is indeed a worthy addition to our understanding of the depth of this exploration. Hel-el could mean God of the Sun, but it more properly means simply 'bright one' or 'shining one', *not* lightbringer/bearer or Venus. Shahar is also coterminous with Ra-Horakte/Khephre, the rising/resurrected Sun, Lord of the Morning (light of dawn). It is noteworthy that gods of the Morning and Evening (aspects of the Sun's Light, i.e. Ra Horakte/ Khephre and Amun) are not the same as gods of the Morning and Evening Stars. The former refer to solar aspects of light, the latter to lunar aspects of light. Typically therefore, our Sun is a 'day star.'

Within the long history of astronomy, the names of planets may be traced back with confidence, to no earlier than 600BCE (sometime after Isaiah). Contrary to popular opinion, planets were named *after* the gods, receiving their associations rather late in antiquity. Somewhere between the 5th and 3rd centuries BCE, Greek astronomers, influenced by their Babylonian predecessors, re-named five planets with deities appropriate to corresponding Babylonian technical forms. Unlike Greek astronomy/astrology, particularly under Stoicism, Babylonian analyses were not deterministic. Mesopotamian astronomers/astrologers nevertheless did record their observations using scientific terms, rather than deific ones. These were appropriated according to conjunctions with other celestial phenomena, reading the whole sky holistically. Nothing was separate from their cosmogonic view. The Greeks did not like this and endeavoured over time to develop a stricter system of dedicated planetary divinities. Stars and other celestial phenomena took a while longer, continuing to reflect loose associations with several deities.

As races and cultures expanded, migrated, conquered and traded in the ancient world, deities became appropriated via their associations with the planets; this acted as the significator for the parallel God form relevant to that planet drawn from the other pantheons. The Romans, however, re-named (most of) the Planets after their own gods, i.e., (Babylonian) *'Rimmon'* became (Greek) *'Zeus,'* became (Roman) *'Jupiter.'* An early Greek title for Mercury was *'stilbon/Apollo'* (shining, glittering or sparkling). Similarly, an early Greek title for Mars was *'pyroeis'* (fiery). Jupiter and Saturn were referred to simply as *'phaethon'* (sic) and *'phaenon'*, respectively; both meaning 'shining'. Venus was simply, *'phosphorus,'* meaning bearer of light/bright light. Hesperus and Eosphorus were also non-deific terms referring more to the qualities of light at dawn and dusk. Another goddess of the Dawn is the Vedic *'Ushas'*, sister of *'Surya'*, the Sun, which makes a fascinating parallel to Lucifer and Venus here. [15]

In his controversial book *Polytheism of the Bible and the Mysteries of Lucifer,'* Frank T. Angelis [16] submits the view that any God or Devil implicit within any biblical (or pre-biblical) passage, belongs entirely to wish-fulfilment of later redactors. Angelis insists that a scrupulous reading of all texts presents nothing more than a reference in Isaiah to the 'Light of Dawn', and is open to myriad interpretations. Accordingly, three patterns developed the character and form of Lucifer as the 'Devil'. The first, of theology, was inspired by Persian dualism suggesting the concept of Satan, as a figure of evil, separate and distinct from God; second, the psychological aspect of free will allowed angels, including the 'fallen', to choose their allegiances, and finally, the historical abuse of myth.

Heaven and Hell as places of reward and punishment inhabited by human beings, rather than realms of upper and underworld gods, was yet another consequence of Persian dualism. Although these views greatly influenced apocalyptic texts and post-exilic apocrypha, they made little impact upon the contemporary writings of the Torah. However, biblical texts and codices derived from these original scrolls have been subject to much interpolation and revisioning in order to maintain compatibility and continuity. Hermetic writings heavily influenced Origen, composer of the Greek Septuagint (LXX) Bible. This greatly troubled Augustine, developer of the inherent theology within the Latin Vulgate Bible later composed by St Jerome. Based only loosely on the Greek LXX, it owes more to the foundational religious teachings of Augustine's Manichean roots than the freer optimistic rational of the Hermetica. [17]

Augustine's soul wrenching grapple with and presentment of extreme dualistic perceptions of good and evil are suggested by Angelis as having been drafted from within Persian conceptions of Ahriman. This shadowy figure presented himself as the perfect candidate upon whom to graft Manichean associations of 'false light,' the deceiver and father of lies. Jerome absorbed these formulae utterly, awarding the name, Lucifer to the Adversary, forever prejudicing this luminary psychopomp. [18] Opposer of Ahura Mazda (Supreme Wise Lord, God of the high noon Sun and all Light on Earth), Ahriman is held responsible for all the evils within the *'getig'* world of mankind in contra-distinction to the (Monist) God of the Hebrew Bible, who in Isaiah 45:7 shoulders all qualities of creation: *"I make well being and create woe."* Heavily influenced by the angelic apocrypha of post-exilic Judaism, Augustine elevates God to supreme creator, even of the angels (not one of them as the Old Testament suggests: psalms 80:5-7 & 86:8), superior to, yet separate from them, allowing the rebel angel to fall from Grace. [19] This Augustine explains as a privation (both in terms of lack and non-awareness) of Good. Evil thus enters the world as the product of another force, a negative space filled with and borne of ignorance.

From such darkness rises the 'prince of light' to distract the unwary from their approaches to God, blinding their vision with his deceptive effulgence. Lucifer or 'little Sun' offered the perfect pseudonym. Some scholars uphold dualism as a necessary consequence of Monotheism in order to explain the origins of evil; but unlike Polytheism, it is not in opposition to Monotheism. [20] Free Will derives from a moral choice, not pre-destination. In its original form, Zoroastrianism (which became the official religion of the Persian Empire under Cyrus the Great), offered a mystical, intellectual cult of existential philosophy opposing the brutality of the warrior classes, warmongering and immoral living. Evil as the absence of good represents the immoral choice, the wrong choice. This faith attempts to rationalise how evil afflicts the world, allowing each individual the opportunity to reject it. Truly we must become our own redeemers. Moreover, it is a cult of life, of living with full pleasure, each moment. Popular opinion asserts a dualism of matter and spirit, though this is to misunderstand the inherent theological complexities of this enigmatic faith. Only Mazda created human life in the material world, therefore the battle between good and evil although prevalent within the body as host, really only exists within the spiritual (menog) and transcendental realms. Purity (not privation) of mind and body repel the spiritual onslaught of Ahriman. Prof. A.V. Williams writes how within Zoroastrian spirituality, it must be understood that the body is the abode, not the prison of divinity: *"The body is the shield of the Soul. Wisdom is the protector of the body. The Soul is saved by the Union of both."* [21] It is easy to see how the concept of 'sins' of the flesh became corrupted from this simple premise. In fact is within Manichean dualism that such extremism developed.

In a legendary account of a Greek myth embellished by Ovid, Lucifer is hailed as the God of Brightness, the Lightbringer. As father to 'Ceyx,' a King of Thessaly, his light shone from his son's face. Ceyx married the daughter of Aeolus, the King of the Winds. Latin and Greek gods of nature (Storm, Wind, Thunder, Lightening) parallel many powerful characteristics of gods from within the variant pantheons of Canaan/Phoenicia/Syria/Sumer i.e. Baal, El, Ud, Rimmon. Above all, Light (lucce/lucre) and Fire (ferra) were pre-dominant, exalted and deified; paradoxically they are prevalent in the name and title - *lucemferre*, or Lucifer, literally, fiery light. It is more than startling to discover then an epithet for Shahar, as God of the Dawn - 'the Torchbearer of El'. Despite its original context, it must have caused considerable consternation for the manic Augustine. The promoters of Jesus as the Christ, the deified son of God, now usurped light/photos, previously reserved for the 'son' of Apollo alongside the qualities of light, logic, and truth. Now, of course, the 'other' light source had to fall, to become 'less than', a 'false light', absorbing all the Bacchanalian traits of a despised Heathenism. Angelis deftly explores how Lucifer gradually assumed his association with Venus, The Morning Star, once known as Ishtar/Inanna. As goddess of the Fates, the Romans (inherited a concept from the early Etruscans who) saw in Venus, an element of good fortune, expressed in the *Jactus Veneris'* the highest cast of any three die - 666. [22] It is rumoured how Roman soldiers cast such die for the robe of Jesus; no doubt this instigated the nefarious association of the anti-Christ with this number and thereby to another erroneous alliance of Lucifer with Venus.

Fundamental to this development is the archaic myth of the Ugaritic Baal Hadad who as 'Rider of the Clouds' and 'Master of the Earth' (with whom the souls of 'blessed' dead were said to feast) is awarded the title *'Melek ha'Aretz'* within Kabbalism. He is a beneficent God of Rain and fecundity, and agriculture, often considered cognate with Osiris (Asar) true spouse to Hat-hor, the Heavenly Cow, even as Baal is the Heavenly Bull. Hadad may be etymologically linked to Hades and his qualities are sometimes confused with those of *Yam/Yaw/Yahu/Iahu/Ieuo* (also Mot), a baneful God of chaos and death. Baal and Yam in other myths are presented as adversaries. In fact many myths involving Baal involve conflict with siblings, but not his father, the High God. Curiously, Yahu (also identified by many scholars with Yahweh) is a theophoric personal name in use today in the form of *'Natanyahu.'* Baal, the dark lord of the Underworld provided a template to represent Lucifer, prince of darkness and false light, rising in the fore of the Dawn, the Sun, the one true light, setting in its wake.

In a theological *'coup de tat'* Augustine had displaced the Mother/spouse and son with the solar logos, the 'light' and the 'word,' all else paling into insignificance. Ishtar became a footnote to history and Lucifer ascended her throne as a beacon of iniquity. All sexual licence and lust, all vice and sins of the flesh, formerly represented by Ishtar as Venus, were now transferred to Lucifer (by popular association as Venus). Combining Persian dualism with Greek and near-eastern Paganism, the ultimate bogeyman was given form, as the Devil himself, representing everything the hated 'body of flesh' signified to the tortured, extreme views of Augustine and St Jerome. The brightest, most powerful light in the heavens was now reserved exclusively for the Christ.

Of course, all Luciferic connections to Dionysus, Orpheus and Pan as saviour and redeemer gods of the mysteries were not lost on the early Church Fathers; wine revelry, dance, intoxication, orgiastic celebration and enlightenment became forever blighted with their association with the blackest demon - Satan. From Sumer to Canaan, Egypt, Rome, Greece and Persia, this eclectic and increasingly malignantly deity developed, representing all the evils of an imperfect race desperate to save itself. Everything from the ancient world of Horned gods, zoomorphic deities and animal sacrifice became embodied in the cultic status of this centralized figure-head of personified evil, the fictional persona of 'Lucifer', now diametrically opposed to everything his name originally meant. Lucifer was not simply a mistranslation of *'Hel-el ben Shahar'* or *'Phosphoros'*; by making it a *'hapex legomenon'* it was a calculated attack, sealing the theological debate on the aspect of the Logos. It is worth re-iterating how no concept of a Devil existed in the time of Isaiah; Hel-el ben Shahar bore no associations with Venus.

This Hebraic phrase is simply a poetic metaphor for the hubris of foreign Kings; Jewish peoples have nowhere in their long history, ever believed in a 'Devil.' Angelis [23] also emphasises a distinction in terms used for daystar/Sun used in both Peter and Revelation, where Jesus is described as *'Stella Splendida Matutina'* (splendid star of the morning/day/dawn) and the term 'Lucifer' used in Isaiah. Clearly, again, they are meant to describe the superior qualities of the former and the pejorative, devolution of the latter. Theology employs to great effect the use of semantics to gloss ambiguities prevalent within annotated texts and codices. Isaiah would not have been remotely concerned with the specifics of astronomy as some elegant but convoluted theories suggest, obsessing over Zeniths and Azimuths of certain stars and which struggle to connect myths pertinent to their orbit and Isaiah's phraseology. No celestial luminary is able to provide a persuasive option, though further exploration is nevertheless rewarding.[24]

Hesiod records in his *'Theogany'* (c700BCE), the myth relating the origins of the all stars and celestial luminaries within the heavens and the winds and forces of nature upon the Earth as products, or offspring of the Divine *'Eos'* (sometimes given as *'Erigenia'*) and *'Astraeus'*, whose subsequent epithets suggest this ancestry rather than their actual form. All light and motion emanate from this divine couple. Thus, Eosphorus, simply means 'light of Eos' (Dawn/East, the place of the daily rebirth of the Sun and the annual spring rebirth - hence 'Eostre'). Homer (c850BCE) too records in his epic, the *'Iliad'*, references to *'Eosphorus'* as the light of dawn. [25] Neither of these authors intended us to assume this implied Venus or the Morning Star. Again, this is an invalid misrepresentation suffered by so many translations of classical texts. *'Hesperus'*, similarly, is an epithet symbolising the simple qualities of the evening/night, wherein all light falls in to the western skies - Hesperides, the etymological root of west, despair and desperate. [26] Star of the Morning (Sun) is not the same as Morning Star (Venus). In fact, a common appellation of Saturn was 'Star of the Sun', the Sun at midnight, with both being named *'Shamash.'*

Historically and mythologically, across the globe, Venus has been almost exclusively female and the Morning Star (there are necessarily exceptions, but these in no way add dispute to the relevance of this generalization). Lucifer, however, has assumed a false association with this planet, which must be suspended in lieu of contrary facts. Venus, a Roman rustic goddess of beauty and cultivation, gradually absorbed the qualities of the Greek Aphrodite, namely of love. As Urania, daughter of Uranus, she is given the epithet 'goddess of the Sea, whose seat is in Heaven' (sometimes shortened to Stella Maris/Star of the Sea), and is thus coterminous with Ishtar and Asherah. Unlike Hermes, whose Roman form lent its name to a planet (Mercury), Aphrodite did not. The Romans referred to her planet as *'Veneri.'* [27] In many ancient myths, the longest association of any deity with the planet Venus was Inanna/Ishtar, the Sumerian/Babylonian goddess of sex, fertility, war, sovereignty and kingship. The 'Horned Crown' conferred by her upon divine anointed Kings was symbolised in the night sky by a shining crescent - of her 'star', poetically referred to as 'the Boat of Heaven.' Isaiah would have been painfully familiar with Ishtar in this and other forms, namely: Anath, Astarte and Asherah, all mothers/spouses of God. To Isaiah, as the Great Whore, she epitomised Babylon herself, the corruption, the Paganism, the divine feminine, everything that was anathema to the patristic priesthood of a biblical prophet.

Reaching even further back into astronomical allegory, we may now explore how the brightest luminaries within the sky: the Moon, Sun and Venus were associated with the status of Sumer's Triadic gods - An, Utu and Inanna, who as Venus was one of the earliest deities to become symbolised by a planet. Inanna's archaic myths were assigned to this celestial body. However Sluij believes these may reflect original associations with the movements of a comet, especially with particular regard to her descent myth. [28] Moving into the realms of mythmaker, Sluij believes that no archetypal relationship existed in the distant past between specific gods and planets, where dedicated identifications are marginal or non-existent. In his seminal treatise on *'Catastrophism'* (which the reader is strongly urged to read in its entirety, especially his exploration of the esoteric value of Saturn as the dark Sun, sadly beyond the scope and purpose of this study), Sluij asserts that all myths existed prior to their later establishment with certain planets and that these were fluid and freely associated to any planet/luminary whose conjunction, azimuth, orbit, size colour or shape, expressed the concept appropriate to it.

Subsequent overlays of myth display a growing awareness of religion, astronomy/astrology, evincing a cross-fertilization of influences from culture and conquest. He does not dispute though, the possibilities of myth inspired by early studies of visible plasma configurations and cosmic catastrophes; these need not reflect the planetary forms later attached to them, but may instead offer clues to other celestial phenomena active in the skies in ancient times. Hence, so many absent or 'lost' gods. Paucity of credible evidence forces us to accept a broken line of tradition between planets and their respective deities, revealing nebulous and tenuous links applied to them over the last three millennia. In particular, Venus, almost universally acknowledged as a goddess, has strong planetary associations that mask her cometry associations and attributes. He postulates how only an extensive study into the evolution of myth would allow us to study it without prejudice and to fully appreciate its original context, a principle that is extremely persuasive.

Typically, gods are often accepted as named for characteristics exhibited by them relative to the planets. Jupiter is the biggest planet, therefore becomes head of the pantheon, rescinding his association with any other celestial body. In reality, mutable qualities were insightfully represented by a variety of celestial phenomena simultaneously and consequentially. History and myth confirm a complex stratum of gods with composite features drawn from a common fount of inherited, archetypal characteristics. Often taken out of context, they are rendered meaningless in isolation. This seriously over simplifies the true dynamic of triadic, triple, twin and sibling motifs prevalent within allied typologies. Sluij cites for example, the Morning Star, typically represented (in the ancient Near East) by many diverse luminaries, planets and even a comet. In almost all cases, these are tentative, subjective and vague. Solar heroes abound, (even within European myth and legend - Lugh/Llew and Balder all represent Light as correlates) of Apollo and Hercules, both of whom are linked to Mercury and Mars, particularly within the ancient texts of Aristotle (384-322BCE) and Pliny. Magically, of course correspondences between Mercury and the Sun are still divisive. Moreover, ancient terminology made no distinction between ben, meaning 'son of', and ben, meaning of, from, or affinity with; context alone revealed pertinent subtleties.

There is no universal gender distinction either between planetary associations; for example, Venus, often, though not exclusively presented as female, receives the epithet *Phaethon* (meaning radiant), it is more generally applied to the Sun and also to Saturn, the Star of Sol. The myth of '*Phaethon,*' places him as son of Helios/Apollo, the Sun God. Yet this appellation to a planet also refers to Jupiter, simply because the word itself signifies a specific quality of light, which does not compromise it as a product of the Sun. Initially, all planets received appellations such as these allowing inconsistent associations until they acquired 'fixed' identities with specific theophoric names of deities. For example, Mars, the God of War was assigned to a fiery red planet, formerly referred to by the epithet '*pyroeis*'.

A myth concerning the Egyptian God Osiris offers controversial revisioning of alternative stellar applications, from a reference to his 'risen' soul in the 'Book of the Dead'/Coming forth by Day as the 'Morning Star of Ra' (nrdwj): *"I come forth, like the Bennu, the Morning Star of Ra."* The 'Bennu' bird symbolises the solar fire, the Phoenix, the resurrected light and power of the Sun. Clearly from an Egyptian perspective, the reference is to the Sun. However, when translated in the Hellenistic period where the Morning Star was (thanks to Pythagoras) now tacitly Venus, an erroneous link was forged. Osiris and Set were also understood to represent the rising/living and setting/dying aspects of the light of Dawn and Dusk respectively. Complexities develop as we also realise how male and female attributes of Venus shift following gender application to either morning or evening modes/aspects. Venus is linked to the Sun as Shamash, but if understood correctly, this becomes: the Sun aspected in the light of the evening star - Venus. Some researchers have also referenced Baal in connection to Venus, along with the Ugaritic Sar (sic) and Salim (sic) [*ibid*]. Sluij also suggests the terms; '*Phosphorus,*' '*Eosphoru*' and '*Hesperus*' could be male gender specific. Again, it is stressed that as they lack the prefix or suffix ast/er/rae, these are qualities of light and *are not* stars. He cites for example, the star of Nemesis - *'ho tes Nemeseos aster'*. The perils of absolute association cannot be overstated.

Natural phenomenon i.e., thunder, lightening, rainbows, planets and stars, all acquired gender eventually, dependent upon interpretation and application of myth within spatial and cultural contexts. They do not, however, indicate absolute form. In fact, many myths equally cast hero and heroine in the same roles; the relevance of the myth remains intact and completely interchangeable. Descent, exposure, resurrection, death, ascent, avatars, are all vehicular praxes around which the myths evolve, acquiring gender superiority. Gender is frustratingly arbitrary and subjective, offering us no clue to the purpose of each myth. In the final analyses, the same truth underpins them all. Myths and legends grow and evolve in the telling; subsequent overlays obfuscate their origins, but not the message. Context however, is vital to comprehension. Sluij [*ibid.*] asserts that if the planets were the prototypes of all myth then they would be conspicuously gender specific, as they are not, then he may well be correct in assuming a later deific assignation for the planets. Despite widely speculative early interest in the skies and celestial phenomena, no reliable astronomical records exist prior to 8th century BCE; therefore we may safely conclude planetary associations to be a late phenomenon. The oldest names for the planets appear to be generic rather than theophoric. Myth evidently preceded them.

Classical astronomy/astrology classified Saturn, Jupiter and Mars as masculine and the Moon and Venus as feminine. Mercury was curiously ambiguous only because its gender was dependent upon the planet closest to it. Sluij places India, Greece, Rome and Mesopotamia within a single mythogenetic zone, outside of which lie the Oriental and Occidental zones whose contrary correspondences offer convincing support for his theory. He emphasises how Mars, Saturn and Venus in particular share many similar archetypal attributes, bearing imperceptible meritable distinction. Nowhere is fluidity of gender and attributes better expressed than within the Kabbalah, analogous with Taoist principles that flow from one 'sphere' to another, all within the One encompassing whole, the unifying, fructifying Creatrix. Saturn/Binah is 'female' as the enclosing dragon, the womb, the underworld, and the primal egg. Yet, we still perceive Saturnian deities as male, the masculine 'Father'. He/she is the great primal sea - 'Marah.' Citing many convincing examples, Sluij [*ibid.*] provides a sound basis upon which to positively re-conceptualise the pre-existence of myth building in ancient times. Zeus, the 'bright one', could in an earlier 'life' have easily referred to deities later associated with Saturn or Mars. Clearly, planetary associations of the gods were originally of only marginal importance. Tammuz, the dying and resurrected solar hero, 'the rising Sun' (son), spouse of the goddess Ishtar (Venus) also retains through his agricultural attributes more ancient links to both Saturn and Mars; a theme axiomatic to celestial correspondence.

Therefore, when researching origins of the Morning Star, specifically to a male Venus, we are on very thin ice. At no time in the history of any culture is there a consistent myth that places Venus = Morning Star = Male; so to add = Lucifer should be considered folly of the highest ignorance. All these points must be considered when making unequivocal identifications. Lucifer, as 'fiery light of Dawn', truly bears/brings the forth the light, mythically, poetically, esoterically, logically and purposefully. Astronomy and Cosmology are fickle modalities, evidenced in the vexing displacement of anomalous vincula extant within our own time. The whole concept of differentiated planetary deities collapses once the full body of enquiry is consulted. Neither colours nor names remain consistently dedicated in description to single planets alone. Metaphor displacement allows us to accept myths as they become transposed from their point of origin to a new *'locus operandi.'*

Ishtar, as a divine goddess manifested her qualities within a whole plethora of symbols, ranging from the planet Venus (with whom her main corpus of attributes were identified), but also in the Moon, stars, heavens etc., down to a related set of earthly simulacra. Described in cuneiform as *'ilu'*, this concept encompassed all that she was and was represented by, yet remained separate from her. By means of the *'ilu'*, she could be approached, propitiated and venerated, utilizing their collective 'power' for divination and acts of magic. In this way all celestial phenomena are understood as symbols of, not indicative of, specific deities. Ancient cultures engendered endless projection where multiple objects symbolised singular concepts that were appropriated at random, subjectively and superlatively. Such mutable ambiguity has deluded many historians, biblical exegesists, mythographers and unwary magi for countless generations. At all times we must re-configure our minds to the cognitive awareness of another world view, of ancient peoples whose lives were inexorably bound within culturally distinct mythos. We may judge and discern them with the full weight and understanding of history and education, but we can only interpret their observations minus the intuition that engendered them.

Celestial phenomena existed as machinery oiled slavishly by fatalistic ancients in order to avert the ever-encroaching powers of chaos. Moreover, to fully appreciate myths relative to each planet we must take into consideration their derivation from prior celestial phenomena, which only later became associated or re-connected with them. For example, there is much evidence to support the original qualities of Venus with the baneful activities of a comet. And let us not forget Kybele, embodied within the black stone/comet, the dark and terrible Mother of all, whose myth recalls how she was once fair and pale, turning black only with the 'sins and woes' of mankind. Among other anomalous myths are those of *'Sata'* (Egyptian) and *'Zu'* (Sumerian) gods of lightening, who similarly 'fell' to Earth.

It is true that we must resist random or superficial selections in order to arrive at a satisfactory conclusion; the data must support a pattern of probability, a series of associated possibilities from which we may empirically conclude. The pattern must fit the theory. *'Science is Mythology applied'* [*ibid.*]. Each generation of stargazers add another dimension to these basic praxes, overlaying occasional anomalous attributes, no longer applicable to their time or culture. New associations take precedence while others fade into obscurity. The aim must ever be one of evolution, the objective being to resist duplication of errors borne of ignorance and limited comprehension simply because they precede us. Rather, we should seek to determine the purpose that underpins arcane lore, working to restore broken threads along which we may complete the Great Work. After all, we now realise fully the true order of all planets in our heliocentric world, so to follow dogmatically a ritual that lists ascension through the realms incorrectly would be ludicrous. The magic is not within that order but within the methodology of moving from one level to another until our objective is reached. If we fail to correct errors, we duplicate for eternity a nonsense, forging a deficit in our magical egress.

Myths move, evolving and progressing along the path of truth, which should never be static. What is true today may be false tomorrow. Only in a single moment of forever is anything really true. Sophisticated modern astronomy allows us to identify Venus the planet as both the Morning and Evening 'stars.' Yet the myths attached to it over time are at best figurative, or worst, erroneous, compounded by repetition. In our time, Lucifer as a concept of enlightenment, shining forth, should and must now be allied with the absolute symbol of fire and light blazing across the skies above - the Sun, the solar Logos, the source and power of all light in our helio-centric world, the heavens and the Earth. A true symbol for the 21$^{st}$ century in which we live, it retains a vital cyclical symbology serving as a constant link to its complex origins.

Having completed an exploration of our three principle modalities, how may we now perceive the pensive words of Isaiah? To whom then did he vent his spleen? Remember, throughout the ancient Near and Middle East, Ishtar in Isaiah's time was the supreme goddess; adopted even by the Assyrians (sometimes in the form of Mylitta). She represented everything loathsome to Isaiah, a constant reminder of female power, of a spouse, consort and mother of God, all things he sought desperately to eradicate from his world. Any King ruling in her name (via the rule of sovereignty) was understood to receive the latent qualities of her mythical son (by El/Anu), aspected in the daily rising of the Sun - Shahar/Baal, the resurrection of his Father, just as Horakte was to Ra. Kings in the Middle East ruled not by *dynastic lineage* as did the Hebrews, but as *God's electives* through divine Kingship. Isaiah's rant is therefore a tirade against any and all current and future oppressors, Kings, and their false gods; not against any later fictional Devil. Jewish people, then as now do not ascribe to evil as a manufacture of a demon, but regard it as a result of the abuse of free-will.[29] Nor is it a reference to celestial bodies, it is simply a mythopoetical, politico-religious statement endorsing the veracity of an unyielding priesthood, obsessed with the fulfilment of its own supreme, autocratic Monotheism over all contenders and opposers.

John's vision in Revelation must also be understood in nationalistic and immediate terms; it describes the immanence of the promised Kingdom of God upon Earth, in which a united Israel shall reside after the destruction of its enemies. War, conquest and destruction will cease, putting an end to famine and hunger. Expressed in the allegorical and mystical visionary skills of Ezekiel, Enoch and Daniel, the emblems of the main tribes, Ephraim, Judah, Dan and Israel are the Bull, Lion, Eagle and Man respectively and represent the full unity of all twelve tribes drawn from each corner of the Earth. Redemption is now sought through Jesus rather than Yahweh, expressed emphatically as the 'Light of the World'. Jesus too has his opposer, found in the body of the state of Rome, the oppressor of God's Kingdom. Context apprehends the lack-lustre tarnish of legerdemain, ever the enemy of truth.

Although my reasons differ from Bouw, Angelis and Sluij, I also do not believe Lucifer is the Morning Star, but the Son/Sun of the Morning Star/Venus. He is the light of dawn itself, the Rising Sun (the resurrected form of his father), the true and effulgent daystar. Lucifer is not Venus, is not the Morning Star, yet the deific spirit of Lucifer as 'light' itself is manifest in all its divers celestial phenomena. By the same process of logic, I naturally refute the implication linking Jesus with the Morning Star as Venus, who is properly, the Mother. Figuratively and metaphorically, both Lucifer and Jesus equate with 'all light.'

Celestial objects were merely symbols signifying concepts, qualities and power of light relevant to appropriate pre-existent myth. Their evidence, despite personal bias evinces no other possible conclusion. In the archaic world of our distant ancestors, myth was greater than science; life was unthinkable without adherence to daily ritual and prayer. Yet even as Isaiah penned his erstwhile polemic, Babylonian astronomy/astrology flourished, awarding scientific (mundane) names alongside divine titles; unhappily, only the latter has survived. Though these were often applied consecutively, they were rarely consistent. All we can ascertain for certain is that 'light', aspected in its myriad forms and terms, imparts the power and might of the creator as psychopomp, guiding enraptured souls toward gnosis and enlightenment. Of course, in the absolute Platonic sense, as an emanation from the One, the Void, the ineffable Creatrix, it has no physical form, remaining an absolute principle. In the sense of a sentient angelic force prevalent within the atavistic manifestations, this is another mystery altogether.

And so, throughout this miasmic labyrinth of nomenclature, it is certain there exists no definitive or absolute term or translation for the word - 'Lucifer'. His mythos is multi-layered, multi-faceted and enigmatic, evolving to meet the needs and requirements of the remaining mystery Schools who retain the insight to separate his truth from the prevailing orthodoxies of past and present. Lucifer as the Morning Star, was never so in the ancient world. This remains an important distinction, more relevant in fact than the 'mistranslation' rationale normally offered. There was an ancient form bearing the name of Lucifer, but that form was 'misappropriated' by the needs and concerns of the Church Fathers. Out of necessity, the power and force behind this critique was that of a Promethean torch, blazing down through the ages, the hermits' lamp, the fools' star, the smiths' fire, all focussing upon the eternal flame, the inextinguishable Light of the Universe, *Lux Mundi'* - Light of the Rising Sun.

> "Let mine eyes see the Sun that I may be sated with Light.
> Banished afar is the darkness, if the light is sufficient.
> May he who has died the death, see the Light of the Sun."
>
> Epic of Gilgamesh

A shortlist of key celestial associations relative to this discourse:

| | |
|---|---|
| Sahar/Shahar | Moon. Supreme (Male) God of Sabaeans (South) and Northern Semites. |

| | |
|---|---|
| Sun. | (Male) Ugaritic and Canaanite God of Western Semites. |
| Shahar | (Dawn) and Shalem (Perfect) and/or (Dusk) |
| Salim/Salem | Evening Star. Ugaritic Semites. |
| Samas/Shamash | Sun (Male) God of the Northern Semites. Consort of the Queen of Heaven. |
| Sam/Shams | Sun (Male) God. Arabic Sun Goddess. Northern Semites. |
| Sapas/Shapash | Sun Goddess. Western Semites. |
| Athtar/Attar | Venus. Son of Sun and Moon. |
| Athtar Sharquan | (Morning Star) |
| Athtar Dhu Qabad | (Evening Star) |
| Ishtar | Venus. Supreme Goddess of Babylon, Mesopotamia, Assyria, subsuming many other goddesses from all over the Middle-East, including Asherah (also the 'Heavenly cow'), Tanit, Elath, Anath and Astarte. |
| Al-Uzza | (Lady) Venus, 'Most Mighty'. Northern Semites. |
| Azizos | 'Powerful', Evening Star. Northern Semites |
| Monimos | Beneficent', Morning Star. Northern Semites |

*"Shining One, bringer of the Light of Dawn"*
*- Lucifer is the Sun/ son of the Morning Star*

# Notes

1. www.paghat.com/libanimyths
2. Marc Edmund Jones & Dane Rudhyar www.**rudhyar**.com/fromhtot_1.shtml
3. Jones & Rudhyar [*ibid*.]
4. Bouw, G.D. www.geocentricity.com/astron
5. Lecture notes from Undergraduate Biblical Studies course by Prof Philip Davies at Sheffield Uni.
6. Notes: Prof. Philip Davies.
7. Notes: Prof. Philip Davies.
8. Bouw, G.D. www.geocentricity.com/astron
9. Bouw, G.D. www.geocentricity.com/astron
10. Bouw, G.D. www.geocentricity.com/astron
11. Leland, C.G. 1892 *'Etruscan Roman remains in Popular Tradition.'* pp146-9. T. Fisher Unwin. London
12. www.paghat.com/libanimyths
13. Notes: Prof. Philip Davies.
14. Siren, C.B. www.pubpages.unh.edu/~cbsiren/canaanite-faq.html
15. Siren, C.B. www.pubpages.unh.edu/~cbsiren/canaanite-faq.html
16. Angelis, Frank. T. www.home.fda.net/~Spartacus
17. Bouw, G.D. www.geocentricity.com/astron
18. Angelis, Frank. T. www.home.fda.net/~Spartacus
19. www.cc.usu.edu/~faith6/bible

20. Prof. Philip Davies.

21. Williams, A.V. 1989 *The Body and Boundaries of Zoroastrian Spirituality.'* In 'Religion' 19. pp231. Academic Press

22. Leland, C.G. 1892 *Etruscan Roman remains in Popular Tradition.'* pp146-9. T. Fisher Unwin. London

23. Angelis, Frank. T. www.home.fda.net/~Spartacus

24. www.spiritandtruth.org/teaching

25. Homer. 1864. *Iliad.'* Book 23, line 215. Routledge and Sons Ltd. London

26. Bouw, G.D. www.geocentricity.com/astron

27. Sluij, M.A. van der www.mythopedia.info/Gods-and-planets

28. Sluij, M.A. van der www.mythopedia.info/Gods-and-planets

29. Picknet, L. 2005. *'Secret History of Lucifer.'* pp22. Robinson. London


KJV Bible & NWT Bible

Previously published in: *The Wytches' Standard* # 4 Litha 2006

*Verdelet* # 17 Summer Solstice 2006

*The Cauldron* #127 February 2008

# 6
# The Profane Art of Masking: A Study into the Darker Elements of our Winter Masking and Guising rituals

*"Masks were invented by Satan: 'It was he who put on the Mask of a serpent in Paradise"* [Gesner]

This 'deception' reveals the root of the early Christian abhorrence for masking and disguise, and one which they believed precipitated man's fall from grace. The New Testament is replete with similar polemical analogies. Such things were proclaimed as lures for the weak [Twycross & Carpenter, 2002:300]. So rigid were these views that even in the 16th century when ladies fashion turned to velvet and lace cauls worn over the face as protection against the severities of winter, the Church bore down on them the harshest of criticisms, claiming them as whims and fancies of Satan [*ibid.* 302]. It was the Devil they feared, not the long extinct Pagan pantheons. His sly 'deceptions' were still to be seen in all acts of impropriety, freedom, indulgence, surrender and joy, especially in sensation. Dualist theological conflict percolated down through all societal levels, forever colouring our perception and more importantly, our reactions to those who choose to change their physical appearance, even temporarily. Concealment abdicates moral responsibility; where inhibitions are abandoned, immorality prevails encouraging a propensity to sin. Ironically, Twycross and Carpenter [2002:308] postulate how the wearing of a 'chastity' veil does in fact automatically present and highlight the licentious and sinful sexuality of the (supposedly) errant female gender!

What is a mask, actually? Magically, a mask is understood to represent three characters: the wearer, the personage it represents and the spirit that synthesises the two. Dramatically, it is considered as the 'persona' (voice carrier, that through which sound is carried) contrived for profit, disguise or deception. Psychologically, in hiding the person, it frees the self, this double face imposes its will, engaging and manipulating the environment to which it is subject. Countless generations of revellers have exploited this expression of power, given free license to act, prompt, cajole, intimidate at will an audience always unsure of the motivation and intention of the figure in disguise. Ranging from animal to supernatural forms, something of their nature is imparted to its wearer. But is it really that simple? Why do people don mask and disguise? History reveals cultural practises that are secular, religious and/or supernatural.

Originally, cathartic dance, mime, drama and divine musing were all held as sacred acts by the ancient Greeks yet they gradually became secularised by the pragmatic Romans into farce and other hellish funereal acts (*fabula atellana*) separating worship from celebration, formerly held as one by their Grecian predecessors. Further east and north, supernatural or magical elements were emphasised as culture dictated. Naturally, considerable aspects of all three practices become synthesised to a greater or lesser degree, and this is typified in various Eastern, African and South American religious carnivals and festivals. However, when assessing the purpose and intent of these rites, academia cautions against the supposition that traditions over time (and more evidently over greater periods of time) remain the same. Traditions at opposite ends of such a spectrum may differ considerably [Twycross & Carpenter, 2002:1].

Masks are the oldest expression of humanity. They retain the element of mystery, inculcating uncertainty within the onlooker. According to anthropologists masking has just one role, to deceive by illusion, either by the gods inspiring them or the alter egos of people wearing them. They adopt a public face by hiding the private one; they transform, protect, scare, intimidate, shock, all by inversion! Masks generate transformation

Mask Diabolique

in the viewers mind, for the wearer of such a tool, this is immensely empowering. It is also liberating. They are the intercessors between the gods and man, hence all the superstitions accorded to them by onlookers. Masks command attention. As an idiom, mask is derived from the Italian word *'masca'* meaning hideous. Culturally, Anglo-Saxons are responsible for our modern concept of the 'Grim Reaper', a psychopomp (and epithet for the Devil, the stealer of souls), formulated from the word for facemask -*'grima'* the root of which originally meant the expression of ferocious or enraged man, which links again the violence and aggression associated with its adopted features [*ibid.*18]. Curiously it is now commonly worn in celebration remembering the dead, albeit in deflection of the spirit it represents, an apotropaic Pagan concept that averts mischief from the wearer.

Mediaeval *'Comedia dell'arte'* descended from the *'fabula atellana,'* and as inheritors of the Christian Roman perception of masks as representations of 'evil,' the first mask made was a caricature of the Devil himself. This was used provocatively in satirical plays to parody the licentious or greedy natures of both nobility and clergy. Also popular was the *'Aliquino'* (Harlequin), the prince of demons. Excommunicated by the Pope, all players became wandering troupes of rogues, players of satirical buffoonery and farce. Subversive potential was further parodied by them as each Italian city and class were masterfully condensed into a character and typified by the artful features of each mask. [1]

In Britain, similar troupes known as 'mummers' would carouse the streets during seasonal celebrations, but more commonly over winter. Folklorist Ralph Whitlock [1978:21] suggests the unlikely meaning of disguised revellers common to Scotland and Cornwall, known as *'guizers'*, is 'geese dancers'; due he claims, to their bizarre propensity to wear rags and skins/pelts of animals. Incidentally, these traditions acquired the socially uncomfortable and normally forbidden aspects of begging, especially amongst children, thinly veneered in the custom of 'soul-caking.'

Apparently though, both adult 'mummers' and 'guizers' would gain entry to homes by an unwritten law, on the pretext of 'sweeping' away the ills of the old year to herald in the new, entirely reliant upon the superstitious need to avert ill fate and fortune for the coming year. Thus granted the threshold powers of Janus, they exerted a protocol which was known and readily accepted. Provided this was adhered to, violence was avoided. The subversive nature and implicit violence of these and similar visiting customs were acknowledged as a double-edged sword. The players brought either a blessing or a curse, it was ever a choice, free-will and all that. Recorded in his 18th century history of Kent, are Edward Husted's comments regarding a similar Wassailing Custom performed by the workers of the orchards, there is: *"an incantation for which the confused rabble expect a gratuity in money, or drink!"* If they are disappointed in both, they will, with great solemnity anathematise the owners and trees with altogether as significant a curse." Throughout the south-east, gangs of men and youths (generally farm labourers, smiths and ploughmen) were known to scour the countryside farms during the privations of winter seeking alms [Doel, 1992:20].

Engineered here, were the interactions between the masked and the unmasked within the liminality of a particular time and space, where such an intrusion was allowed without retribution. Festooned in paper or rags, faces blackened by charcoal or caked in flour, suggesting absence of identity rather than disguise, they were more generally given to 'cross-dressing.' These disguises represented transgression, a flouting of normality. They were not 'role-playing,' trying to appear 'female,' but had crossed accepted boundaries, signalling inversion, mob rule (even if rarely realised) and chaos. In fact, they have become as ghosts. The need to appease superstition continued tentatively into the 20th century; thinly disguised as folk traditions, few survived the colossal upheaval of two world wars. Fewer still (if any) were in any way sacred; they had become a means to an end [*ibid.*]. The niceties of the late 20th and 21st century revivalist traditions are a far cry from those of the medieval and later periods. Or are they, really? Disguise is after all an open invitation to unacceptable behaviour.

Extreme cases highlight this potential vehicle of the saboteur. In 1993 masked (protestant) gunmen in Derry shouted out 'Trick or Treat' during a Halloween procession before opening fire into the crowd of celebrants. Seven died and thirteen were injured, most of whom were Catholic.[1] Excessive violence has here been suggested as a cleansing force, purging from the perpetrator any sense of imposed inferiority, despair or impotence. And so the natural vehicle of celebration of inversion that carries the spirit of misrule generates the opportunity for such acute challenges to the life and liberty of others. The underlying element of chaos is latent; 'chance' decides whether such activities will be victimless. The mask is the liminal doorway, its wearer stands on the threshold, his/her boundary temporarily blurred and indistinct, poised to herald in and unleash the forces of chaos, often playfully, generally unruly, but always the threat is inherent.

To cover one's face is alluring and motivates intrigue, it cultivates curiosity and fear; it arouses suspicion and often engenders unease. We cannot see through the mask to the face beneath and are unsettled by our reactions to that. Subtle expression, the guide to comprehension, is denied by the blank stare from a static mask: the poker-face, the dead-pan gaze of void-less emotion. We cannot know our tormentor, entertainer, anarchist; they remain shadows to our senses. These disturbing reactions assert the need to recognize the social and cultural complexity of masking and disguise, remaining mindful of their practise and purpose, from the past through to the present. There is no full communion between masked and unmasked, interaction is restricted. We are simultaneously seduced and repelled by it. The mask and disguise invites an intimacy that is at once a barrier, paradoxically enforcing separation. This duality sets the viewer on edge, considerably disadvantaged by the wearer.

Such a psychological advantage has been the vehicle by which a performance engineers a shift in our reactions at odds with the instinct it arouses. Movement and speech become grossly articulated, exaggerated, expanding the unreal. Visual images processed in one side of the brain, conflict with stimulus by words and aural information, processed by the other. Robbed of our wits, we are tormented by an alien foe. We are confused. Are we entertained or the entertainment? Do we project our fears or receive theirs? We are thus at their mercy and apparently defenceless. We know them not and therefore cannot hold them to account; essentially they are beyond the bounds of Law. Do we ask or answer the puzzles and mysteries suggested by their antics and posturings. Do we imagine they are pointing the finger at us? Can they read our minds? Surely we agree, but why then do we shuffle, is it because we are unnerved in spite of the humour. Is this folklore, history or myth? Is it satire, protest or anarchy? All of them; assuredly? Fascination weaves its spell and we are engaged, hooked by the mesmerising magic of theatre, the immanence of something 'other'.

Mundanity is vanquished, momentarily banished in this small suspension of reality. We are drawn into an alternative worldview, and we believe it, just for a moment. We have become juxtaposed to our environs, severed from our comfort zones, cajoled into a spectacle of manic behaviour, amused by farce, within which we feel a distinct shift. For a few brief moments we experience euphoria, elation whilst riding the tide of unease. Friction or fiction? Their success depends upon our willingness to engage. Fight or flight. Adrenalin rush either way. This is pure magic and heady stuff. So where and how did all this devolve?

With the exception of medieval mystery and morality plays which continued to display elements of religiosity, most theatre was seen as secular. Unlike true shamanism, where the shaman mediates through the supernatural spirit of the mask the use of masks in secular activities is quite dissimilar. Here, the mask signifies the mundane and earth-bound nature of mankind in all his various guises. We have ceased in general to be a culture of the word, but of the image, the symbol of which, the mask endorses a narrative via its visual impact upon the psyche of the viewer. The psychological and emotive responses cannot be overemphasised as our propensity to suspend belief is extended even further by the timing of these events. Almost always they are enacted around twilight; subtle nuances and shadows dramatically pronounce the surreal and organic performances unfolding before and around bewitched spectators. Strange creatures lurk, zoomorphic and bestial. We are lured into the dark world of phantasmagoria. These are the physical, social and temporal contexts essential for true comprehension and study of these contentious activities according to Twycross and Carpenter [2002:6]. We need now to consider more fully the socio/political aspects of masking and guising throughout history, in which there is no place for either speculation or sentimentalism.

Despite heavy settlement by the Anglo-Saxons, Norse and later Normans, all of which have left their indelible mark upon our culture, our winter festivals and celebrations are especially according to Geoff & Fran Doel [1992], essentially Roman. Three specific festivals encompassed the festive period from Saturnalia (17-24th December); Sol Invictus (25th December) and finally, the Kalends (first days of January) which was the civic celebration of the New Year. Asserted throughout is the escapism these festivities generated, from hardship, privations, mundanity and restriction; but most significantly from one's identity and responsibility. They posit a melee of variant folk practices divorced from original culture and context that accumulated over time subject to wars, famine and plague in addition to religious conversions that eventually bear little resemblance to their associate sources. What they additionally underline, is how the overall and continued relaxation of civic law over these 'Roman' periods lead to virtual license to beg, steal, borrow, protest, carouse and most especially gamble, all activities forbidden at all other times, always under disguise and which eventually developed into English and European social traditions.

During Saturnalia, the woollen bonds that fettered the feet of the ivory cultic statues of Saturn were loosened to symbolise the liberation of this dark God of chaos and misrule. In 217BCE, a public and orgiastic banquet was introduced and it became the most popular festival of the year. Declared a public holiday, business was suspended and gambling was allowed in public, open to all classes, even slaves. Apparently, the Emperor Commodus (192CE) was strangled in his bath even as the festivities continued outside his palace. [3] Abandonment of the self was expressed most commonly through the exchange across gender of clothing and the wearing of animal skins in mock bestiality. These provided simple disguises for the poorest classes of society and provide insightful clues as to their true purpose, which was not to adopt another's persona, or character, but to hide their own.

'Burchard of Worms' infamous 'Penitentials' inveighs against the capering about in animal skins, likening them to the Kalends, bemoaning the folk custom commemorating the dead in which, during 'Wakes Weeks,' 'sinister' masks were worn by the participants. But were these performed out of fear or in mockery of the spirits? This activity is also recorded in a Ludlow Register circa 1284 [Twycross and Carpenter, 2002:51]. Conversely, in 12th century France, the 'Feast of Fools', a Church sanctioned festival lasting twelve days that was supposedly the direct liturgical heir of the Kalends (which now phases out of record) was introduced for the lower orders of the clergy; yet it retained all the apparent free licence of the forbidden rites of Saturnalia, especially popular in the Netherlands [Twycross and Carpenter, 2002:39]. Within it, the *'Asinaria Festa'*, or Feast of the Ass, revives the eventual triumph of order over the Egyptian Set animal, the ass, representing chaos [Fergusan, 1996:48] allegorically enacted by the 'holy family' riding it as they flee into Egypt.

The ass of the holy fool as guardian of the liminal threshold, either real or metaphorical of Saturn is also emblematic of the 'Lord of Misrule'. Speaking oracular heads were fashioned under the celestial auspices of Saturn by medieval magicians fascinated by the expansive occultism available to them, and Jackson [1996:643-4] suggests this forges a tentative link to *'Baphomet,'* enigmatic and provocative symbol of man and beast conjoined. Animal disguises exaggerate the baser elements of man's nature, in terms of both sex and violence. Certainly escalating violent behaviour necessitated the halting by the Church of these unsavoury activities and even the Pope had to intervene to prevent devolution into anarchy in 1249 when riots broke out during this increasingly insubordinate celebration [Jackson, 1996:64].

However, cross-dressing, make-up and much horse-play characterised these informal seasonal festivities which by the High Middle Ages had extended into the general populace, becoming institutionalised as the 'Carnivals' (licence before privation) in which excessive eating, drinking, fornication and yet more gambling were the order of the day, varied only by local custom. Prostitutes dressed as men in order to gain the freedom to ply their wares in public during Carnival. Men dressed as women to escape the social mores of *'macho'* responsibilities. Twycross and Carpenter [2002:65] suggest these freedoms were liberating acts in a society of strict roles and demeanour at all other times, rendering the celebrant intoxicated by the cathartic energy and pleasure of release. Germanic sources of the 16th century regard such behaviour as erotic, giving vent to orgiastic activity, akin to the Roman Saturnalia. Though even here, many cases of violence are recorded. Typically, in the spirit of primeval theatre, we move from sex to death to appreciate how the spectral dead were traditionally represented by a blackened face, known by an old English pun as *'grime/grima'*, which eventually just meant 'mask'. Personified as 'devils', by pious clerics, these supernatural 'fright' masks are dutifully recorded, but not as remnants of heathen cults. It is clear that good Christians also comported themselves in this unsavoury manner! [*ibid.* 341] Nevertheless, they remained fearful of the implications of such irreligious and licentious acts.

Worthy here of inclusion, but which must remain brief, again of necessity being beyond the scope and purpose of this particular study is the thorny issue of the ultimate disguise, as a beast, replete with horns and skins. Cawte [1978:195-7] cites the vehement proscriptions by 5th and 6th century Bishops against the vulgar antics of the *'cervulus,'* asserting the possibility that the 'Little Stag' dance (*'cervulus facere'*) could be linked tentatively to the *'Sorcerer' of 'Les Trois Frères'* (which is, itself a contentious issue also beyond the remit of this study) and thus by default to the 'Hobby Horse'. Yet this dance was ambulatory, visiting houses bringing good-luck, much as the Abbots Bromley Horn Dancers do even now. Yet the record is silent regarding the 'Hobby Horse' until at least the 14th century. Flemish manuscripts depict gleeful revellers prancing abroad upon hobby staffs, accompanied by pipers and musicians, in mockery of the

'*Pagani*' as entertainment. [Twycross and Carpenter, 2002:32-33]. By the 15th century hobby horses were firmly entrenched in the folk scene and social calendar, being employed in the raising of funds for the parish church, generally removed from all Pagan association within the minds of the performers, in spite of any actual or original symbolic significance [Jones & Clifton, 1997: 8].

In Iceland, the '*Vikivaki*' custom (documented since the 16th century) held over winter is a dance and banquet at which the chief guest is a curious 'hobby' beast, possibly a goat [4] or even a white stallion, whose bawdy antics are strikingly similar to the Irish white mare (Lair Bhan) in the 'Lifting the Nag' wake tradition also employed at weddings to induce fertility within the newly-weds. Its fee was a good bottle of whiskey, without which it was given over to lamentable violence and harrowing of all guests until enumerated [O' Cathain, 2001:231-237]. According to Druidic and 'Celtic' lore, the colour white is generally associated with all anthropomorphic, zoomorphic and theriomorphic forms. In discussing the legendary and Grand '*Ooser*' or '*Wooset*,' Jackson [1996:27-31] posits a Saxon origin in '*Wodwas/Wudewasa*,' which he interprets as the master of the forest, the wild green spirit of prophetic ecstasis. This all too often aggressive Christmas Bull was a totemic beast of great significance within each village. Under the guardianship of one particular family, he would be sported with great pomp and ceremony at all civil protests against oppression and injustice. He signified the power of Saturn to overturn conventional boundaries of law, ushering in those of chaos. Eventually, this authority fell into use only among more general social and domestic issues until its eventual disappearance. This powerful symbol of anarchy thus attains links with the Black Bull deity of the Pyrenean Basques, themselves great political activists of no mean degree [*ibid.* 49-50].

It has been suggested how regional variations of the hobby horse have manifested in the form of other more regional once totemic/tribal beasts, giving rise to a whole range of animals including a bear, a bull, a stag a goat and the notorious (derby) ram, also known as 'Old Tup.'[2] This creature of immense size has significance to the peoples of the Midlands, covering Sheffield, Derby and Nottingham, whose notable geography reveals settlement by Danes and Anglo-Saxons, known as being distinctly not 'horsey' people. In common with other legendary beasts, 'Old Tup' has correlations aligned to extrovert creation myths whereby a giant totem beast such as Ymir is slaughtered and whose carcass feeds its needy people. Of course this theme again centred upon midwinter privations, is reflected in the song and legend of this enormous prize ram![5] Accompanying the grand procession of this 'malodorous head' is a Morris troupe, of blackened faces, dressed in tatters and a team commonly comprising of a butcher, an old man and woman and 'devil doubt;' less common are the smith and his enigmatic 'brother' [Cawte, 1978:113]. The wearing of horns and animal skins as representative of an actual animal can be easily traced back to Pagan rituals of 9$^{th}$ century Norway. By the 13$^{th}$ century, even in these remote areas, it is now believed that masking and the wearing of animal skins was entirely theatrical, especially with particular regard to spectacular and dramatic games.[4] Peripatetic dances and performances generate strains of fertility and resurrection, no matter how degenerate, but again, academia cautions against the conclusion of Pagan survivals [Pegg, 1981:99]. The former glosses of Victorian sentimentalism are now shunned in favour of realism where context is vital.

Cawte [1978:208-17] advocates an open mind regarding the origins and purpose of these 'hobby' beasts (citing the speculative Dutch, 'hobben' - to move up and down), and within his own highly discursive study he proffers these may be found in either the tourney pageant horses of the medieval periods or the even earlier 'mast' style which has ancient correlations in Neolithic totems. Yet 'Hob' is well known within folklore as a reference to the Devil [Harte, 2004:24:40:66]. Intriguingly, it has been suggested that 'Oss' infers a concept of 'deity' and there is no doubt this beast has and is considered to be representative of a variety of gods both male and female [Peter, 1997]. Something curious is being 'masked' here. There is also a curious legend that relates the ability of animals to pronounce 'prophecies' via oracular powers gained at the birth of Christ. This belief may have influenced the supposed oracular activities of some of the winter totem and hobby beasts at play over the winter period (as mentioned previously), but others believe this a much older concept [Pennick, 1998:87]. Certainly, it was known amongst earlier Pagans, who did indeed perambulate an animal skull or head upon a pole for this divinatory/oracular purpose and is dutifully recorded by Tacitus (who also mentions vigorous but stylised sword dancing by naked Germanic warriors! in the 1st century CE, another curious and possible origin of yet one more of our winter customs). Skins were also worn, especially bull or ox hides for divination [Doel, 1992]. Even the totemic horse has been reduced to accompanying other masked guisers, players and dancers over the centuries, procuring doles and charity, such that its original purpose is now obscured, although alms are still considered a magickal charm for good fortune bestowing health and wealth upon both giver and taker. Some researchers are keen to promote the divine imperative in association with the 'Oss' and divine prophecy in the absolute sense through the Horseman's Word. The secret 'word' of God was said to be concealed within the horse's mouth along with the means to achieve it. Such a word is believed to precipitate self-empowerment and ingress to gnosis.[6]

Adjunct to this, in England, even as John Gladman's insurrection of 1443 exploited the grand 'masque' of Carnival to incite rebellion against the Prior of Norwich, further records reveal a high incidence of gang warfare, social bullying, and racketeering along the urban centres of the continent. Robberies and blood feuds were given free reign under the mantle of Chaos adopted by these nefarious celebrations. A royal decree in 1485 forbade the painting and disguising of the face by poachers and mummers alike. No distinction in the criminality of both cases was considered [*ibid*.7]. Any attempt at public disguise was seen as a breach of civic order determining the intent to deceive by concealment of the features by which each of us may be known and recognised The Puritan, Phillip Stubbs bewails in his 'Anatomy of Abuses' numerous reports of masking and mummery leading to grief and bedlam [Fergusan, 1996:45]. During the Interregnum, masking and any form of disguising was strictly forbidden (masks, specifically were banned during the Reformation), as were all 'performances' being perceived as the domain of the Devil. Many, though by no means all these customs including the Masquerade (from Europe) and the Pantomime were gradually restored after the re-instatement of the Monarchy under Charles II in 1660 [Pennick, 1998:21].

Though highly popular in Southern Europe, the core component of revelry turned from the sophisticated and stylised art forms of Carnival and *'Commedia dell'arte'*, into the Mumming and Guising Folk Traditions of Britain and Northern Europe, enjoyed in smaller, localised centres, often, though not exclusively, rural. Spectacular carnivals, executed on a large scale continued to represent the sophisticated aspects of cosmopolitan city life. Similarly, in England the Mock Kings and the Lords of Misrule were the province of wealthy and privileged celebrants, hired specifically for entertainment over the winter period. This is another important distinction; they were, in spite of their elaborate disguises and masks perceived as entertainers, not as Pagan revellers! Though even these were certainly not exempt from unruly public posturings and in

1570, the Archbishop of York took out an injunction against disruptive behaviour when these activities had encroached religious celebrations [Twycross and Carpenter, 2002: 43-45].

An act of Parliament in 1511 had previously forbidden masking and guising in England after a desperate effort to keep the peace by 'policing' public events failed [*ibid.*83]. Bands of cheaply disguised marauders, faces blackened with soot/paint/polish, even moss, roamed menacingly around the streets attempting to gain access to homes and public houses for the express purposes of drinking and more importantly, gaming which for the servant and peasant classes was forbidden at all other times! The privileged classes were the preferred sport, having a more profitable purse to win by dice in games of chance. Thus anonymous could a servant fleece his master. The host is obliged to entertain his 'guests,' to provide food and drink and an opportunity to try their luck. Despite the strict rules of conduct, power is levied on the side of the disguised caller, of whom we are never sure. Redolent of the 'Kalends', 'Order', invites 'Chaos' over the threshold. Confrontation is implicit. In contra-distinction to much later records (circa 1738), no 'Mumming' plays are known from this period [Hutton, 2001:8]. Rather, they were said to keep 'mom/mum'; articulation was entirely gestural. Art or artifice? Cass & Roud [2002:16] adds an interesting but cynical view even to the later practises of Mumming play performances as being the product of the 'mountebanks' scheming opportunism to sell cheap cures to unwitting bystanders! In general, whether this is true or mere speculation, records do reveal the same group of performers jealously guarding their patch, year after year in villages and rural areas. Land enclosures between 1740-1840 led to the tragic 'Swing Riots' wherein battling industrialists clashed with rural independents, decimating local Crafts which resulted in extreme poverty and deprivation. [6] Town performances after the industrialisation of the countryside inculcated an even bleaker though more diverse form of disguised behaviour of a noted menacing and ominous manner, especially when attitudes towards beggary changed after the 1880s [Cass & Roud, 2002.51].

Equally rowdy and unsavoury were the medieval *'Charivari,'* whose discordant rough music haunted the streets at night, seeking to expose and pronounce their equally rough justice amongst the populaces of France and Italy. Social and political commentators, these rowdy 'musicians, sporting grotesque masks of specific 'demons' (termed - *'larva'*) and wild animal costumes were given free licence to carouse the streets in the belief that they represented the deceased 'spirits' of husbands protesting against the remarriage of their wives. This disapproval, could naturally, be waived for a fee! [Twycross and Carpenter, 2002:47]. Sinister, unrecognisable, full of malevolent intent, they are free of restraint or reprisal. Again, numerous cases of injury to victims are recorded. In England, this practise, known as 'riding the stang' or *'skimmity'* was much less sinister, though no less provocative, and was generally performed unmasked. Even Plough Monday gatherings during the 16th century were forbidden due to the rising extent of the drunkenness and brawling in the streets; in fact many popular festivals came under increasing restraint due to the riotous nature of their celebrants [Hutton, 2001:89]. Europe too was prey to anarchic factions, and Pegg [1981:21-33] provides numerous chilling accounts of escalating hostility, murder and executions in his seminal study of brutality exerted during 'Carnival' and other guising and masking activities, including the *'Haxey Hood'* game! Pegg [133-140] concludes them to be far from harmless customs in which racism and nationalism are also frequent motivations for retribution and reprisal in recent centuries.

Thomas Urquhart wrote of the wild release and excess intrinsic to the 'Misrule' celebrations of the 17th century of his time. Billington [1991:35] explores this theme tenaciously, positing the very real challenge to normality as pre-requisite for stability. Moreover, she asserts, the upsurge in interest of philosophy, occultism, cosmology and the arts valorised the extreme wonder of the magnificence of our universe, tempering the riotous behaviour of all classes of society. Particularly cogent was the cessation of the anarchic actuations of the 'Mock' King, which after the beheading of Charles 1st and Louis XVI in France were deemed unacceptable expressions of folk celebrations. Known as the *'Saturnalicus Princeps'*, this 'Mock' King role was not entirely facile. His function designated him a Master of the Revels, which chiefly involved the organisation of convivial courtly masked balls, the vain purpose of which was for clandestine affairs, venial assignations, Machiavellian machinations and other sundry nefarious practises. These disguises were a cunning confection of concealment and conceit. More importantly, his role was to secure the more lucrative and at all other times discouraged, gaming activities of gambling and betting in which the anonymous winner could literally claim all. The removal of the Mock King at the end of his short term, once again symbolised the return to standard law and order, not in any way connected to the Frazerian concept of sacrifice, death and resurrection. Billington [1991:257] reiterates the very real problem for the monarchies of this time in regaining public order, which devolved further during this troubled time. Political and religious upheavals gave vent to extremist behaviour advantaged during these times of celebration when certain laws of conduct were lax. Leaders of these unruly acts were apparently named 'captain' as derivative of the Latin, 'caput', for 'head', in a parody of the King, insinuating that both are equally outside the Law [*ibid.* 15].

Other titles reflecting this euphemism were awarded instigators and rebels, often of an agrarian flavour, suggesting a less than noble root to these social problems. A popular selection of these names included, 'Jack Straw', named after a leader of the peasants revolt of 1381, the 'Earl of the Plough', and 'John Sheep.' Ronald Hutton [2001:9]in explaining how the extensive ban between the early 1400s and 1560 on public masking to deter criminal activity, impresses upon us the distinction between the anarchistic activities of the lower orders and those of the nobler classes, which he presents as being more theatrical, satirical and inclined to general buffoonery. In spite of the divergent origins of these domains and their motivations for unruly behaviour, this explanation somehow implies an artificial and less intimidating manifestation of social unrest and economic depression. Prosecutions were indeed rife within all classes. Increasing polemics against religion and social dissent trickled downwards from high society role playing 'mummery' of the court to the less privileged classes taking form in the Mystery and Miracle plays of Tudor England in which animal masks naturally signified the more bestial vices of human nature [Twycross and Carpenter, 2002:231-234].

Yet the Theatre, ever precarious due to the caprice of governments and Monarchies, was increasingly an ideal platform for the expression of grievance, grudge, injustice and retribution, cleverly executed under choice plays performed by heavily disguised, masked and costumed actors of the acting guilds and touring companies; *"freedom comes clothed in a clownish garment....freedom is the man that will turn the world upside down"* [Billington, 1991:254]. We must concede this was a public forum 'par excellence,' often hi-jacked by more subversive factions of the populace. This bears out the huge drive towards pageantry at all levels in a vain attempt at staving the forces of chaos and destruction corroding the wealth and health of an ailing climate. [Hutton, 2001:65]. Of particular and striking importance is the stress placed upon the contrast of the summer customs to those of winter. Again, Billington's [1991:254] erudite research exposes the encouragement given to the summer customs by the Church in support of much needed revenue. Morality plays were elaborately performed public spectacles in no way associated with the glorification or ratification of Paganism, but were designed to highlight the folly of sin, and to appreciate the loftier principles of eschatology and duty. These were in sharp contrast to the savage rebellions and biting satire of those of the winter festivities. The polarised 'mood' of these extremes is axiomatic to purpose and opportunity exploited by the darker factions of human nature and those who ride its tide. The 'Gag' Acts of the later 18$^{th}$ century again curtailed the abuse exercised by trade unionists and other revolutionary activists among the working classes objecting to poverty and injustice seeking a voice amidst the mayhem of public chaos [Pennick, 1998:46].

Certainly during the 17$^{th}$ century, English public records do reveal winter folk activities that more closely resemble those former Roman/Continental methods of celebration, especially in the wearing of masks, popularised during the Middle Ages in spite of the several Penitentials between the 4$^{th}$ and 8$^{th}$ centuries condemning that practice. Commonly, it is suggested this may have been due to their desire to stamp out whatever they perceived as superstitious rural customs of the *'Pagani'* [Twycross & Carpenter, 2002:24-25]. Interestingly, the masking rites of the 'Pagani' ridiculed and satirised the 'human' antics of their gods. Early Christians too joined in these processions as exemplars of this 'mock' piety! Succinctly, humanity at its most bestial is an inconceivable affront to divinity, Pagan or otherwise. Pertinently, this is extremely relevant to this study because it calls to attention the often overlooked yet vital reasons why animal guising and masking was considered such an abomination by the Church offering a contra view to the popular and over simplified anti-Pagan view as mentioned previously. So sacrilegious in fact, it was rendered the worst offence simply because it mocked nature, God's perfect creation, it violated the divine, in both Pagan and Christian celebrations during *'mundus inversus'* (the Earth inverted) that is, when it is ruled by the Devil! [*ibid.*, 27]. St Jerome in attacking Classical theatre, inveighed vehemently the horror and insult to God in the concealment of our natural state, the form He chose for us. Ironically though, Jerome had shown his supreme ignorance because, within Greek theatre, the Mask expressed or revealed 'Truth', personified in stylised conceptual forms to avert corruption by the actors' human features! [*ibid.*, 285] Let us not forget; all theatre is illusion.

Deception is made real by our own belief in it. Magic manifests in our acceptance. Moralists and fanatics of the medieval period in openly citing the opinions of their predecessors during the early and formative years of the Church, especially in regard to the Kalends and Saturnalian celebrations, have erroneously forged a spurious link that is commonly perceived as revealing a continuity of practice of those festivals throughout [*ibid.*, 296-7]. Hutton [1997:329] concludes how revelling, masking and the exchange of clothes redolent of these ancient festivals, were always an indication of secular, not religious practises, wherein a relaxation of the normatively stringent laws surrounding the liturgical year regarding the sacred, asserting that even in ancient Pagan times, these secular activities were always understood as being outside these rules, beyond their bounds in fact, not worship in any way, given over to free and abandoned public license. Geoff & Fran Doel [1992] also avidly refute the survival of Paganism within these rites, despite the disparate and obvious elements discernable within them. Being more incidental than instrumental to the activities, they insist these minor issues have been awarded far too much emphasis by indiscriminate folklorists. They assert that revival must not be mistaken for survival! Especially, they are keen to emphasize how typically, for example, Christmas remains for many of us a mainly secular festival bearing little resemblance in form or meaning to its practise of a thousand years ago.

Yet it could be effectively argued that despite latent barbarism and carnality synthesised with free licence common to both ends of the spectrum and throughout the fourteen hundred period between the third century to the seventeenth, there lies inherent the archaic and epic battle between the forces of Chaos and Order, exemplified within the Rites of *'Zagmuk,'* the Babylonian New Year. This highly stylised, ritualised and formal 'Festival of the Fates' lasting twelve days reversed the social order, plunging the city states into anarchy - a pure state representing a time before 'the Beginning'. The Tutelary God of each city state would abdicate (and then regain) his position, by proving his worth, in order to stave the forces of chaos manifest in the female figure of 'Tiamat', the Dragon Queen. This sense of the sacred, of piety, wholly lacking from the inane secularisation by the Roman machine, changed forever the methodology of celebration in the western world. It is absolutely vital to distinguish between the customs of Church and State, which is not to say that the latter do not contain religious elements, but that they are enacted in spite of them, not because of them. If masked folk practises survived the processing by Christianity, they regrettably did not survive in the records. Not until the British witch craze of 1400-1700 was suggestion made of nocturnal worship of sinister Pagan gods, dressed in masks and animal skins. Even the Penitentials and law codes are bereft of such reports. [Twycross and Carpenter, 2002:23-31].

So many customs reflect a cultural need, found only in a group identity, and this more properly explains the underlying recurrence of similar human principles than unsupported suggestions of 'Pagan' survival. Many festivals and rituals have found either their origin or continuance within liturgical calendar customs. But few can with certainty be said to be genuinely 'Pagan.' Communal rites were not generally perceived as magical or divinatory, therefore not connected to any heathen practises of the past [Hutton, 2001:71]. Owen Davies [2003:185] astutely remarks how by the medieval period, in spite of residual elements of Paganism within inherently Christian celebrations, all vestiges of pre-associated belief and religion had been utterly removed. Folklorists have frequently been remiss in their analyses of social anthropology and have grossly underestimated the efficacy of their observance in the negative feedback system [Pegg, 1981:140].

The practice of masking and the wearing of disguise has permeated all cultures across many diverse demographic and time zones, most commonly finding expression in magical and/or religious activities. Sacred divine theatre, primarily acts of devotion, morphed steadily into riotous acts of parody and irreverence. Within this transition a vehicle was discovered and shrewdly exploited and which many commentators have found offensive, anti-social and disquieting. This radical exposition has explored the mask, not as a reflection of the divine, but as the dark and all too human psyche of man; a perspective often glossed over, or ignored. We are after all matter and spirit, and the mask has been utilised interchangeably to effectively conceal one whilst displaying the other. More than artifice or illusion, the mask is a medium of projection, of control, exposed and manipulated by the less than scrupulous actor within a theatre of his own devising. It has provided the opportunity for social display and comment on a lavish and unmitigated scale.

Society of the 18$^{th}$ century was itself a virtual stage where every facet of society articulated a volley of role-playing, intrigue, deceit, sex and violence, flourishing behind the anonymity of the mask. By the 1780s these fancies were officially banned in England as immoral, but continued in spite of it. It literalised society defining the freedoms that loosened conformity and restriction. All of this was accomplished even as it entertained and enthralled both participants and voyeurs. All drawn into a surreal and fascinating world of the other, the alter ego, the self disguised, hidden yet free. Most popular in European high society were the androgynous black cloaks worn with simple white masks (*'en travesti'*).

Sweeping industrialisations initiated in the late 18th century were further exacerbated by the rise in continental warfare, bearing witness to a decline of many once lavish and gauche activities. Those of the poorer classes were soon to follow, eventually falling into decline during the First World War. It is cruelly ironic that the middle classes who once fought the hardest to suppress these delinquent working-class practises in the 1940s are now striving for their survival! Though today, the motivations are entirely unconnected. These acts are now performed for pleasure and nostalgia, rather than hunger and anger, and are rarely fully masked or concealed [Cass & Roud, 2002]. Nevertheless, throughout it all a common thread can be discerned; an underlying motive which offers an uncomfortable profane causality. From the Kalends of Rome to the Hogmanay guizers of the early 20th century, the most common activity of all the lurid practises throughout, affirming the prime root of all evil - is that of money, in terms of power or need, either in the form of gambling or begging. This is not incidental, but primary, engendering the opportunity for excessive violence and abuse.

This is an extreme claim and yet historiography is a maze of semantics and hierarchical subjective analyses. Each skilful argument persuades us with artful and erudite revelations. Do we respond to this rationally and objectively, or subjectively and emotively? Experience in the field is the only key; active responsive visceral reaction. Again, each of us must decide. How do we feel amidst masked revellers, joyful or uneasy? If we perform, wearing a mask or disguise, do we feel empowered or weak and anonymous? The 'voice' is guaranteed in either case to project a dual sense, a dichotomy of potential. So do we exploit this, or withdraw?

Ethics of nature once typified in the bifrons mask of Janus, revealing simultaneously the duplicity and neutrality of concept, became abandoned by the 16th century in favour of the open, bare and unconcealed face. Virtue presents its own true face, that it might be known and recognised, whereas sin and corruption are the measure of concealment. [Twycross and Carpenter, 2002:257-8] These are inherent, intrinsic and implicit principle dynamics of the Medieval Theatre and drama both secular and religious! So were the Christian moralists right to condemn masking and guising? Was it or can it ever be, just harmless fun? Are we drawn inexorably towards aggression, depravity and decadence when immersed in our darker natures? How are such things determined and measured? Is it liberating and edifying or intimidating and oppressive? Surely it all depends from which side of the mask we view the world?

"All the world's a stage, and all the men and women merely players…"
(*As You Like It*)

# Bibliography:

Billington, S. 1991 *'Mock Kings in Medieval Renaissance Drama'* Clarendon Press. Oxford.

Cass, E. & Roud, S. 2002 *'An introduction to the English Mummer's Play'* English Folkdance and Song Society. London.

Cawte, E. C. 1978 *'Ritual Animal Disguise'* Redwood Burn Ltd. GB.

Davies, O. 2003 *'Cunning Folk: Popular Magic in English History'* Hambledon & London. London

Doel, G&F. 1992 *'Mumming, Howling and Hoodening: Midwinter Rituals in*

*Sussex, Kent and Surrey'* Headly Bros Ltd. Kent.

Ferguson, D. 1996 *'The Magical Year'* Batsford. London

Harte, J. 2004 *'Explore Fairy Traditions'* Heart of Albion Press. UK

Hutton, R. 2001 *'The Rise and Fall of Merrie England'*. Ox. Uni Press. England

Hutton, R. 1997 *'The Pagan Religions of the British Isles'* Blackwell. UK

Jackson, N. 1996 *'Masks of Misrule'* Capall Bann. UK

Jones, E. J. & Clifton, C. 1997 *'Sacred Mask Sacred Dance'* Llewellyn. Pub. USA

O' Caithan, S. 2001 *'Irish Hobby Horse and Icelandic Horse Dance'* ('Northern Lights') Uni College. Dublin Press. Ireland.

Pegg, B. 1981 *'Rites and Riots: Folk Customs of Britain and Europe'* Blandford Press. Dorset

Pennick, N. 1998 *'Crossing the Borderlines'* Capall Bann. UK

Peter, T. 1997 *'The Cornish Obby Oss'* 1997. Oakmagic Pub. Penzance.

Twycross, M. & Carpenter, S. 2002 *'Masks and Masking in Medieval and Early Tudor England'* Ashgate Pub. Ltd. England

Whitlock, R. 1978 *'A Calendar of Country Customs'* Batsford. London

# References:

1. http://aspen.conncoll.edu/politicsandculture/page.cfm?key=448#
2. www.folkplay.info/confs/Pettit2002.pdf
3. http://Penelope.uchicago.edu/~grout/encyclopaedia_romana/calendar/Saturnalia.html#archon1162795
4. http://jol.ismennt.is/english/gryla-terry-gunnell.htm
5. Derbyshire Miscellany. *'Origins of the Derby Ram'* Vol 2. No 1 pp221-228 October 1959.
6. Richard William Parkinson, (private correspondence 22nd Oct 2008)

# 7
# 'Witch Blood'
# - A Modern Heresy?

The following essay is in two parts: the first is presented by my esteemed friend and colleague Christopher R. Reibling and the second is my own response to it. Both were inspired by themes touched upon within *'A Man for all Seasons'* regarding the highly controversial aspects and opinions on the 'substance' and 'value' of 'witch-blood'.

## Grist for the Oatesian Heresy:
## Or, More Doubts about the Witch Blood

This is in response to Shani Oates': *'A Man for All Seasons'* [*The Cauldron*: 02/07#123] in which readers were invited to participate in an open discussion on the witch blood and its implications for Modern Traditional Witchcraft.

In deference to Robert Cochrane, Oates avails herself in this instance of a thoroughly contentious pronouncement, a 'heresy' in fact, concerning the existence of a bloodline or, more specifically, a blood *type*, unique to witches and their historical claim to 'difference'; a claim cherished not only by Cochrane but - by extension and no less passionately - by other avatars of the modern Craft: *'Isn't it time,'* she asks, *'that all this nonsense was laid to rest?'* [1]

I am indebted to Oates not only for her invitation to further reify this heresy, but for her permission to reproduce portions of our private correspondence [02/07-10/07] in the following pages.

Initiatory experience and/or an intimate familiarity with the subject of this writing is definitely to be assumed here, though no particular witchcraft lineage is intended to serve as its focus. This is a *general* attempt to evaluate the myth of the blood and its implications at the widest possible level/s: (historical, metaphysical, experiential). The following opinions, consequently, reflect my *own* knowledge and experience of this phenomenon as an ex-communicant Gardnerian practitioner residing in Toronto, Canada. I do not propose to speak for initiates of *other* initiatory bloodlines in this matter or, indeed, for other Gardnerians however much I might welcome their opinions and response.

It is not my purpose here, moreover, to re-state well-known biographical and/or autobiographical material/s examining claims to the blood made by all or any of the Craft's most visible progenitors: Robert Cochrane, Alex Sanders, G.B. Gardner. This task - especially in Gardner's case - has been exhaustively undertaken elsewhere. [2] Suffice to say that each of these men - all without question founding fathers of discreet witchcraft lineages - claimed a connection to witch blood which - while ostensibly metaphysical - was *implicitly* genetic and biological.

One's willingness to accept the validity of all or any of these claims is, of course, entirely subjective. What *is* important, is that each of these men - independently and of their own accord - felt the need for this connection so acutely that they were willing to ignore scientific fact and engage in self-delusion in order to secure it. Be this as it may, and given the willingness of these *modern* men to turn a blind eye to the possibility that their blood may have been as mortal as any, certain questions nonetheless remain, namely: was the blood to which each of them lay claim common to a single (ie. *indivisible*) hereditary source, or are we to believe that - by the mid-twentieth-century - the witch blood *itself* (via. inherent haematological volition) somehow managed to sub-divide into separate initiatory 'lines:' (i.e. Gardnerian, Alexandrian, R.B. Tubal Cain). Surely it is ludicrous to think so?

And yet ... and yet ... witches of various ilks continue to insist upon their 'difference,' not only from humanity at large, but from *each other* as initiates of competing branches (blood-types?) of the same Craft. A Darwinian scenario *('survival of the fittest')*, typically mortal and not in the least metaphysical, springs to mind here, and one all the more regrettable in its implications as the Craft continues to factionalize and squabble itself out of existence.

The problem, of course, is that the lore encountered by the founding fathers of witchcraft and - by extension - their initiates, posits not only the existence of a bloodline unique to witches, but a line which - in mythical times - existed *outside* the parameters of the human gene pool. This crucial idea, accessible to *all* aspirants to the Craft for well over a century now through the *Book of Enoch,* tells of vast, Angelic beings ('Sons of God') who, upon mating with the daughters of men, seeded the human race - or portions thereof - with magical powers.[3] Romantic and aesthetically pleasing, this remote legend retains its power as an unassailable 'given' of modern witchcraft - a mystery whose validity might more aptly be defined as an *act of faith*. The contention that this mythical seeding may have escaped detection across the millennia by science or - more damningly - the appearance of even *one* avatar in whom its haematological properties might be *physically observed,* remains one of the Craft's weakest bids to credibility. Shani Oates comments: [4]

> "Man's curiosity for his origins has spawned many theories, the most popular of which (in a mythical sense) is very similar to Robert Cochrane's and concerns some ancestral progenitor seeding humanity with superior DNA (from one source or another dependant upon belief). But ... if this is accepted, then we must

also accept that this DNA is now dispersed throughout the whole of mankind in minutely varying degrees. It is scientifically impossible for it to have remained within any one racial or 'belief system' group. This is absolute nonsense."

Given that the validity of witch blood as anything but myth or metaphor can be seriously contested at both the genetic and/or biological level/s, it is nonetheless astounding that its existence as *literal reality* remains deeply entrenched in the imaginations of otherwise sentient twentieth-century witches. The longevity of this factitious and thoroughly disruptive myth has been enabled, moreover, by the attendant belief that, upon initiation, one joins/re-joins a bloodline stretching back to mythic times. The words of recognition spoken to G.B. Gardner by members of the 'New Forest Coven' are revealing to recall here: '*You belonged to us in the past. You are of the blood. Come back to where you belong.*' [5] Indeed, the terror of setting one's foot on the path of witchcraft, which ends for many a worthy aspirant in a fruitless search for 'authenticity,' is that one might fail to make contact with a group or individual possessed of sufficient blood connection to legitimize one's initiatory status. Referencing the praxis of certain groups within the UK (and the slavish obliteration of personality required to join them) Oates observes: [6]

> "Who's who (in witchcraft) depends entirely upon who initiated you. No more no less. No name? Well, then, you are nobody, bereft of all knowledge and rights thereof."

But the damage perpetrated upon the Craft by an unreasoning and unreasonable belief in the value of witch blood does not end here. Particularly evident in North America, but by no means uniquely so, I would assert that something *happened* to the blood when it made its way to North America from the Old World. Namely, that it underwent a material transformation which reified *even further* its value, not as an article of spirit, but as a *commodity* which might be exchanged - even offered for sale in some instances - to would-be initiates desperate to possess a blood connection to the Craft. Witness, for example, the 2,690,000 internet sites presently on offer pertaining to 'witch blood;' (i.e. advertisements for board games, cocktail mix, horror movies, spa treatments, pulp fiction, music groups, wiccan 'blogs' … the reader is encouraged to undertake his or her own search of this thoroughly *materialist* domain). There is nothing *magical* about blood such as this, though its efficacy as a coercive and/or political tool in the hands of many an all-too-human Priest or Priestess has indeed entailed a certain wizardry!

Materialist underpinnings notwithstanding, continuing to insist upon the magical validity of a phenomenon which - ironically - is as Christian in concept as the 'Apostolic Procession,' [7] there are surprisingly few witches in North America or elsewhere, willing to unmask the witch blood for the fable it truly is or, more contentiously, to embrace its function as a (fictive) means of engendering a sense of shared heritage and belonging which, in reality, has nothing to do with genetic aberration. Explicating the role played by such fables (rites) in so-called primitive societies and - by extension - the modern Craft, Oates opines: [8]

> "anthropological studies have revealed these (rites) to signify a unity on the *mortal* plane linking a (very real) *physical* ancestry, the celebration of which denotes a particular tribe or clan ship. *Modern* witchcraft (GBG and JGD et. al.) replicates this act in order to impress a psychological association of all those generations of witches with whom we (supposedly) share a commonality of belief and practice (scant and incredulous in reality we know) in order to induce a sympathetic sense of unity among the 'brethren.' It is a *desperate act of theatre* designed to induce a sense of belonging, of continuity, at

least psychologically. But we are not tribal peoples inducting members of our own families; we are disparate peoples from the length and breadth of the planet. This is why in such 'created' communities we strive to call each other 'brother' and 'sister,' to consciously remind ourselves of this artificial 'link.'"

Impeding a consensus among witches which might redeem our understanding of the term 'witch blood' from the plethora of medieval ideas in which it presently lies mired, has been a backward-gazing insistence upon orally-transmitted 'teachings,' hand-copied (i.e. subjectively edited) 'Books of Shadows,' and other material/s as *'Holy Writ.'* Redolent of fundamentalist Christianity with its blinkered emphasis on biblical scripture as *literal* truth, no portion of this battered legacy may be changed or questioned since, to do so, is to fly in the face not only of 'tradition' but - far worse - of the God/s themselves. (That these Titanic entities might prefer truth to fiction in their respective belief systems does not seem to have occurred to Craft priesthood and remains an enduring taboo!) [9]

Further undermining the possibility that an inclusive re-definition of the blood might necessarily be undertaken by those who should know better is the fact that - in North America at least - all pre-eminent 'authority' pertaining to the Craft's inner teachings (including blood provenance) originates - or indeed continues to reside - *elsewhere*. In this regard, and however well-meaning the avatars who carried the Craft to North America might have imagined themselves to be, their efforts have resulted in a form of colonialism which - impacting adherents at the most basic (initiatory) level - has made it all but impossible for Modern Witchcraft to evolve beyond its pseudo-medieval trappings and simply 'move on.' Too often, the crux of the matter, the truth, the 'real goods' concerning our heritage are said to lie hidden in the experience of some long-departed elder or in some forever unobtainable 'Book of Shadows'

- the myth of a lost '*ubertext.*' (And this is *not*, be it understood, an attempt to make a plea for the horrors and insubstantiality of the '*New Age!*' Indeed, the growth of this thoroughly materialist enterprise serves only to underline the need for a more rigorous look at our origins and the nullifying devaluation of one of our most *potent* metaphors at the hands of unscrupulous opportunists on both sides of the Atlantic).

And yet ... and yet ... is not the idea of a blood which stands apart, a blood which separates the witch from everyday humanity a glamorous and seductive fiction to be sure? Does it not compensate us, at a level requiring no ill-advised hex or curse, for centuries of misunderstanding and persecution? Little wonder, then, it should prove equally attractive to persons of weak mind ... the desperate, the gullible - those who come to the Craft seeking 'family' in the absence of family elsewhere? Sadly, such individuals open themselves to manipulation at the hands of those for whom a claim to witch blood signifies not only power, but '*power over.*' Indeed, little imaginative effort is required to envision how an unscrupulous priesthood might use this claim as a means of control over initiates willing to accept the myth of the blood at face value. In such instances, practices such as the 'taking of the measure' (i.e. a measure of blood), assume dark and malevolent import as acts of 'psychological terrorism' and/or forms of 'cultish paranoia' – weapons to be used *against* the initiate should he or she elect to leave the coven contrary to the will of the 'group mind' or reigning priesthood. [10]

It will be argued, of course, that this response to Oates' pioneering call to re-formulate our collective response to one of witchcraft's most cherished beliefs constitutes a 'worst case scenario' which does not reflect the true praxis or philosophy of the Craft. And yet it cannot be denied that abuses of power – too often informed by the authority of the blood have indeed occurred, *and will continue to occur,* until a far less literal understanding of this myth has been achieved. Only witness the damage done by priesthood who have employed the blood (i.e. subjective recognition of its presence in a potential initiate), as a 'litmus test' to decide who *is* and who *is not* a witch. Ironically, and in the absence of elders capable of evolving beyond a mythic fundamentalism so obviously divisive and undesirable, the much-disparaged option of 'self-initiation' into witchcraft assumes an all-new credibility!

In deference to this admittedly radical point-of-view, the time-worn adage: *'One cannot be a witch alone'* belies the effect an insistence on various bloodlines has had upon the Craft's validity and coherence as a spiritual path. One need only recall the pettiness which attends any occasion where diverse bloodlines gather (i.e. the ostensibly well-intended 'pub-moot') to perceive that this is true. Surely we are all of the *same* blood, which is to say blood of the human variety? As Oates attests, to believe otherwise may in fact be tantamount to calling down upon ourselves renewed misunderstanding and persecution: [11]

> "I feel we present a greater risk for a return to times of persecution if we insist on holding on to the premise that our blood is different in some way to that of others. This is an alienating and dangerous premise that could be easily utilized against us. But if we can educate people by showing them we are all basically the same, that we are not a breed apart, that only our faith separates us, then we offer a greater hope of tolerance."

Looking back on the contents of these pages, I am indeed aware of the gigantic leap of faith called for in postulating a re-consideration of the witch blood no less blasphemous, in extension, than the one initiated by Shani Oates. It is difficult for any of us, myself included, to relinquish faith in cherished beliefs, and yet, transformation is of the essence … the nature of the universe is change.

Yes?

The debate continues …

## Notes

1. 'A Man For All Seasons' by S. Oates, *The Cauldron*, 02/07, #123:25. All further references are to this publication.

2. For relevant biographical data re. Gardner's claim to the blood see: *Gerald Gardner and the Witchcraft Revival: The Significance of His Life and Works to the Story of Modern Witchcraft* by Philip Heselton (Capall Bann, 2001: 384-387). For confirmation of Gardner's claim, see Gardner's own text, *The Meaning of Witchcraft* (Magickal Childe, 1991: 11) and/or his discussion of the hereditary powers of the witch in *Witchcraft Today* (Magickal Childe, 1991, II: 31-40). Alex Sanders' claim to the blood is described at length in *King of the Witches: The World of Alex Sanders* by June Johns (Coward Mc Cann, 1969: 12-17). Also, Shani Oates provides a representative statement from Robert Cochrane in her article: p. 24: *"I cannot die until I have passed my virtue on. I carry within my physical body the totality of all the witches that have been in my family for many centuries. If I call upon my ancestors, I call upon forces which are within myself and exterior. Now you know what I mean by the burden of time."*

3. Relevant passages from *The Book of Enoch* are provided by Paul Huson in *Mastering Witchcraft* (Berkley Publishing, 1980: 9-13). The complete text can be found in *The Other Bible: Jewish Pseudepigrapha, Christian Apocrypha, Gnostic Scriptures, Kabbalah, Dead Sea Scrolls* ed. Willis Barnstone (Harper Collins, 1984: I/Creation Myths: 3-9).

4. Correspondence: 01/02/07.

5. G.B. Gardner, *The Meaning of Witchcraft*: p. 11 as cited above.

6. Correspondence: 08/03/07.

7. Discussing the role of the Catholic Pope in the Apostolic Procession, Cyrus Shahrad writes: "at the pontifical high mass in St. Peter's Basilica, when the choir calls to him 'Tu Es Petra' ('You are Peter'), it's a reminder that he is also first in a direct line leading all the way back to the original bishop of Rome, the Apostle Peter, and thereby to Jesus himself. The reaction of many (wailing, weeping, falling to their knees at his blessing) is a sign of just how powerful a link this is." *Secrets of the Vatican* (Capella Books, 2007: 50).

8. Correspondence: 05/29/07.

9. My use of the term 'truth' in this context is intended to signify *empirical* truth: that which can be *shown to be true* by means or evidence beyond personal experience, faith-based affirmation and/or pure speculation. I am aware that this definition does not satisfy or pertain to post-structuralist thinking about the nature of 'the Truth' as my correspondence with Shani Oates (01/02/07) hopefully shows: "As I'm sure you know – our concept of 'the Truth' as an unassailable 'given' has slipped and slithered quite considerably in recent years thanks to the writings of Jacques Derrida and his ilk."

10. Correspondence: 29/05/07. See Oates' comments re. 'the measure.'

11. Correspondence: 01/02/07.

## Witch Blood: A Modern Heresy?

The following paper is a response and conclusion to the debate opened by Mr Reibling, which as noted, was inspired by comments raised on the subject of 'witch-blood' by this writer in the article 'A Man for all Seasons.' [1] For the benefit of all current readers, relevant paragraphs from that article have been selected and are herein quoted verbatim to facilitate an introduction to the concepts and context of Reibling's commentaries.

> "But I disagree with Robert Cochrane's opinion that divinity and spirituality are products of the '5$^{th}$ art' - a 'blood' heritage: I cannot die until I have passed my virtue on. I carry within my *physical* (my emphasis) body the totality of all the witches that have been in my family for many centuries. If I call upon my ancestors, I call upon forces that are within myself and exterior. Now you know what I mean when I speak of the burden of time." [A Man for all Seasons]

This cherished belief, refers more to personal and family virtue within Hereditary families, being but a small cog in the greater cog of humanity and therefore ultimately of God. Rather, I believe our true legacy to be a spiritual one, and thus we are created 'spiritual' heirs. Another heresy?

> "Moving backwards quickly in 'time' (to Ancient Egypt) to cull another sacred cow – Pharaoh didn't marry his sisters and daughters to acquire a 'blood' inherited power, but to maintain political control of his empire. Once this practice ceased, his power base crumbled and the rise of the Priesthood contracted a grip that even the 'heretical' reforms of Akhenaten (during the Armana period) was unable to eradicate. Furthermore, not until Pharaoh and his (chosen) Chief wife had undergone certain rituals and proclaimed specific oaths, anointed by the (King-making) Priests, was the spirit of Horus (God) believed to reside within him. Contrary to popular opinion,

he was *not* born with this divinity inherent, but had to *acquire* it by rite and priestly sanction. Only then was he awarded his office and sacred duty. So many diverse dynasties ruled Egypt; Pharaoh simply 'inherited the title along with the divine *spirit* of Horus from his predecessor. This is the true 'divine' right and legacy of Kings, not 'blood'. In this way, Joshua was elected as the spiritual heir of Moses taking precedence over his own sons. The practise of the Tibetan ascension of the Dalai Lama may be similarly viewed. His spirit may re-incarnate anywhere in any person, of low or high birth. Again this is not a heritage of the blood, but one of spirit." [A Man for all Seasons]

"Science heras proven that everyone is not only related to one another, but to the first humans. This means that, short of in-breeding to the point of extinction, all of us somewhere possess 'Witch-blood' from some ancestor however many genera back. Therefore by Robert Cochrane's reckoning this affords them "the ear of the gods". Yet we know this simply isn't so. Many children born into 'witch' families heed not the call of blood, while other, apparent outsiders, rise from divine inspiration to become teachers, prophets and mystics in their own right. Sadly, the need to conform to this fiction also inspires contrived 'bloodlines' as proof of worthiness." [A Man for all Seasons]

Significant comments were tendered by Reibling[2] in his challenging response to the main issues outlined above, and I was cordially invited to continue the debate. Prompted thus to expand upon certain points raised during our consequent and private correspondence, I now feel able to better articulate and convey the true 'occult' significance of 'witch-blood'. Further investigation is requisite in my opinion, to expose this disingenuous idiom - 'witch-blood' and its popular but often inapt application within the Craft.[3] The revelation of these fallacious associations will hopefully engender a greater understanding of what Reibling refers to as *"the curious effects of spirit on mortal blood in mortal time."*[4]

Cherished beliefs provide solace, comfort, security and most pertinently with regard to 'witch-blood', a pre-requisite sense of identity, of belonging. Understandably then, for many, the culling of sacred cows, especially this one, is a slow, protracted and considerably tentative enterprise. Ultimately, false beliefs, crucial to religious dogma impede or withhold completely spiritual and intellectual fruition. Some of these may simply be outmoded superstitions - the common ignorance of natural causes;[5] others, for example, are more complex, sinister acts of *'hocus pocus'* (doggerel Latin for *'hoc est corpus meum'*) which means somewhat ironically - this is my body, viz. matter, in which the *transforming* spirit has or will descend. The powerful evocation of Spirit, invested in the transubstantiation of the Catholic Eucharist, where Christ's presence as the 'bread of heaven' is acknowledged (again) as a *spiritual* food, imparting some measure of Grace via ingestion of 'presence', remains one of the greater mysteries of the Catholic Church.

Yet even here, the difference between theory (of intent) and practice (of belief) enforces the realisation of the gulf between the beauty and grace of the *original* concept (not affirmed as a theological tenet until 1215CE by the Fourth Lateran Council) and the somewhat challenging credulity of the primitive cannibalism of its divergent general practise. Here I wish to highlight the *process* by which such a change in the 'substance' takes place (wishing to avoid the thorny issue of what exactly what has changed into what!!!) i.e., the invocation of *spirit* by the officiating priest, and its true import and impact upon that substance, irrespective of 'what' it is believed to be. Significantly, neither orthodox nor heterodox doctrinal philosophies are aligned at 'ground level.' [6] Attendant aberrations to fundamental tenets are in fact analogous to those evident within the equally erroneous concept and expression of 'witch-blood'. Very often, what people believe they are doing is considerably distinct from what they are actually doing. Continued ignorance of this reality further discredits all religious belief and benefits no-one to perpetuate. In the past, this has led to bigoted dissent, and if unchecked, will once again erode credibility to a paralysing sterility.

Within occultism, mystical or poetic terms that reference 'witch-blood', or 'the blood', as it is more commonly referred to, do so metaphorically and/or metaphysically. Confusingly, these have become forged into a rallying call to the faithful and should not be taken as a <u>literal</u> statement of fact. As a statement, 'witch-blood' declaims recognition, an acknowledgment by and of the enlightened and initiated. Both these states of heightened awareness are effectively induced by spiritual interaction, further emphasising the shift away from corporeality. Mankind being animated by spirit, seeks its reciprocity. Generally this search is generated culturally, sometimes politically, and less frequently personally. One could argue that it is the enlightened and re-incarnated soul that is able to discern more favourably, on a personal level, their choice of religion or spiritual philosophy. This gives purpose and support in this life for the next, extraneous of ancestry.

Absolute enlightenment is a spiritual achievement, acquired only when one is finally able to release all reliance upon matter. We need to realize that an insistence upon *matter*, as a mark of distinction, is utterly erroneous. Everything organic is generated by spirit, irrespective of whether or not it is possessed of blood, and upon death and decay of its corporeal host, is recycled separately from it. Consciousness is a transferable state and is entirely independent of blood; a profound belief typified in Buddhist, Neo-Platonic and Hermetic philosophies.

Regarding these contentious matters of the 'blood', my purpose here is *not* to denounce hereditary practises or family bloodlines whose nurturing of specific mythopoeia and idiosyncratic modus operandi are invaluable to understanding the historiography and integrity of the Craft. Yet, I believe the misconceptions surrounding such 'Clanships' to have unwittingly complicated the question of 'witch blood.' Of course, a mitigating factor in this is the propensity of some individuals to view their command of this 'Virtue' as either sorcerous or mystical; the former tends to award more credence in terms of 'heritage' than the latter. However, it is mankind as a *species* that receives the 'birthright' of ascension, grace and re-incarnation, a realisation of our absolute destiny, actuated in the form of an initiatory priesthood, the keepers of the mysteries. Hence its dissemination throughout the occult body politic. Polluted and corrupted, its true virtue and veracity is now in question.

Furthermore, elementary elitism has eroded and disintegrated treasured ideas into unacceptable dogma, forcefully suppressing seekers of the truth. Witch blood is more properly a 'state of mind', a thought process, albeit one of spirit; it cannot be a literal *physical* reality, it cannot be invested by corporeal means. If one witch is born of another then they could be (if wished) loosely described as possessing 'witch' blood, but only in the same sense that a doctor might claim reception of a medical heritage, or indeed a Christian, their belief system. There is here an imperative to distinguish between the rights to knowledge afforded by birthright, viz., birth *advantage* arising from family trade, practice or belief which is passed on (via nurture, familiarity, tutoring, etc), and knowledge inherited (allegedly) from within the actual gene structure itself. In reality, being born of another witch confers nothing *extraordinary*, emotionally, physically, spiritually or mentally. Such things are determined only by the incarnating <u>soul</u> (which is not genetic) and the teaching the child may receive in life, a fundamental principle I shall return to shortly.

Another elitism coterminous with 'witch-blood' is that of 'blue blood'; a parallel belief that somehow, royalty and aristocracy possess a different strain of this viscous life-giving fluid to everyone else! More nonsense propagated to secure privileges denied those not ranked by its measure. We have become distracted with the pursuit of 'authenticity' rather than truth; the former, signified by possession of a 'correct' blood-line of course, the latter, though intrinsic to the former, is deemed subjective and honed to suit quite specific agendas. It is said, the nature of the mysteries is a paradox, such that, the truth is everywhere revealed and concealed, open to discovery by all sincere seekers, not only the supposed elite, or approved few. It could be argued of course, that the act of seeking itself marks those individuals with prior distinction and may be counted as a spiritual vocation that may or may not be hereditary. Certainly, in reality, such a calling does manifest indiscriminately.

From this supposed 'elitism' we may easily discern how the concept of 'witch-blood' as a distinguishing feature or mark of distinction has acquired the unwarranted status akin to Holy Writ. As Reibling [7] asserts, it is redolent of the apostolic succession of Catholic Popes descending from St Peter. Apostle literally means a 'teacher' or 'messenger' and interestingly, the succession here is one of the *Word*,[8] not blood, not even spirit. This authorized lineage and approved succession of oral transmission simply dictates and preserves, as doctrine, those *teachings* of the first fabled men, Peter and Paul, no more, no less; supposedly. They claim their connection to and within the Holy Spirit keeps this 'original' knowledge pure, untainted by the corruption of encroaching heresies. [9] In other words, only the Catholic Hierarchy have the authority to determine, demonstrate and deliver 'truth.' Everything outside their remit is deemed false. Consider carefully the following facets of dogma common to both Craft and Christianity. Valid ordinations (initiations), the right to 'spiritual' comfort within the tradition (access to and protection by the Egregore) and definitive liturgy (authentic 'Book of Shadows') [10] reside with an auspicious (elite) body. Clearly, between Church and Occult traditions there emerges a disturbing and uncomfortable parallel that emphasizes the paralysing and suffocating grip executed through their respective authorities and laities.

Priesthoods by distinction *are* however, incontrovertibly elite; simply because their *knowledge* sets them apart from normal society. Particular individuals with more than a passing curiosity in the Craft/Occult worlds are easily recognised in all traditions and cultures. These exceptional and gifted people have an intrinsic awareness of the 'Truth' and a burning desire to pursue it, utterly divorced from any ludicrous bias of lineage in any material sense. Clarification is an essential imperative; spiritually acquired gnosis is entirely distinct from other redoubtable hereditary skills and faculties, many of which, in times past, were in fact trades and crafts maintained as secrets to ensure continuance of livelihoods. Knowledge is power, in every sense of the word. It is a sad truism that the drive for gnosis has exposed many people to exploitation and abuse by unscrupulous egotists of primitive and sinister dispositions. In reality, there can never be a definitive 'Book of Shadows', or a 'pure' line of hereditary witchcraft. Every avatar brings his/her unique message, but it is only part of the whole; it is never complete. Each individual must fulfil this achievement for themselves. All knowledge, however acquired, is but a springboard from which we must launch ourselves, driven onwards by our own diverse and subjective experiences.

Even so, independent of either experience or knowledge, every 'Witch' is driven to trace a 'biological ancestor from whom' it is supposed 'the errant liquid' is 'inherited.' [11] Astutely, Reibling [12] suggests a 'scientific study' of the molecular make-up of this viscous fluid in our endeavour to expose this popular myth. But even here there is conflict within the field. Evolution at the macro level is not yet a proven fact, despite all contemporary exploration into the human genome. The human gene pool is suffused with consistent variation; aptly named, 'genetic drift', it is alleged by some to increase further over time, eventually obliterating all evidence of origin.[13] Recent scientific research also expresses the differences between all humans as being around 0.03%, a figure responsible for the 'transmission of (physical) hereditary traits.' In fact, irrespective of its modified Darwinism, this remains a theory traceable to Hippocrates and Aristotle, and one that has been largely unchallenged outside the scientific community.[14]

Caution is strongly advocated, especially when re-viewing some of the more speculative research into biological ascendancy, for this inculcates a negative catalyst of unprecedented magnitude. These investigations defy common-sense, ignoring even the most basic of all natural laws. Though let us not forget, DNA testing is primarily for the detection and isolation of *physical* and *psychological* variations in (perceived) racial typologies within anthropological studies. Another, more appealing theory proposes that every human being has within their bio-molecular make-up 'silent genes', engendering exceptional metamorphosis: i.e., flower petals from leaves, proving that evolutionary traits exist *prior* to their expression. [15] This radical theory seductively asserts the pre-existence of latent genes, lying dormant awaiting activation! Naturally, the *process* of activation is not automatic, neither is it hereditary [16]. Rather, it requires stimulation *via an external prompt*; it requires specific engagement with a force 'other' than that acquired in the natural reproductive processing of genes and chromosomes, be that 'supernatural' in cases of 'random' genius or of inherent divinity, as in the example of the Dalai Lama, or even symbiotic in those where 'inherent' Will is developed under initiatory status and prolonged exposure to the metaphysical 'other'. Even though our origins may be currently untraceable, we *remain* nonetheless, an homogenous species. The significant differences are distinctly 'other'; they are clearly 'metaphysical', and they defy empirical analysis.

Clearly then, what we do share, as 'witches', within this metaphysical alchemy, is '*blood dedicated*', offered to the service of the occult gene pool, as manifest beings in pursuit of more spiritual quests. Our gifts (as psychics, mediums, healers etc) are merely random; equally so is an impulse towards asceticism. Spirit and matter conjoin within the heart and mind of an old soul upon the singular path towards gnosis. Body and soul are dedicated to this end. The 'arte'[17] is the format in which the rare individual of virtue and promise is deemed a suitable candidate to initiate, to teach and explore the mysteries. Great masters, past and present have immeasurably diverse knowledge to share with all students, privileged only in the presentation of such an opportunity and whose real work is accomplished by their own merit and singular dedication to their path. Unwelcome as this is, such knowledge is not given, is not passed on, nor is it ceded by any known rite. It is certainly not 'seeded' in the blood. Children are gifted much by their biological parents, but not with spiritual wisdoms and experiential gnosis; most especially not wort-cunning, alchemy, astrology or spell craft. These have all to be taught and remembered, and the aptitude for these arts is as variable as the people who pursue them. Within the First Nation traditions of both the USA and Canada, it is understood that only limited knowledge of things such as herbalism can be passed on between father to son, or mother to daughter; the real gifts are manifest within random individuals who mediate as exceptional (non-hereditary) connections to spirit.

Rudolf Steiner [18] expresses this eloquently in his 1906 lecture on the 'Occult Significance of Blood' wherein he unambiguously postulates:

> "it was an important moment for humanity [...] when alien blood was introduced, and when marriage between relations was replaced by marriage with strangers, when endogamy gave place to exogamy. Endogamy preserves the blood of the generations through the entire tribe or the entire people. Exogamy inoculates man with new blood, and this breaking down of the tribal principle, this mixing of blood which sooner or later takes place among all peoples, signifies the birth of intellect, of <u>external</u> understanding."

He goes on to explain how tribal clairvoyance pertaining to legends and myths constrains the mind within the ancestral train, and how, through exogamy, this link was severed: *"thus in an unmixed blood is expressed the power of the ancestral life, and in a mixed blood the power of personal experience."* This, Steiner [19] asserts, is the positive drive towards intellectual evolution and self-realisation within the greater consciousness, a development denied our primitive tribal forebears who ardently clung to the concept espoused within their own legends, which affirms *"that which has power over thy blood has power over thee."* Dispersal and dilution of this venal fluid extinguished man's capacity for response to this covenanted ancestral summons bound by the purity of its untainted source. Nowhere is this better expressed than within the legend of Faust, to whom Mephistopheles exhorts the signing of a pact with his own blood *"then shall I have drawn thee over to myself."*

Steiner astutely concludes that mastery over the blood equates with mastery over the man himself, the Ego in fact. What the gift of exogamy reveals is the freedom of the individual soul (ego) when released from such bonds. And as the world of the senses and the intellect are the expression of the spiritual realms (axiomatic of Hermetics), the blood is thus the total expression of the 'I' or ego, for *"blood is a very singular fluid."* [20] The impetus of all blood related phenomenon is fundamentally one of spirit, according to Steiner. Certainly as the bicameral brain developed, the distinct sense of 'I', developed even as the group soul connection receded, thereby losing its connection to the ancestral unit. The 'I' is the singular expression of the innate divinity of the soul. By the osmotic action of spirit into the blood via the astral and etheric bodies *"here then begins that monologue, that soliloquy of the soul whereby the divine Self announces its presence when the path lies clear for the entry of the spirit into the human soul.."* (I am that, I am!). [21]

Yet this does not deny heritage of a remote gene donated from forebears of remote ancestry (both witch and non-witch) delineating our origins as a species and more significantly, our primal progenitors; though I advise caution and rationale within a pragmatic examination into its <u>real</u> effects and indiscriminate dissemination throughout its diaspora over time. Creation myths, however perceived, whether, religious, spiritual, metaphysical, mythical or anagogical, must be honoured and preserved. But this should not bind us in ignorance, nor blind us to reason. Few isolated tribes have in fact retained a significant percentage of their original gene pool material; yet even whilst preserving substantial cultural traits, such tribes consistently fail to produce or generate hoards of witch doctors, shamen, seers, or prophets. Rather, these exceptional souls are procured as and when they are required in relatively small numbers, chosen for their 'natural' talents and trained accordingly.

Mankind <u>is</u> generic; his skills, beliefs and faiths are not. We elect these choices; some may be impressed upon us, others are vocational; we heed 'the call', driven by something 'other', deep within our psyche (soul). It is a summons of the spirit, the ingress of carnation, which draws us back to the fold, in awareness of the primal genetrix. At best, these returning souls could be considered 'wise' souls, whose connection to the source is deeper than most. But these are far and few between. This is why I say that *"some of us are born knowing, others may die still searching."* The occult world attracts many wondrous folk, including some I would be proud to call 'kindred', some I would not! Spirit inspires us to seek out the 'other', either in the flesh, the ether or the astral. In this too we must be aware that all of us carry latent genes that may become kinetic when activated by self-realisation or initiation by human or non-human agents. To avoid confusion, it is vital we separate the *function* of genes as (paired) carriers of *past* data within the blood from that of the etheric charge that animates it and which *essentially* connects humanity to the greater pool of *evolutionary* consciousness. Put simply, this means matter is reproduced indiscriminately *ad finitum* until transformed by a random essence into superior form. We are all complex carbon based units in which the original spark of divinity resides severally, connecting us to it and to each other. Essentially, there is no purpose in the fruitless search for what Reibling[22] eloquently describes as the *"iconography of signature,"* undetectable by the human eye.

Much is claimed in order to validate and valorise both purpose and position within the Craft, yet, curiously, no other occult path exalts such alleged 'gifts' of lineage, nor do they require them. Initiation activates and stimulates the latent potential within those of us who are of sufficient occult persuasion to recognize the reality of something 'other' within 'witch-blood' and its incumbent implications within an alternative creation myth. Nothing less than spiritual alchemy engenders the initiatory experience, a harmonic infusion, which, if imparted correctly, quite literally changes us forever. Witches can and do birth non-witches just as non witches can and do birth witches. Nature reigns undisputed. 'Born a witch or made a witch?' - a hoary chestnut analogous to the lore ascribed to that of 'King making'. Even a swift excursion into history of regnal power, brutality and corruption will convincingly reveal how succession was originally dependant upon (s)<u>election</u> (the heritage being one of position and title) and not a 'divine' birthright as later claimed. This lucrative idea was later developed by power mongering factions with self-serving agendas. Again, such developments are uncomfortably comparable to those which might be cited from the Occult World. Necessity is, after all, the mother of invention!

Throughout history, guilds, lodges and later unions have protected the rights of trades-people to retain the jealously-guarded and discretionary rights of practice, normatively awarded within families. For example, a blacksmith will pass on his trade to his son, as would a stone mason, a tanner, a printer, an apothecary/herbalist/chemist et cetera. It is thus easy to understand how the arts of spell craft and wort-cunning would similarly be kept 'in-house', quite literally, within the family. Purkiss [23] makes the clear and valid point that early modern culture had no 'concept of genetics' or 'congenital causes'. Inheritance was due to moral reflection, hence the phrase - 'bad blood will out', or attained by bequest, in which case it was 'passed on', that is, given in trade or apprenticeship. The blood shared (by everyone) was generic and tainted by the sin of Eve. In support of this, Purkiss[24] quotes the case of Elizabeth Frauncis who *learned* the art of witchcraft at the tender age of 12 from her Grandmother, who *taught* her all she knew.

Owen Davies[25] admirably exposes this natural practice as less an inherited quality or birthright and more of a skill acquired, despite claims by cunning-folk to the contrary. *"As in any other trade, it was not unusual for the sons and daughters of cunning-folk to take over from their parents or other family members."*[26] Germane to this, Davies [27] astutely highlights the superstitious regard with which these skills expressed as 'blessings' or 'gifts' from the faerie or elven-folk were widely upheld. But of course, if business really boomed then apprentices were called for, who by necessity had to be sworn to secrecy - for obvious reasons.[28] Charmers[29] too considered themselves as custodians of a *'God-given gift';* yet knowledge of their secret charms was quite often withheld in life, being passed on almost as a death bed confession! Additionally, Davies demonstrates the very real need beyond the 17th century for Cunning-folk to resort to occult lore from books and all available tomes for 'crucial information'. [30] Knowledge is here taught! It is *not* hereditary in the sense of the *blood*. If this were so, then every scientist could produce an Einstein, every opera singer a Pavarotti, every artist a Rembrandt and so on. Science, music, the fine arts…all of these are crafts, and the 'arte magickal' is no exception. Contrary to popular opinion, the word 'art' originally defined a skill, and not an aesthetic phenomenon.

Many psychically gifted people can be found in the fields of Tarotmancy, Clairvoyance, Mediumship, Healing et cetera, many of whom would never consider themselves to be witches. Nor is their 'arte' vocational; for the most part, they just happen to have a (random) gift for it, the material potential of which they fully exploit. Many are those in the Craft who even after many years of study and practise are never able to achieve the abilities of these (spiritually) 'gifted' people. Again Davies [31] is at pains to assert how even in centuries past, such folk practised separately from those who might be known for 'witches'. Owing little in fact to the supernatural, nature and nurture combine to form the individual, and superficially at least, spirit alone provides that ephemeral 'otherness', separating its beneficiary from those not in receipt of this 'blessing'.

Cogently, the whole concept of 'bad blood' was formulated by the Christian Church to explain man's propensity to 'sin,' a vice allegedly 'inherited' from the errant Eve! Thus is the notion of blood as the prime courier deeply engrained within our consciousness and culture. What defines us as witches must surely be our world view, at least that is, regarding the natural or phenomenal world. Though in this consideration, I personally believe that nothing can be said to be 'supernatural' in the sense that nothing can exist outside 'nature', for all that exists can be known, understood and experienced. Significantly, in the metaphysical world, where we are introduced to the realms of the numinous, psychic 'gifts' and other inexplicable phenomena are objectively revealed; for everyone there, regardless of race, creed, faith or belief receives of these 'gifts' freely and indiscriminately. Clearly then, such phenomena are <u>not</u> confined to, nor are they the soul domain of - the witch! As far as the cosmos is concerned, there is nothing special about being a witch. We have no powers above and beyond anyone else on this planet.

Our distinguishing world view however, is upheld by belief in the re-incarnation of old souls from Palaeolithic cultures across the globe, where primitive forms of animism and proto-'shamanic' practices as found in Daoism, Voodoo, the natural beliefs of the Australian Aborigine and the First Nation Peoples of America, remain extant to a greater or lesser degree. Within the West (where various forms of Wicca now flourish), these once pure ancestor-revering beliefs have largely degenerated and the history of this within the Craft is not a pleasant one. Few among us would really choose to be a witch in the 'traditional' historical sense of the term, viz., a *'malefici.'* [32] Again, many claim to be answering the 'call', returning to beliefs held in a former life, remembered and re-affirmed in this one. Others are simply drawn to the power, glamour and secrecy it facilitates. In the last century, controversial claims were made (many of which are still hotly debated) that attempted to link hereditary factions to modern 'Wicca' in order to establish a continuous link with these older traditions; a gesture that instigated the much exploited allusion to the virtue of the 'blood'. Lamentably, this erroneous perception has become a catalyst for much angst on both sides of the Atlantic. Davies [33] remarks:

> " the desire to find an ancient inheritance has led some modern witches to accept seductive but entirely unsubstantiated claims, which have only served to undermine less sensational but more reasonable connections between popular wizards of the past and the witches of the present" - namely that of practice, or 'nature of business'!

People who can accept this are the true heirs of witches of yore, advises Davies. [34]

Moreover, in matters of the 'blood', generations may be skipped even as others may turn up unexpectedly across the socio-historical spectrum. There is no logical pattern discernable in those who heed the 'call'. These are complex mysteries some of which are revealed in congress with the indwelling daimon as an act of self subsumation - of the self to the True Will. It is of necessity that the soul answers the 'call', for it alone burns with the need to return; it alone seeks the 'other'. To some, this phenomenon denotes the 'Mark of Cain' which is no more than the desire of the soul to return to its origins and to acknowledge the 'spirit' of the wanderer both within themselves and those who live outside societal norms, cursed for their progressive views and knowledge of that significant 'other'. Shifting the focus from matter to spirit in no way devalues 'witch-blood'; it merely re-evaluates it, dismissing such misconceptions as impediments to truth. Our real heritage, of gnosis, is priceless, it was and is worth dying for and must never be abandoned to the illusions of the ignorant and foolish. The Craft is wrought with many pitfalls. It is a labyrinth of falsities and egocentric anomalies. Humanity elevates that which is dearest to its heart. Spirit alone carries the lamp.

All claims to Craft lineages, traditional or hereditary remain problematic due to the many issues surrounding the mythos of the 'blood'. Gerald B. Gardner, [35] for example, instigated an initiatory line of 'witches' who are able to trace their descent through a link activated by the combined wills of priest and neophyte during initiation. In the USA and Canada this system is understood confusingly as 'Traditional Craft' and aligns all witches in the 'blood'; yet in British Craft, this system is known as Wicca, being quite distinct from both Traditional and Hereditary Craft practises and beliefs. Factionalising terms of nomenclature regarding the blood (obsessed over by our cousins in the USA and Canada) and Initiatory status (obsessed over by British Traditionals and some Wiccans) widen the schism with every breath. Our naming and use of the loaded term 'witch' does indeed beg for re-appraisal. It is a long defunct title. How then are we to determine or classify the 'genuine article' among witches et al. Who is deemed worthy enough to test the density of our viscous life-giving liquid for that elusive quality of witch-dom? Who is the quality control manager? And who gets to decide who is 'in' or out? But even more importantly, why is this myth perpetuated? For power and control – vainglory, no more, no less! Reibling [36] avidly attests to this:

> "...I also understand the damage which has been done over the last 50 years or so by elders who've used ideas about 'the blood' as a litmus test in deciding who is and who is not a witch….it wasn't pretty or honourable or founded on anything more solid than jealously and/or subjective choice."

Robert Cochrane[37] who was an atavistic genius in his own right, shares company with many who have, in their own time, perpetuated a necessary fiction - the myth of a distinction in 'blood', that secures this 'belonging', a 'return' within an elitist framework wherein we may be recognised as 'special'. This identity unites us within the significant 'other' that binds us to it; the neumenon that acts as a catalyst for our beliefs.

Neither arcane knowledge nor skills in the 'arte' needed to acquire it are exclusively germane to any ill conceived precept of a qualifying 'witch-blood'. So clearly, we need to reassess our understanding and appreciation of the *human* need to belong relative to a *spiritual* awareness of our evolving gnosis. To remain fixated on manifest causes or corporeality is to regress, denying evolution, both intellectually and spiritually. It goes without saying of course that proclaiming yourself a witch will not make you privy to the mysteries! For just as every Christian is not a priest, neither is every witch a mystic. Perhaps I may suggest that we all accept instead a heritage of consciousness, wherein we are enjoined to fulfil the evolution of archaic animisms upon which our cultural and demographic interpretations have foisted an unnatural separation of belief and practise. By this naïve and simplistic suggestion sentience alone becomes the foremost reason for all existence, and the focus of our quest without concern or regard to wasted efforts negotiating who has rights to what. And this is really more than enough.

## Notes & References:

1. *The Cauldron*: no.123, Feb.2007
2. Personal corres: 1st Feb 2007
3. Craft: an all encompassing term used to describe distinct occult activities and beliefs within variant pre-dominantly pre-Wiccan, Traditional witch practices in the UK, though increasingly used now to include Wicca and all other neo-Pagan practises, especially in the USA and Canada where, the term 'tradition' may further separate these Wiccan and even neo-Pagan practises from others provided there is a verifiable initiatory lineage established!
4. Personal corres: 25th March, 2007

5. http://en.wikipedia.org/wiki/Superstition

   Superstition is a belief or notion, *not based on reason or knowledge* (my emphasis), in or of the ominous significance of a particular thing, circumstance, occurrence, proceeding or the like. Primitivisms.

6. Reibling quote discussing the principles of Transubstantiation. Personal corres: Nov/Dec 2007

7. [*ibid.*]

8. In the interests of comprehending a more enlightened exegesis, my expression of the term – 'Word', is utilized to counter the popular but misguided literal understanding of its application, here eloquently explained by Reibling (in private correspondence Nov/Dec 2007) as: "*the lineage, despite etymological 'meaning' of the word 'apostle' is widely understood/experienced on a more literal level: when Xist* [sic] *broke bread / shared wine with his disciples at the last supper he [quite literally] shared his BODY with them … his blood flowed into their veins … he now lives in them [supposedly] … not only through them! The so called 'BODY OF XIST'* [sic] *exists [again quite literally] in the BODY OF THE CHURCH [represented on Earth by his apostles, the Popes]. THE WORD MADE FLESH!*" I would argue that, theologically and metaphysically, the 'Word' made 'Flesh' is again <u>not</u> meant to be literal - like so many other things, this corruption is generally accepted, but then in the Middle Ages, many believed the Sun revolved around the Earth - belief does <u>not</u> make it so!

9. www.catholic.com/library/Apostolic_Succession.asp

10. The term 'Book of Shadows' is commonly used to refer to definitive liturgy, an authorised 'canon', passed down in succession from the founder of (modern) Wicca, Gerald B. Gardner.

11. Personal corres: 1st Feb 2007

12. [*ibid.*]

13. http://bioinfo.med.utoronto.ca/Evolution_by_Accident/Random_Genetic_Drift.html

14. http://sandwalk.blogspot.com/2007/09/nobel-laureate-thomas-hunt-morgan.html

15. http://www.brainmind.com/astrobiology_chapter.html

16. http://www.brainmind.com/astrobiology_chapter.html

17. 'Arte', a deliberate archaic spelling used deferentially in literary occultism to distinguish either authenticity or long established tradition, which infers specifically a technical skill, opposed to the (recent) modern association implied by the generalised spelling - 'art' that intimates something more ephemeral, aesthetic, and possibly even illusory.

18. Rudolf Steiner, 'The Occult Significance of Blood' (Public Lecture - 25th Oct, 1906) Berlin. 1978. Rudolf Steiner Press. London.

19. [*ibid.*]

20. [*ibid.*]

21. [*ibid.*]

22. Personal corres: 8th Feb.2007

23. Purkiss, Diana. *The Witch in History* pp146 Routledge. 1996 UK

24. [*ibid.*]

25. Owen Davies. *Popular Magic: Cunning - Folk in English History*. pp70-2 Hambledon Continuum. 2007. NY

26. [*ibid.*]

27. [*ibid.*]

28. [*ibid.*]

29. Charmers - a distinctive term used to denote practitioners of folk

magic, more generally of a 'simpler' kind (specifically of healing) than the more sophisticated practices employed by the Cunning-folk, and which are frequently and mistakenly used indiscriminately in reference to both, interchangeably.

30. Owen Davies. *Popular Magic: Cunning-Folk in English History.* pp83. Hambledon Continuum. 2007. NY
31. Owen Davies. *Popular Magic: Cunning Folk in English History.* pp74-76. Hambledon Continuum. 2007. NY
32. Malefici - acts of malice exacted by supernatural means to inflict harm.
33. Owen Davies. *Popular Magic: Cunning Folk in English History.* pp194. Hambledon Continuum. 2007. NY
34. [*ibid.*]
35. G.B.G.- Founding Father of Modern 'Wicca' in the wake of the repeal in 1951 of the last Witchcraft Act, which was replaced with the 'Fraudulent Mediums Act', actively facilitating greater freedom in the general press.
36. Personal corres: 1st Feb.2007
37. Robert Cochrane - Traditional witch, mystic and (late) Magister of the Clan of Tubal Cain.

# 8
# Sin Eating
# - Its Relevance to the Craft

Many readers of occult material will I'm sure, be reasonably familiar with both Robert Cochrane's 'Ritual Observance to Candlemas' [1] and the idea within Folk-Magic of Sin-Eating. The link between them is obvious or is it? Somewhat enigmatically, the opening instructions to this particular Rite (and in fact the Rite of All Hallows) begin with: *Confession, Expiation and Purification*. Before launching into an esoteric explanation of this process, tempting as it may be, it is necessary to first address other matters relating to context. Candlemas reflects ever deepening truths within the mysteries and is one of the primary rites by which they are revealed. Certain folk elements of medieval (Christian) Craft beliefs and practices are maintained within them, in addition to some archaic precepts that predate them. As mankind slowly became distanced from his true origins, the loss of primal spirituality led to increasingly unfamiliar seasonal rites that offer little or no essence of Grace. Faith, if it exists at all has devolved into variant Paganisms.

This Candlemas Rite reflects those needs, drawing out physical and mental obstacles that hinder our progress (sin), allowing us to purge them (expiation), before moving on to celebrate our desires both physical and mental on all magical and spiritual levels through the stimulation of 'anamnesis' – literally re-remembering (an ecstasy), affording us the insight to honour deity in a truly devotional manner (through prayer and supplication). It should be noted that 'light' is affirmed as the tool of focus by which we are encouraged to 'ascend' all material 'sins' or concerns that anchor us to 'terra firma.'

The theme of Purification within this ritual is achieved in three stages:-

- Expiation. 'Sins' eaten by the Magister as the sacrificial aspect of deity

- Blessing. Anointing by Magister as the priestly representative of deity.

- *Unio Mystica*. Receiving the Light of gnosis, presented as 'Compassion,' the magical child. Deity is the light, the manifestation of truth, revealing the way of devotion. Emerging from this dark, the 'light' of our own humanity manifests as 'Truth' and 'Beauty,' metaphoric appellations for the divine spirit. She is the Crowned and Conquering, the Whore and the Holy One, celebrating the 'Light' (Lux, born of Nox) - the divine consciousness. This is realised Grace, or Absolution, a sacred gift of spirit, rendered visible by force taking form within the prepared Host.

Before exploring the consequential directives of Robert Cochrane's beguiling opening quotation: "*be thou the bearer of my sins*" and why it is pivotal to this whole essay, it is first necessary to clarify the importance of the remaining document which will periodically be referred to as appropriate. Moreover, though the subject of sin-eating itself will be discussed, it will be in the context of this particular Candlemas Rite and not as a critical treatise on its generic practice, which is both outside the remit of this essay and irrelevant to it. The efficacy and veracity of this praxis may be one for others to consider.

What then is Sin? What is Expiation, and how do they lead to Purification? Terminology appoints and distinguishes conceptual principalities germane to an inherent theology regarding the mythos as determined by Cochrane's presentation of his tradition. For some, this necessitates an uncomfortable exploration of many themes associated with concepts of religion and spirituality not in conflict with those of Dual Faith persuasions, as Cochrane herein exemplifies. Understanding these will prompt awareness of certain practices within some Traditions. Without full comprehension of these tenets, Sin-Eating will make little sense. Esoterically, all of the following dictionary definitions encompass a complexity of meanings infinitely more purposeful, accurate and relevant to any magical path.

Mundane Dictionary terms:-

♦ Absolution - part of the Sacrament of Penance and Reconciliation attainable after confession to a 'Priest' through whose mediation the unmerited favour of 'Grace' is then manifest.

Importantly, Male divinity offers Mercy, whereas Female divinity offers Severity (a theme consolidated within the Kabbalah). Grace may be expressed as the pleroma, an expansive force for our spiritual evolution. Curiously, this is acquired from the divine feminine Creatrix by devotive surrender of the male principle to Her Will: Love under Will. Expiration of 'odic' force, or breath is neutralized through the sacerdotal office of the mediating priest, 'hearing' confession. Prayers and invocations infuse the primacy of divine force into the now cleansed spirit.

Signs and gestures generate symbolic acceleration of this principle. Prayers pronounced by the 'penitent' achieve pardon through word and deed; though only if contrition is sincere. Mercy is deemed to alight only upon the 'pure.' It is otherwise an empty and pointless gesture, reconciling nothing. True heartfelt Confession and its reciprocal gift of Absolution are said to return the Penitent to the Baptismal state of Grace, the Primary purificatory undertaking any one soul may seek in a single lifetime.

Sin-Eater

Normatively, this gift of oneself dedicates the self to the primary Source and is generally awarded upon Initiation or Confirmation. In fact, these are common precepts that form the core of many other beliefs across the Globe, and are not the sole domain of Christianity.

- Altar - Communion (sharing) table. Block for offerings to deity.

- Atonement - (to make) Reparation, compensation, redress, redemption. Process of acquiring pardon for 'transgression.'

Within Judaism, the 'Kohen' (High Priest) performs Rites of Atonement once a year at Yom Kippur to ritually cleanse the community of 'sin.' In more ancient times, this ritual required the passing of sin to a goat, that was then released into the wilderness as a 'Sin' offering in order to procure forgiveness. Adopted from the Babylonian practice involving high gestures of appeal to deity for removal of unfortunate fate bound to both willful and unwitting error.

William Tyndale[2] invented the word 'atonement' (restoration of primal unity) in the 16th century to express the Hebraic concept of propitiation and forgiveness, leading to – at-one-ment, or a state of Grace. Christianity, whether through the mediation of a priest within Catholicism, or without, through acts of self contrition under Protestantism, proclaimed a possibility of reconciliation through the sacrificial act of the Christos (Love surrendered to Will).

Pierre Abelard[3] in the 11th century offered the remarkably enlightened view of elevation through healing made possible by an act of contrition; Grace is considered here a literal infusion of spirit, the transforming virtue of Mercy (Love).

- Expiation - from the Latin '*expiare*'. Meaning to make amends.

Greek '*hilesmos*' - to make acceptable that which will draw one closer to 'God'. To pay a penalty for 'sin' (error), devout actions.

It is accomplished through the act of sacrifice itself, an act that profoundly changes the one making it. Importantly, it stresses the need for each individual to become as or like 'God' – that is 'pure' in thought, which means focused and dedicated in service to the divine, viz, without distraction - complete surrender. It is a self aware act.

- Propitiation - from the Latin *'propitius'* (to make the gift of) appeasement.

Favourable, auspicious, to volunteer oneself, placate, pacify, assuage, mollify. Sumerians performed acts of propitiation to honour their deities, through humility and conciliatory gestures. This is a God-aware act.

- Sacrifice - Surrender of possession; an offering (often of self) to deity; act of prayer. Thanksgiving, or penitence as propitiation; devote to…Slaughter of animal or person for one of above functions.

- Sin - from the Greek *'harmatia'* – Missing the mark/falling short (striving to but not quite making enough effort). An obstruction.
  Unacknowledged dross of mundane life.

Tragic flaw - this refers to the fate of the hero, whose descent into misfortune is pre-determined by an inherent handicap i.e. ego, pride, greed, hubris etc., this exhorts us to be mindful that even excess of virtuous qualities can be a 'sin' leading to inevitable downfall. Originally, *'sin'* was the act of subscribing to illusion (viz, the belief that we are separate from divinity); thus it is a transgression against divine law.
'Sin,' has neither moral judgement nor guilt attachment. It is merely those things that obsess us, that keep us from our spiritual argosies, in fact. This places us 'in error.' Simply put, sins are what keep us from egress and evolution. The things we allow ourselves to consider more important, more pressing, more urgent, more demanding. Art reflects life, for just as in within Greek Tragedy, these errors and/or character flaws engender a fated descent into misfortune, not necessarily in a material sense, but one of psychological despair; at worst - the dark night of the soul, at best –

meaningless life and ritual. This is why Robert Cochrane insisted that only in overcoming fate are we led to the Grail. This means we all need to work, and work hard on those flaws, those obsessions, those errors that keep us constantly 'missing the mark.'

- Extreme Unction[4] is the removal of the heavy burden of unredeemed 'sin' within Catholicism. Often given at the point of death, it absolves all sin, leaving the soul free to ascend.

Administration of Unction, in addition to invocatory prayers, consists of oil anointed upon the 5 sensory orifices and to those places of the body most likely to have succumbed or performed sinful acts. Given as the feet, hands and loins (men only), the sensory actions of the body should be more properly understood as distractions and not attributed to any perceived force of 'evil.' This vies effectively removes obsessions with material issues of the corporeal plane and helps focus upon other more spiritual needs. Grace is once again imparted through the medium of the priest, through his connection to the divine Source. Origen (2nd century Father of the Church) spoke of the laying on of hands, (much akin to faith healing) accompanied by prayers etc to save a dying man, to remove /extract his sin, to become shriven, ergo, light enough to cast off this realm. Luther considered it historically superfluous. Calvin went one step further, declaring that as most Priests were in fact corrupt and sinful, the act had become an 'histrionic hypocrisy.'

According to some theologians, Unction offers (supernatural) bodily healing only (through the agency of the Christos), and not of the Soul. It was rejected on these terms as unnecessary by the Albigenses, whose pious lifestyle and attendant philosophy qualified them as: *'perfectii'* – the (perpetual) pure ones. The Waldenses similarly described Unction as *'ultima superbia.'* Though not always officially recognised as a Sacrament, it is insinuated by the others. To become a Sacrament it must be proven that it is administered under divine authority for spiritual *and* bodily benefit, resulting in Grace. This would then imply the eschatological premise that Unction is performed primarily to save the *soul* from death, denuding the body as a minor consequence.

Because Protestant Reformers abandoned this Sacerdotal Rite in the 17th century, many people turned to those persons within the occult community willing to revive this rite of appeasement. Known as 'Sin-Eaters,' they operated outside the bounds of the Church, taking a fee for 'eating' the sins of the deceased. This freed the over burdened soul, allowing it to transcend the confines of this mortal plane, condemned otherwise to traverse it as vengeful wraith. Problematic to even the early Church who were obliged in 829CE to reprobate this popular resort to magick for removal of maledictions Jonas, Bishop of Orleans wrote in his 'Institutio Laicalis': *"It is obligatory on anyone who is sick to demand, not from wizards and witches, but from the Church and Her Priests, the unction of sanctified oil"* (anointing oil used in the Rite of Extreme Unction). [5]

Fifteen crosses, symbolising the (five) senses and the All inclusive form of deity (trinity), are anointed with oil for use in this most elusive of Rites. Theodulf, a Saxon Bishop of Orleans in 789 elevated the Jacobean Rite (of Unction relative to bodily healing through Grace) into a Sacrament, stressing the literal essentiality of Unction represented in terms of 5 and 3. Significantly, another vital Craft connection can here be demonstrated in the enigmatic directive by both Robert Cochrane and E. J. Jones [6] to consider the Totality, not as eight, but in exactly those terms of 5 and 3. Five represents the senses as experienced throughout the 'Round of Life' (birth, youth, maternity/maturity wisdom, death) and three is of course the triune Godhead. Effectively, it is the ultimate rite of exorcism and uses oil, ash, water and wine to cast off corporeal bondage. Once again, these substances are denoted by E. J. Jones [7] within his description of the transposition of the Three Moats in the Rite of the Castle of the Four Winds. In both contexts, invocations are made to Spirit, expressing a vital element within this processing of form to force.

Seven priests at one time were required to perform the act of Extreme Unction, worked in the name of the One Force (seven + one). Seven archaic (wind) spirits from a distant era in time and space, of Babylon, used in exorcisms, are similarly invoked through the priests. One priest for each spirit/wind. Used in the Medieval Church to curse and banish as well as to absolve Sin, it was ministered upon danger of death. Unction, that is, primal restoration through the banishment of corporeal elements from the soul, 'enlightens' it, such that it may ascend unhindered to await The Final Judgement. Before it can be administered however, the Sacraments of Confession (of Sin), Absolution (of Sin) and Penance (for Sin) must first, where possible be executed, originally over seven days for increased impetus! This 'supernatural' invigoration of the soul [8] removes the temporal punishments of guilt or grief attachment assigned to the act of Confession. To sustain the soul in Purgatory, the soul is strengthened through Absolution; finally, the office of Penance affords the renewal of bodily health and some theologians argue that this like Unction cleanses the soul. [9]

This completes the first section relating to *Confession, Expiation and Purification* of the Candlemas Ritual used by way of example to highlight coterminous associations between superficially dissimilar expiatory praxes. After this, in point two, the 'Blessing' is listed as follows:

"*This is made before the Altar stang.* (note, this is the Cuveen stang and is distinct from the personal stang belonging to each member). *No lights. The form of self-blessing should be used as per Mask. It is the assumption of the Magical personality. Major key is used by Initiates.*"[10] Suffice to say that here, a specific prayer is used; the form is known to Initiates who are enjoined to build its manifest force during its recitation by the Magister, who acts as the mediating priest. We will return to the remaining aspects of this ritual in due course.

Another contemporary practice of 'Sin-Eating' mirrors the lofty modality of the Church, offering visual, yet still profoundly simple pragmatism; this is an earthier and seemingly more 'honest' approach to the problem of 'Sin.' It has long been recognised in all its carnate forms as something undesirable, a hindrance that weighs heavy upon the soul. Its banishment is universal. According to a modern practitioner [11] whose witness to such profound acts among the Peruvian peoples of the Andes, re-educated her (mis)conceptions regarding sin and expiation, a fact she explains as subject to their healthy synthesis of Catholicism and indigenous animist beliefs. [12] She expresses this as being in 'accord' with 'higher forces of the universe,' an act of mediation for alignment of the self to a primal cause. It regards our spiritual evolution towards the assumption of true gnosis. Service of the non-self embraces spirit connection in a dialogue of transmission that reveals the prospect of mastery of one's fate.

Again this is completely in line with other more enlightened views on 'Sin' and its removal for acquisition of the 'Grail.' Submission and sacrifice to that cause is not Wilcox insists, to be misinterpreted as subjugation or subsumation, but as a transmutation of Charis. Almost medieval, this pantheistic view of nature draws from the tenets and creed of St Francis, who pronounced in favour of a manifest 'saviour.' Within Andean Cosmology, such a being is *Lord O'olloriti,* 'who removes all 'sin,' or obstruction to egress, without contradiction or conflict with their synthesis of belief. This indigenous expression of a son of the Sun and daughter of the Moon who taught the arts of farming and weaving, finds a comfort in the many parallels known through the Church.

For the Andean peoples, disease and pestilence are consumed, digested and transformed via a sacred catalyst within the body of the *'Q'ero'* (healer) through his or her special relationship with the Mountain spirits. Having many parallels with the 'Charmers' of English Folk tradition, the *'Q'ero'* claim mediation through ancestral tutelary spirits across the three worlds of their philosophical world-view. In keeping with many, though not all Traditional Craft working praxes, they shun the use of drumming, entheogens and dancing to access the oneiric ('dreamtime') levels of consciousness. Their 'arte' is won through personal trials under the spiritual tutelage of both carnate and incarnate guides who teach them how to read omens, divine and how (and when) to invoke and banish spirit forms.

Andean culture recognizes a mystical 'right hand path,' (acting through the logos) that includes the more analytical linear faculties of a greater magical seership as male mysteries, drawn from the land/mountains and the Sun. But more intriguing yet is their belief in the 'left hand path,' (acting through eros) the more pragmatic and magical female mysteries here are borne of the sea and the Moon. In common with Cunning-folk, a true 'priest' is able to utilize both streams of 'virtue.'[13]

To aid them in such work, fetish (*gris gris*) bags known as *'mesa'* (meaning table or altar) or *'despacho'* (generic medicine bag) containing any number of charms, simulacra and impedimenta, which must be organic, are regularly fed with *'pisco'*, a pure alcohol (100%) to appease the spirits to cleanse the dense unwanted energy forces known as *'hucha'* that inhibits egress and gnosis and restoration of (original) virtue. The *'mesa'* bag is drawn across and through the 'aura' of the body as if to draw out the illness caused through an imbalance of *'hucha.'* Prayers are incanted during this process to establish two links, one with the patient and one with the spirit healer the *'Q'ero'* is mediating through. In accordance with their dual-faith Catholicism, these ancestral spirits are recognised as 'Saints.' The breath is the fundamental vehicle for this energy exchange, rendered pure for such transport via the chewing (not swallowing) of coca leaves. In this way, the refined body is able to receive the lighter, spiritual *'sami,'* or 'God-force' energy. Once again, no guilt or moral value is placed upon this energy. Having no perception of duality in their belief system, it is not perceived in any way negative; it simply obstructs evolution and is therefore incompatible with Grace. Clearly, these superstitious praxes are comparable to the many folk practices known within many western cultures.

Holy Mother Mary stands in for the manifest form of *'Pachamama,'* who taught the first *'Q'ero'* the art of herbalism/root doctoring and breath-work involving sacred coca leaves. [14] Within the Norse Tradition it is notable that Freya taught Odhin similar techniques. Three leaves are selected for use through which the spirit of Mother Mary or *'Pachamama'* may be invoked. Through the mediation of her 'son' the Tutelary 'father' or great mountain Spirit, *'Apukuna'* is summoned. At this juncture it is prudent to bring attention to points three, four and five of the Candlemas Ritual.[15] Here, the Rite specifically mentions the 'Old Woman,' who elevates a platter to the Moon upon which three Herbs (of Grace) are bound, before being offered to the 'pot' (symbol of the regenerative belly of the Mother), seething over the waters of creation. Invocations are made, prayers petitioned and gestures are exacted. Each person then imbibes this transformative brew, receiving some measure of Grace.

In point six of the 'Ritual Observance to Candlemass' (sic), [16] 'fear' is mentioned in the context of a mindful directive that may on one level express our obsessions relative to corporeal concerns. Fear is considered a primary emotional obstruction that advances *'hucha,'* weighing down the body, preventing the absorption of *'sami.'* So, just as Cochrane is moving through a parallel process, variations provide insightful clues as to the psychology that underpins such actions. As an alternative to *'mesa'* bags, skilled *'Q'ero'* may 'draw' or capture, the *'hucha'* from the body directly, consuming it for digestion within his/her spiritual stomach - the *'qosqo'*[17] for ritual purging via its storehouse of *'sami.'* This is cognate with the more familiar *'hara'* centre, or sacral chakra for anyone au fait with these terms. Accompanied by prayer and invocation, this highly ritualized action named - *'mikhuy,'* or spiritual ingestion is importantly one that filters away unwanted *'hucha'*; it does not remain within the body, but is drawn through it. The flow is split, allowing *'sami'* to rise to the head/crown and *'hucha'* to fall through the feet where it is offered up to the tutelary spirit for absorption into 'Pachamama,' the great Earth Mother. Further North, in ancient Mexico, the Aztec goddess *Tlazoteotl'* had cleansed all souls by eating their cumulative debris. Perceived as 'living' energy and in no way a pollutant, but rather as a source of disharmonious or incompatible energy within the body, it is considered a gift to Her, for Her continual acts of creation. It is an act that empowers the patient, the healer and the Earth. However, in order to remain a pure source (channel) for healing, the *'Q'ero,'* may occasionally need to fully purge, physically; this also saves time where instances of extreme illness or epidemics occur.

The *'Q'ero'* recognize four important energy centres throughout the body, listed as: sacrum, solar plexus, heart and crown. The *'siki nawi'*, or black belt (Kundalini) resides in the 'eye' or sacrum of the *'yana chunpi,* otherwise cognate with the auric field. Transpersonal skills such as channelling and manipulation of the life-force require strict discipline, especially with regard to the honing of will. In order for the *'Q'ero'* to be effective healers, they maintain a vigorous regime of self-cleansing. In their world view, the act of service facilitates absorption of the refined and more spiritual *'Sami'* in each individual, and is not to be associated with any form of psychic vampirism. *'Sami,'* may be equated with the more familiar 'ki' or 'prana' of the Far Eastern and Indian cosmologies that represent the 'life force,' or 'virtue'; a sentient essence of animation.

By this definition, *'hucha'* is simply an absence of *'sami;'* it is a binding of negative 'karma' in the sense that it devolves the soul through its inappropriate actions devoid of right speech or thought. A *'kukuchi penitente'* [18] is one whose *'hucha'* has entrapped the spirit, rendering it earthbound, having died 'un-shriven,' that is within a state of unresolved 'sin.' Unequivocal similarities here draw obvious parallels to beliefs shared within Catholicism regarding Extreme Unction, but also to the folkloric renditions within non-Catholic cultures.

Exceptionally gifted 'priests' known singularly as an *'Alto mesayaq'* manipulate *'sami'* through will in order to bring abundance and pure knowledge to his/her people. They carry the authority and intuition to discern the use and merit of casting adverse charms, including that of the 'eye.' More importantly, through their distinct measure of *'k'ara'* or spirit virtue, they have the knowledge when and where to imbue the coca leaves in a shared communion with *Pachamama* or *Apukuna* (Father). Facilitated through discrete interaction with ancestral and tutelary spirits, *'Akalliy,'* is a sacred imbibement of air/breath, moisture and coca enhances their own virtue (*'sami'*) and gnosis immeasurably. Supernatural mountain spirits of *Apukuna*, named 'Nusta's' (black lights of the mountain), being specifically female are mediated by male priests, whereas, female priests mediate the animistic wind spirit messengers of *Pachamama*, collectively encompassing the three worlds of Andean Cosmology. [19]

Neither female (nusta) nor male (apu) potencies can be apprehended directly, but must be linked through *'k'ara,'* or specially appointed totem spirits, usually animal. Moving into the realms of the western cunning arts of the 19th and early 20th centuries, they appear to work mainly through visions and dreams in which their dedicated 'spirit' guides act as conduits for mystical union. Priests of *Apukuna*, undergo selection by means of a trial by lightening. Survival of its close proximity marks that person a *'qoniruna'*, thereon in directed to a Master for intense training that may easily span a decade whereupon they become the *'Atum- Cheqaqs,'* the Men of Great truth. Included in their teaching is the instruction that salt and smoke are vehicles for *'hucha.'* [20]

Ross Heaven[21] who claims to have been taught by possibly one of the few remaining 'Sin-Eaters' in modern times in Hereford during the 1960s, expounds that every living thing has a relationship of service, which he is at pains to distinguish from servitude. In apparent confirmation of Andean belief, Heaven describes in particular the use of salt and smoke within the Sin-Eating Rites concerned with healing and absolution. Heaven names his tutor as 'Adam,' and claims for him an inherited parentage of Cunning, although his working methods are keenly expressed as folk arts or 'Charming.' [22] Nonetheless, Heaven describes his own work in more modern and contentious terms as 'shamanic soul retrieval.' Critically, for our purposes, he also asserts his practice as one engaged in equilibrium, of at-one-ment, the acquisition of the primal or 'pure state.' Cognate with stipulations penned in Leviticus 14:21 & 16:21-22 that refer again to the scapegoat rites of Israel for the necessary atonement of a nation's un-cleanliness, we may study them in lieu of the previous contexts of *'hucha'* and *'sami'* recognising a more sensible subtext for this grossly misunderstood practice.

Modern Buddhist monks in Tibet continue the traditional spring cleansing of their 'sins' via transposing them onto a skull mounted upon an effigy after which it is ceremoniously burned - banished amidst much noise and stomping.[23] In ancient Greece, propitiations were enacted within the harvest rite known as the *'Thalysia.'* According to Homer and

Theocritus, bread was offered to Demeter upon her altar, the threshing floor itself, but in Attica, a more aggressive version of this act was dedicated to Apollo, where the bread, named the *'thargelos'* had thrived on the previous season's blood-offering. This entailed the flogging, then expulsion or death of a specially selected criminal acting as sin-carrier, who, by this act of expiation became the *'pharmakos'* or healer for the annual cumulative hubris of the city.[24]

Heaven relates how the etheric body becomes tainted as it passes through life, corrupted by mundaneity. Trauma consumes the soul at a startling rate. Emotional debris creates psychological fall out; both necessitate psychic cleansing. 'By our sins are we defined'! Sorcery is likewise considered to act as a spiritual virus, becoming a parasite to be un-cleaved. Heaven further explains the role of sin-eater as being in some part equal to that of confessor and psychologist; this is clarified through their ability to remove corporeal obfuscation. Failure to observe the need for expiation increases the burden each soul must bear. In 2002, a Unitarian Reverend expressed his concern for claims made for 'vicarious atonement,' stating his perplexing belief that no-one can be responsible for the sins of anyone else! Yet this is exactly what the Sin-Eaters profess to do, now as in antiquity, here as in the Andes, though under various cultural guises and perceived variently by those outside them. The role and import of Expiation now clarified, reveals its essentiality within Craft practice. Within my tradition, life is considered a preparation for death. Obsessions distract and anchor us in the now, even as the future slips away from us.

Heaven[25] discusses a four-fold order of humanity reflecting a hierarchy from which numerous priesthoods have evolved. Beginning with the level of priestly ministers and mediators, he shifts downwards to levels peopled by those who may be aware, yet choose to oscillate between requisite discipline and corporeal distractions, including those who later abandon those disciplines, to those who have not yet acquired the capacity for such choice. None of these levels infers negative associations, simply an indication that many simply fail to make the 'right choice;' this being the true meaning of 'sin' of course. It is therefore to be understood as a failure to align oneself with divine accord. Remembering that philosophically speaking, there is no such thing as evil, it being merely an absence of good (again when viewed in the sense of *'hucha'* and *'sami,'* this makes better sense), it is moot to consider the occult maxim: *"there is no part of me that is not of the gods."* [26]

Although few references have been made to Sin Eating as a common occurrence in the West, there are other writers of note who have substantiated this as a popular enough folk- practice, particularly common during the 18th-19th centuries, possibly even from antiquity.[27] Similar observances were undertaken across much of Europe, Africa and South America. Primarily, a Sin-Eater is required to remove the weight (of emotional and psychic angst) that binds a soul to the earthly plane. Once restored to a pristine state, it achieves at-one-ment, becoming 'light' enough to ascend, to balance the scales of Maat, offering the promise of re-birth rather than limbo.

Described by Heaven as a process involving the laying on of hands, Christian prayers, invocations to various Saints and spirit breath-work, residual heaviness is drawn from the etheric body, consumed and then expelled through a cleansing purge. Occasionally, sins are written down and expunged through fire in an ash bowl set aside for that purpose. A mild emetic is self-administered inducing a dry-retching, often into an area of cleared ground set aside for this purpose, which is commonly the base of an old yew tree. Again this western 'Charming' method mirrors the Andean redistribution of dense energy to the Earth. More importantly, it echoes Craft mysteries where the 'true priest' is none other than the

Magister, the leaper between, who hovers between the roles of king and leper, the bridge and guide between the worlds.

Sin-eating is by definition a solitary practice, determining a location of a practitioner outside the civil bounds of society, within the peripheral 'shadow lands.' Careful orchestrations engender anamnesis; realization brings clarity of true purpose and the soul is reified in preparation of at-one-ment. Heaven further confirms sin extraction by either absorption or consumption, and its requisite purging thereafter; salt is suggested as the most effective cleanser, though a seven herbal tonic is also given to cleanse both body and soul. [28] Comprised of 3 fluid mediums of the Fates, Mothers and the Graces, one sweet, one bitter and one neutral as found in honey, vinegar, water; added to two bitter herbs in hyssop and rue and two sweet herbs of rose and coriander, these seven correlate with the bundle of herbs strewn into the pot within the Candlemas Rite (point 6). Used as tonics, or for asperging, herbs are commonly listed among folk medicines and find good use in faith healing. St John's Wort is apparently of especial value in warding un-warranted enchantments.

Baptism, as one of the seven sacraments, effectively removes 'sin.' Herbs are often used to assist in this office that ultimately seeks to confer 'Grace,' the single act of divine at-one-ment. By comparison, Robert Cochrane's Mask Prayer, given at Candlemas by the Magister as a baptismal blessing to his cuveners, exemplifies his belief that through confession and expiation, we are cleansed of our 'sin' (in the sense of dense or corporeal obstructions) to become pure enough to receive the conference of Grace, administered through a shared sacrament gifted within the Eucharist of the Cauldron, the womb and the tomb of the Ambivalent Creatrix, whose benign countenance is at once the dark and terrible Mother.

As a boy, Heaven was instructed by his teacher to be open minded, to consider 'sin' in the context not as Catholic doctrine has misrepresented it, but rather, as *an error* in judgement. In addition to fear, illusion is also universally recognized as an obstruction. Both bar the gate to evolution. As illusion, sin becomes the primary lapwing, drawing us ever further from our quest. Yet fate is not fixed, it is not pre-determined. Intent acts upon its subtle threads – weaving the promise of gnosis and revelation, for those who first know where to look.

Aside from healing, the Sin-Eater is required to perform the last rites - post mortem. A description of this act is given by Aubrey for historical purposes, to mark the acknowledgment of this enigmatic profession. Prayers, including several psalms from Old and New Testaments have proven popular choices for the blessings during the gravid task of sin-eating having the dual purpose of an invocation to remove the guilt or apathy of the mourners and a plea for absolution for the deceased.

> "... In the County of Hereford was an old Custome at funeralls to hire poor people, who were to take upon them all the sinnes of the party deceased. One of /hem, I remember, lived in a Cottage on Ross-high way. (He was a long, leane, ugly, lamentable poor raskal.) The manner was that when the Corps was brought out of the house and layd on the Biere; a Loafe of Breade was brought out, and delivered to the Sinne-eater over the Corps, as also a Mazar-bowle of maple (Gossips bowle) full of beer, which he was to drinke up, and sixpence in money, in consideration whereof he tooke upon him (ipso facto) all the Sinnes of the Defunct, and freed him (or her) from walking after they were dead ... The like was donne at ye City of Hereford in these times, when a woman kept many yeares before her death a Mazar-bowle for the Sinne-eater; and the like in other places in this Countie; as also in Brecon, e.g. at Llangors,

where Mr Gwin the minister about 1640 could no hinder ye performing of this ancient custome. I believe this custome was heretofore used over all Wales . . ." [29]

This is later supplemented by a related rite, allegedly witnessed by Heaven as a young man. To prevent the soul from becoming an angry wraith, water, bread and salt were consumed straight from the corpse's body. Heaven describes how extensive breath work is required to draw off the heavy etheric matter shrouding a corpse. He also mentions the tradition, now largely forgotten of passing a drink of whiskey over the corpse to each witness, family members first. It is to be remembered that not only is whiskey an alcohol, and therefore a suitable offering to spirit, but it carries the folk appellation, 'water of life' or *Aqua Vitae*. This infers the transference in some way of the (now) purified essence of the corpse into the family mourners for continuance among the living generations.[28] Curiously, perhaps in some expression of dispensation or jurisdiction for his office, the Sin-Eater is described as having his face daubed thickly in black soot and ash from the holy oak and the accumulation of burned ashes from his 'confessional bowl.' To fully ensure the transition of 'sin' from the corpse to the person hired for the job, corpse silver is given over the body, lifting any residual spirit, left by ineptitude or apathy, witting or otherwise. Silver is of course an excellent conductor, and this payment sealed the act.

In Shropshire, the last recorded Sin-Eater Richard Munslow, was said to enjoy warm plum cake and spiced ale as his sin-offering.[31] Funeral feasts and wakes in Bavaria require the next of kin to eat a similar corpse cake as their ransom to 'sin.' Corpse cakes made in the Balkans deliberately resemble the shape and form of the deceased. This act of Charity absolves the deceased through the willingness of a family member to assume the etheric karma of their kin. However, this is viewed by the family as an honour in that the essence or virtue of the deceased is passed into a new host, leasing cumulative ancestry through them. Cornish custom once encouraged small children to 'kiss' the corpse in order to receive from it their measure of 'virtue,' perceived as vigour and strength. 'Soul caking' is a folk tradition derived from the combined beliefs of transference through coin and cake as ransom for 'sin.'

Customs developed increasingly sinister associations during the late Middle Ages connected with 'corpse watching.' Known as 'wakes,' these were once solemn vigils for the dead held over a three day period for signs of life. Thereafter, the corpse was deemed to have 'given-up the ghost,' that is the spirit of animation, which is distinct from the virtue or soul. But perverse customs, including alleged acts of necromancy were expressly forbidden by the Council of York in 1367. Liberties with the corpses denied them due honour and the Church expounded the deliberate response that all vengeful and returning spirits haunting the populace was the direct consequence of these violations. In truth, many of these acts were simple but rombustuous acts of horse-play designated to relieve the tedium of their austere vigils. Nevertheless, corpse-watching was a lucrative business and in 1916, it was recorded that £2 a week and no mean sum, could be earned from this profession.[32]

Given that fire and candles feature heavily within the preparation for the corpse for burial, it is unsurprising then to learn that the word funeral is derived from the Latin: *'funeralis'* and the root *'funis'* meaning torch. After the three day vigil, torch lit funeral processions once took place at night along designated corpse roads, the one clear path of light to guide the spirit to its final resting place. Linked to this was a curious custom accompanying wakes involving a proscription against lighting any of the corpse candles one to another, nor of lighting anything from a corpse candle.[33] This oddity may be explained through the belief in spirit transference using the medium of elemental fire as host. Similarly, no ash was to be removed from the fires within the house in which the corpse was laid out, until it had been buried or burned.

All attendees were enjoined to carry salt in their pockets to deflect and absorb any unwanted attention from spirit entities surrounding the corpse at this time. Reed canes (rush-lights) were placed around the coffin in certain talismanic patterns to ward off external unwanted spirit intrusion: "a circle of five was an effective protection from the powers of darkness." [34] In one of his letters Robert Cochrane also talks of position 'five' and 'six' relative to oneiric travelling. [35] So far then, certain ingredients have been highlighted significantly in relation to this association with the dead. Salt, ash, water and wine, herbs of grace, prayers, blessings and invocations, consumption of the Eucharist and atonement. These all feature heavily within two specific rites attributed to the late Robert Cochrane known publicly as the twin rites of Candlemas and All Hallows. Also traditional in the ancient world were masked rites, transfigured into an art form by the Romans. Wailers and Mourners would wear ever more elaborate disguises ranging from totemic beasts to fearsome daemons. The import of such guising is marked by E.J. Jones specifically regarding the use of masks for rites that summon and honour the ancestors. [36]

Absolution is awarded to the penitent whose sincere contrition has burned' off the heaviness of their burden (sin) during their period of penance that begins in confession and ends in absolution. In between, they make expiation and propitiation - At-one-ment. Sin is also expressed as disloyalty, or indifference and confliction. Esoterically, At-one-ment is the renewal of loyalty through a feudal Covenant. Christians believe that The Christos laid his hand upon those heavy with 'sin,' breathed upon them and thus absolved them of this obstacle to their own ascension. These are clearly the same actions mimicked by later Sin-Eaters. In the

Craft and particularly within the Clan of Tubal Cain, we recognize the comparison between this act and that expressed through the Mask prayer. Grace is the imperative here; 4th to 7th century texts on Extreme Unction stress exemplary use of breath and 'sealing' by hand the blessing upon the soul of its recipient in preference to the body.[37] It is a spiritual Baptism of Renewal.

Relevant to this unfolding of the mysteries, is the succinct tale of one particular Bishop in the 13th century, who rasped out upon his dying breath that he had no need of Extreme Unction, exclaiming that over the course of his life, the seven sacraments had revealed to him the 'mystery' of death and he feared it not. Moreover his sincere attrition had induced the requisite Grace, removing the need for its bequest by the flurry of priests surrounding him.[38] Robert Cochrane explored the boundaries of a parallel system of seven sacraments within the Clan of Tubal Cain. These are Five from the 'Round of Life' and two more, one each given at Induction and Full admission. These are as follows: Birth/Life for Penance; Youth/love for Confirmation; Maturity/Marriage for Marriage, Wisdom for Ordination and Death for Extreme Unction. Curiously these five equate with the sacraments dropped during the Reformation. Two only were retained by the Protestants – those of Baptism and Eucharist/Holy Communion. These two priestly Sacraments were taken up by Cochrane's Clan and re-instated as mentioned previously at First and Second admission respectively.

It is noteworthy that those supposed as being in a state of sin, ie, 'the penitent,' are denied the Covenanted renewal in spirit of the Eucharist until absolved, of that 'sin.' In other words, they are in an unfit state to receive it. Catholicism pronounces that we *"do not give what is holy to dogs!"* Use of aggressive metaphor aside, semantics again obscure the issue here. For what is being stressed is not how unworthy a person is but how unable to absorb it they are. From the Andean perspective, the necessity for the removal of *'hucha'* before *'sami'* may be transmitted suggests an ingenuous and acceptable alternative. Ironically, within the narrative of the 'Child's Play' poem attributed to Robert Cochrane [39] is the line *"that feeds the hound,"* referring to the hound as psychopompic guardian. If the 'work' done in the 'Mill' is unproductive, insincere or sour, then the 'hound' is said to have turned his nose up at the 'cake'! In other words, the offering was unacceptable and insufficient to attain communion.

Throughout the broad spectrum of occult practice and belief, salt, wine and bread have become synonymous as the ritual Eucharist, or Houzel. Bread and salt are offered and consumed by all in sacred awareness. Bread as significant of the Host has been discussed previously, but not so salt. Salt represents many things within all magical praxes. Here are some of the most important:

- Salt    Symbol of man's labour (of self worth and love of the Gods)
- Salt    Symbol of incorruptibility as it preserves organic matter from decay.
- Salt    Symbol of Sterility as it makes all living matter barren, hence its efficacy in rites of purification for use in magic, medicine and spiritualism.
- Salt    Typifies friendship and wisdom.

Most of us will be familiar with the first three, but not many the last. To eat another man's salt is to establish a mystical bond between giver and receiver. The pact, if accepted is regarded as inviolate, a bond that cannot be severed with impunity or safety. To eat the salt of your 'King' is to owe him the utmost fealty and fidelity. Eating bread and salt together is to make an unbreakable bond of friendship and camaraderie of the highest degree, hence its use in all higher magical orders and alleged rejection by witches. It is noteworthy that many modern Pagans have replaced the consumption of bread and salt with the more palatable but spiritually sterile offering of biscuits or cake (no salt). Some traditions exist for good reason and should be maintained even where our social desires or sensibilities conflict. So a renewed understanding of these should serve to heighten every aspect of our spiritual argosy.

Nevertheless, certain foods are consumed in continuance of particular archaic traditions regarding widely spread sacred cannibalistic acts once connected with the dead. Eating the 'flesh of the dead' is a high ritual contested by some, is spite of an abundance of contrary evidence. This superstitious yet magically potent act imparted the living with sustenance of body and soul. From this we may secure links to taboos through forbidden consumption of tribal totem animals, said to represent the group soul of its people. Strict censures involving bones, fetishes, banners and heraldry gave birth to a vast array of Craft practices dispersed and disseminated through migratory cultures of the 17th and 18th centuries, all of which underpin the current revivalist practices of modern Craft modalities. Historians of the Craft have been both fascinated and appalled in their search for the roots of our modern practices. Of these, the Eucharist from the Greek *'eucharistias'* meaning to give thanks, to rejoice, remains the one most profoundly linked to this divisive act. [40]

Many Pagan (totem style) altars were of wood symbolising the Tree of Life, or divine presence and the point of transformation and renewal through integration. For Hebrews, 'the Altar of Perfumes' is the operation of Grace for the elements. An altar is also the place of re-union with deity by means of *sacrifice*. It is noteworthy that our own (portable, wooden) altar, the Stang, represents the Clan's tutelary deity. The Magister of the Cuveen as his representative becomes a living embodiment of the above principles. Therefore, any true sacrifice or 'sin' offering offered through him reciprocates a state of Grace manifest in the anointing of oil during the Mask Prayer Blessing. The Altar is regarded by Catholic priests as the Cross, that point of Sacrifice, or manifestation, and this is why we too place the Houzle, or bread and wine in front of the Coven Stang, as noted in point 3 of the Candlemas Rite - the Place of Presence. We remember that presence through our experience of it.

Contrary to popular opinion, a true Eucharist or *'pain benit'* blesses *deity*, it honours and celebrates the provision of the sacrificial elements of divine Grace present in the food and wine for our consumption. Through it we share a moment of sentience, of at-one-ment. Unio Mystica. The corporeal substance is consumed in mindful awareness of what it represents and how we acquired it. It celebrates the renewal of that bond; that Covenant. Our reciprocal sacrifice is total submission to divine guidance, through reconciliation, the offering of the self to divine Will – expiation ! Sacrifice preserves this symbiosis, our pathway to immortality. Our life is forfeit, surrendered, ransomed in fact to our progenitors, Blood for Blood, Life for Life, in Unity, Love and Devotion. The renunciation of impediments establishes a link between the supplicant and their notion of the divine in which all ritual becomes 'prayer.'

Modern rituals are the result of archaic sacrificial techniques of positive propitiation. Through consumption of 'bread' and 'wine', we receive the word/logos or fructifying essence of deity, literally and figuratively; not through a contested act of transubstantiation. Remember that *sym-bolic* actually means to bring together as One! It is therefore opined that all reality is simultaneously symbolic and mystical. We can eat the bread and the flesh without prejudice or contradiction. Equally so with the wine and the blood. This, is the real mystery! Sacraments are to be understood as an oath or pledge from one's tutelary deity, and as demonstrations of allegiance.[41] The Eucharist, as the crown of the Sacraments, mediates divine favour, generating apotheosis. Within the Candlemas ritual of Robert Cochrane, points 7, 8 and 9 is expressed, unambiguously, this symbiotic manifestation. These three points present the Eucharist, the manifestation and the blessing of Grace imparted through the Renewed Covenant.

The Ritual for Candlemas began with Confession and Expiation, as prelude to the active process of Sin-Eating or Purification. Absolution is confirmed in the final line of the Closing Blessing by the Maid:

" May Old Tubal Shepher ye all, Blessed, thrice blessed, be…"

## Notes and References:

1. E.J. Jones. *'The Roebuck in the Thicket'* Capall Bann pub 2001 p143:
THE RITUAL OBSERVATION TO CANDLEMAS

i.  Confession. This should be willed to the Master, if felt.
    Expiation. "Be thou the bearer of my sins."
    Purification.

ii. The Blessing
    This is made before the altar stang. No lights. The form of self-blessing should be used as per Mask. It is also the assumption of the magical personality. Major key is used by initiates.

iii. Drawing of New Moon into Cauldron
    According to major Sabbat star…Enter Old Woman and others.

iv. Elevate platter to Moon. Place contents into pot. Enter Old Man.

v.  He plunges sword into Cauldron. S…

vi. The Sacred Bread: Old Woman passes round the cake, saying, "You eat this bread in the Devil's Name, with girt terror and fearful dread…"

vii. Old Woman to cuveen, after entering -

"Rejoice! A child is born… Her name in Compassion."

viii. The Maid is lead forward by the Magister, uncloaked and offered to the cuveen. The cuveen offer white candles and a kiss.

viiii. Maid: "Blessed is the plough, the Mover of Earth[...]May Old Tubal Shepherd ye all, Blessed, thrice blessed be … Feast …. loving Cup.

2. Wikipedia-atonement

3. Wikipedia-atonement

4. Wikipedia-extreme unction

5. Wikipedia-extreme unction

6. E.J. Jones. *The Roebuck in the Thicket* Capall Bann pub 2001 p80

7. E.J. Jones. *The Roebuck in the Thicket* Capall Bann pub 2001 p76

8. Kevin Knight 2009. *Catholic Encyclopaedia* – Extreme Unction

9. Kevin Knight 2009. *Catholic Encyclopaedia* – Extreme Unction

10. E.J. Jones. *The Roebuck in the Thicket* Capall Bann pub 2001 p144

11. J. P. Wilcox. *Keepers of Ancient Knowledge* Vega 2001- intro.

12. J. P. Wilcox. *Keepers of Ancient Knowledge* Vega 2001- p70.

13. J. P. Wilcox. *Keepers of Ancient Knowledge* Vega 2001- p98.

14. J. P. Wilcox. *Keepers of Ancient Knowledge* Vega 2001- p92.

15. E.J. Jones. *The Roebuck in the Thicket* p143/4 Capall Bann pub 2001

16. J. P. Wilcox. *Keepers of Ancient Knowledge* Vega 2001- p36.

17. J. P. Wilcox. *Keepers of Ancient Knowledge* Vega 2001- p131.

18. J. P. Wilcox. *Keepers of Ancient Knowledge* Vega 2001- p92.

19. J. P. Wilcox. *Keepers of Ancient Knowledge* Vega 2001- p178.

20. J. P. Wilcox. *'Keepers of Ancient Knowledge'* Vega 2001- p114-5.
21. Ross Heaven. *'The Sin-Eater's Last Confessions'* Llewellyn 2008- intro
22. Ross Heaven. *'The Sin-Eater's Last Confessions'* Llewellyn 2008- p19
23. Time-Life Books: *'The Mystical Year'* Amsterdam 1994/5 p106
24. E. O. James. *'Seasonal Feasts and Festivals'* Barnes & Noble USA 1963 pp138-39
25. Ross Heaven. *'The Sin-Eater's Last Confessions'* Llewellyn 2008- p48
26. Liber XV Gnostic Mass http://en.wikiquote.org/wiki/Aleister_Crowley
27. Ross Heaven. *'The Sin-Eater's Last Confessions'* Llewellyn 2008- p7 (Bertram Puckle in 1926; Prof Evans – 1825 in Carmarthen Historian and several others in: Sacred Texts. All quote from John Aubury's definitive description)
28. Ross Heaven. *'The Sin-Eater's Last Confessions'* Llewellyn 2008- p88-92
29. Quote from John Aubrey 1688: Dr Huw Walters, B. Lib. *'Sin-Eating in the Amman Valley'* Carmarthen Historian, Vol. XV (1978) pp 70-76 & http://carmarthenshirehistorian.org/cgibin/twiki/view/Historian/HistorianVol15
30. Ross Heaven. *'The Sin-Eater's Last Confessions'* Llewellyn 2008- p195-8
31. Ross Heaven. *'The Sin-Eater's Last Confessions'* Llewellyn 2008- p203-5
32. Sacred Texts: Chap. IV Funeral Customs: Wakes, mutes, wailers, sin-eating, totemism and death taxes.
33. Sacred Texts: Chap. IV Funeral Customs: Wakes, mutes, wailers, sin-eating, totemism and death taxes.

34. Sacred Texts: Chap. IV Funeral Customs: Wakes, mutes, wailers, sin-eating, totemism and death taxes.
35. E.J. Jones. [ed] Mike Howard. *'The Robert Cochrane Letters'* Capall Bann Pub. 2002 p121
36. E.J. Jones. [ed] Chas Clifton. *'Sacred Mask, Sacred Dance'* Llewellyn 1997 p67&XV1
37. Kevin Knight 2009. Catholic Encyclopaedia – Extreme Unction
38. Kevin Knight 2009. Catholic Encyclopaedia – Extreme Unction
39. E.J. Jones. *'The Roebuck in the Thicket'* Capall Bann pub 2001 p136
40. Robin Pary – A Theological History of the Eucharist: www.saltlight.org/europe/resources/theology
41. Robin Pary – A Theological History of the Eucharist: www.saltlight.org/europe/resources/theology

# 9
# Traditional Witchcraft for the 21st Century

By any other name, Witchcraft is as old as
the history of mankind.

Before we begin, we need to understand the context wherein witchcraft is placed and practised, and also the terminology used to describe it - if we neglect context, then we will fail utterly in grasping the reality, rather than the illusion of this much maligned and misunderstood practice, by critics and exponents of this arte both past and present. Modern academia is currently closing the gap between fact and fantasy, in a readily accessible way, such that in the near future there will be no excuse for any ignorance of the origins, the meanings or practises of witchcraft. Professor Owen Davies humorously, yet succinctly highlights this estranged reality in his excellent book on the role of Cunning-folk in English history. I shall read the following passage from it, in order to initiate 'context'.

> "Situations vacant. Only the following need apply: men and women with prior working experience outside the business, and entrepreneurial acumen. Must have competent literacy skills, possess own books of the trade, herbal experience, good divinatory skills, practical knowledge of conjuration, and intimate understanding of witchcraft. Working knowledge of astrology desirable. Own transport advisable. Formal dress optional. The candidate will work from home, but must expect to be on call at all times and be prepared to work

with animals. Lack of scruples no barrier. Start of employment: when sufficient numbers of people complain of bewitchment once again."

This wonderful quote typifies how all too easily, we are defined by what we do. Yet a label is meaningless unless the description fits its wearer. This in turn begs the question: 'Should we even be labelled at all?' The answer to this lies in whether or not you have truly understood the meaning and significance of the label in the first place, in order to make what should be, an 'informed choice.'

In the 21st century we desperately need to re-examine the meaning and use of terms for which our modern practises, in reality, bear little resemblance to those of the distant past. Let us then examine in particular, the terms Tradition and Witchcraft. Tradition implies old, ancient or even archaic, yet it needn't be.

## So what is Tradition?

The word tradition has a Latin root which simply means to 'hand down' and is used throughout much of the world to denote beliefs or customs taught by one generation to the next, orally, in the form of stories, be they myths or anecdotes, or by example, that is, in practise. Information and knowledge passed in this way is thus preserved, becoming established as 'Tradition'. Established custom can in fact be as little as one generation old. Wicca for example is now considered 'Traditional', especially in America. Tradition can also refer to specific customs within families, culture or religion, expressing the way in which people view, celebrate, enact or perceive subjective phenomena that typifies racial, tribal or otherwise idiosyncratic distinctions.

It is a common misconception that for a Tradition to remain valid, it must continue unchanged, without alteration in form or content. This is not so. Traditions must service the needs of their time. They must be flexible to evolution. Everything shifts, from Law through politics to religion and belief. Many philosophers and mystics have commented on the importance of ideas and beliefs remaining relevant to all students, be they theoretical or practical. When they fail to be so, they simply fail. Any Tradition that fails to meet the needs or demands of its heirs, is abandoned with impunity. History is littered with many such instances (Christianity, being the largest exemplar). Self-destruction surely follows those who are slaves to outmoded truths.

Here we may take a moment to analyse a simple example of a tradition found in dancing, that provides through analogy, the variant states that are all served by the ubiquitous term - Tradition. Morris dancing has been a popular expression of folk style for many centuries. However, many of the dances fall under the categories of authentic, revived, or stylised.

- Authentic dances are those mimicked to the very step, reproduced exactly, as pieces of living history, in continuous unbroken succession.

- Revived dances are largely based upon remnants, generally after a lacuna of at least one generation, and faithfully retain the style, intent and expression of the original dance.

- The stylised dances however, simply preserve the style of the historical dances they are based upon, yet are interpreted in new and exciting ways to which the modern viewer can relate. The narratives expressed may change in content but not intent. This distinction is important because it highlights the need for relevance. The dance steps too adopt subtle nuances that symbolise facets of our modern lives that we can instantly recognize.

Evidently, tradition is a term more complex than it first implies.

Nostalgia is indeed comforting, but few of us in this modern age are able to relate to a completely rural way of life, of famine after the harvests have failed, or the fear of disease prior to the wonder of modern pharmacology. Tradition then, lies in purpose, in function, meaning and intent, and not necessarily in its practises. In force then, not form.

## What is Witchcraft?

It would be very glib of me to say this can mean many things to many people, and that both in theory and practise it has changed considerably over the last millennia especially. And so, I would rather beg your indulgence as I attempt to summarise the historical position of witchcraft in order that you may better appreciate how best to take it through this century and into the next. In social and anthropological terms, witchcraft as a malefic practise, as we shall see, has sustained a negative reputation, and proscriptions against sorcery, known to have existed for over four millennia, throughout both Pagan and Christian cultures, have been in many cases, falsely levied at this, its most basic and widely practised form.

Much of what we think we know of witchcraft has been written retrospectively, and by people with quite specific agendas. In many cases where translations have occurred, words have been substituted for those with quite explicit significance relative to that particular time-frame. Take for instance the familiar biblical phrases 'the witch of Endor', and 'suffer not a witch to live'. In both cases, the words originally used, more properly describe the practitioners of sorcery. It is also commonly assumed that the later classical world was also replete with 'witches'. Again, not so; in the majority of translations, the word 'witch' is substituted for a variety of terms that range from sorcerer to necromancer. Moreover, the persons ascribed to such activities are quite frequently and surprisingly male.

Nevertheless, the most famous so called 'witches', Medea and Circe were in fact highly skilled divine Pagan enchantresses, labelled by some poets as mere witches in order to debase both their status and magical abilities. Other poets glorified and exaggerated their abilities to exemplify the fantastic; an effective breach of poetic license. According to one academic, when carefully scrutinised, even Dido is in fact, rather fetchingly portrayed as an Oriental Faerie Queen. These are super women, and not meant in any way to represent the more grotesque and innocuous hag, shriven by her own spite and malcontent. Yet history has labelled them all, quite indiscriminately as 'witches'.

Magic too has proved just as illusive, ranging from *'theurgy'* to *'goetia,'* that is from the higher forms of mysticism to the lower or base acts of sorcery. But let us look more closely at the word *'goetia,'* which again has been used extensively to describe witchcraft. In fact, it does not. Moreover, both fraud and deceit are implicit in its true meaning. Its root, *'goes'*, means incantator, who was quite literally, a person (usually female) who could sing the spirits of the dead into the Underworld. The rituals assigned to this procedure, necessitated invocations to Hekate, the supreme psychopomp of all departed spirits, who would ensure the spirit made a successful transmission. The astute of you will have already recognised this as a form of exorcism, but, would you also make the leap to the next step, which is of course, necromancy. If the spirits could be sung out, they could also be sung back in.

Communication between the living and the dead, for the purpose of personal gain or profit was strictly abhorred, by the theurgists, the priests and the magoi. Deemed as totally devoid of any religious principle, it was summarily consigned to the ever increasing list of the 'dark arts', meaning acts of extreme impiety. Removed from any sacred purpose or application, such acts of magic were eventually labelled as witchcraft, a progressively inclusive term for all the undesirable and unprincipled acts of both amoral and immoral turpitude.

Witchcraft could include necromancy, sorcery, weather magic and Rites of Divination (that is, more properly, divine notion) once quite profound operations, which were originally performed to learn the will of the gods, to ensure harmony, and not for personal trivia or general mundanities. The techniques sustained by these so called 'witches' were obviously not dissimilar to those employed by priests and magoi, except that is for the lack of religious aspiration which had rendered them quite unlawful. In reality, the rites enacted by both practitioners of 'goetia' and theurgy for mediating with the spirit world were the same, only the intent and purpose were different. It is easy to see how witchcraft acquired its reputation for all things negative and malefic, hence the archetypal associations with all things dark or sinister and even with 'black magic.'

Narrative history once again stepped in to cast the necromancer in an astonishing mold, far outreaching the reality, ascribing to them the roles of violent aggressor, child eater, demon killer and stealer of souls! Undeniably, necromancy does suggest the desecration of corpses and therefore did breach the sensibilities of the pious. Necromancy was considered a polluter of the living that reversed the natural order and thus the natural law, for which it was believed immense retribution would occur. Necromancers were understandably perceived as the great opposers, of law, order, fertility and growth; and once created, this monstrous literary figure haunted both the real and the fictional worlds with equal dread, first in the Pagan world, and then, more latterly in the Christian world. This horrific figure, now invariably female, epitomized and represented misfortune, becoming an elaborate device to personify all the ills of the world, and a means of social control, especially of status. All acts of sorcery, including necromancy, were condemned due to their baneful and malicious use of spirits, or rather demons, as they were now termed. A theological shift transferred the good daimon of theurgy, into the negative demon of sorcery. An irreversible moral judgement had been proclaimed.

Finally, one more group would join this ever expanding coterie of perceived evil, to be denounced as witchcraft; these were the herbalists and root cutters, wise-men and women whose immense pharmacological knowledge fed the vivid imaginations of the grand poetry and narratives of the classical world. All these alleged subvertors of society gradually evolved into the nightmare image of the strega, the night-hag, of dark shapes huddled over their noxious brews, of potions and poisons. It may be a false image, but it has survived for over two thousand years and it has served its purpose well.

As an aside, both religion and magic are based on belief and tradition, whereas science is not. Therefore, as witchcraft works with the weirder but more logical aspects of superstition, it is ironically closer to natural magic, and is therefore more scientific, than religion. Yet there existed no distinction in the antique world between magic and religious rites. Witchcraft in later periods has also been linked inexorably with the Cunning-Craft, especially prior to the modern Pagan revival of the 1960s. Yet for the most part, despite sharing certain basic rudiments of practice, their function and purpose remain quite distinct.

Cunning derives from the Anglo-Saxon root *'cunnan'* - to know. Wizard, similarly derives from the Old English *'wis'* - meaning wise, hence wise-man. These were individuals who were seen as being in some way 'different' from those around them. They had knowledge and gifts, that in times past were perceived as hereditary, or even obtained from a supernatural source, generally from the Fey, the Faerie folk. In their world, folk custom and tradition provided the context for their everyday lives, for their beliefs and superstitions, and for which we have no parallel in this century. It is impossible to estimate the saturation level or the import and influence these values instigated. This is completely alien to the modern mind. Early Viking and Anglo-Saxon accounts describe these 'Cunning-folk' or wise-men under the blanket term 'Wiccan', believed to have been pronounced *'Wichen'*, that has since devolved into the more derogatory term 'wytch.' Encompassed within the term *'Wiccan'*, were the variant practises of hexcraft and *'drycroeft'*, that covered all manner of sorceries, divination, healing and spell craft.

Importantly, many of the charms used, were later recorded in medical 'Leech-books' blending herbalism, folk magic and Christian observances, involving relics and scraps of liturgy, together as forms of healing. Of great interest, specifically, are the abundant charms for protection, against witchcraft: how to lift a curse, how to deflect a hex, and how to cure visitations of malscrung (all acts of malice). Of course there are other charms for the procurement of love, or how to find a thief, and for healing, most of which required the talents of the Cunning-men (or women), better known by their primary function as 'un-bewitchers'. Additionally, wherever sorcery and witchcraft have existed within a society, primitive or otherwise, then the witch-doctors, shaman, medicine-men or Cunning-men (or women) have existed to counter them. But do not for one moment look upon these figures in the past as benign or altruistic. They were neither. They were in fact, greatly feared. Furthermore, the boundaries between witches and Cunning-folk blurred ambiguously, especially as the latter were also known to have been necromancers, treasure-seekers, exorcists and in some cases, even pimps!

Perpetuated in oral tradition, the almost legendary magical expertise of these Cunning-folk as they came to be known by the 15th century, ranged from simple acts of folk magic, to complex sorceries and enchantments, and were often regarded as the most unsavoury and unscrupulous of persons. They enjoyed a precarious existence, teetering between the overtly illicit and condemned practices of malicious witchcraft, and their own counter practices that were commonly sanctioned or tolerated by the civil authorities, yet which frequently engaged the same methodologies. Naturally, a few fell foul of the system, but by and large they survived it. In reality they healed, or cursed, equally devoid of religious or spiritual aspiration. It was a job, and they executed their services quite efficiently, for which they received substantial fees. Their secrets or tricks of the trade were closely guarded, often preserved within the family as a trade or business, just as a blacksmith or carpenter might. Most significantly, these practitioners were nominal Christians! They were not Pagans! Both witches and Cunning-folk fulfilled their roles in society, anterior to religious vocation.

Magics both high and low were explored within the confines of the Christian faith, as it too evolved through the turbulence of the Middle Ages. It is imperative that it is not assumed that witchcraft has a history of anti-Christian sentiments, or that it pertains to any form of Paganism except in pre-Christian and non Christian societies, wherein its practitioners were of the religion of that culture (for example, Roman, African or Norse). As charges of heresy and diabolism entered the field of witchcraft towards the end of the 16th century, bills were passed in parliament (1563CE) as a bulwark against conjurations and witchcraft in an attempt to curb the rampant and disreputable practises of necromancy and sorcery. This shift in emphasis released the pressure from Cunning-folk and their dubious practises, as the courts turned their attention instead to the alleged witches. Again, the name may have been different, but the practise rarely was. Yet, it was the name, the title or label that facilitated this distinction and their persecution. Rightly or wrongly, names carry particular kudos, and a certain stigma.

Of course, at the zenith of the witch-craze, everyone with even a remote connection to any form of magic was liable to prosecution; many were tried indiscriminately, and many received the capital punishment, with which we are all too familiar. A curious note of caution is veiled here, for, in the ensuing hysteria, many medical students and surgeons, not associated with any form of witchcraft, were nonetheless, also caught up in these prosecutions, on charges of necromancy, for the theft of corpses required for their research. For a while, everyone was suspect. Petty rivalries, neighbourhood disputes, debtors and the greedy land grabbers all fuelled the fury. And when the storm cleared…the Cunning-folk, who had largely survived it, were back in business. Where there exists a hex, there is a need for its removal…ad finitum…

Witches were deemed evil, but the Cunning-folk, having a greater repertoire of practice and services were considered useful, that is at least, by the ordinary folk. The witch simply hexed. She (and it was nearly, though not always, a she) was malicious, no more, no less. She was therefore an undesirable member of society. Whether she was just a nasty, cantankerous, foul mouthed old woman, or a person of real power and volition, people were naturally uneasy with it. These then, were the 'traditions' of the people at the ground level of society, the everyday folk who had all manner of toil and misfortune with which to contend. It was but a simple matter for the law courts to condemn and discourage the only recourse available to them. Yet by the 18$^{th}$ century, the age of reason dawned, bringing with it industrialisation and urbanisation, thereby diminishing greatly the need for, and belief in, witchcraft and its attendant superstitions. It survived mainly in rural pockets, where family communities were largely isolated from the spreading socialization, the modern disease. It lingered, finally withering in the wake of two world wars, devolving into quaint but tenacious traditions, quietly in the shadows.

Then in 1951, Gerald Gardner shattered the peace with his vision of a Pagan revival. He re-styled the archaic practise of *'Wicca,'* and launched it onto a world nostalgic for customs and traditions of the past it believed lost in the decimation of war and creeping intellectualism. The New Age had begun. An old idea took new form, presented as the new occultism, the presentable face of Paganism. This movement had in fact begun much earlier within 18th century art and literature, by Romantics hungry for arcadia, a false hope in a grim world. This had been the primary intellectual motivation that pushed forward into later Victorian occultism, all of which remained distinct from associations with witchcraft. Again, many of its exponents were practising Christians.

Gardner especially, astutely distanced his Pagan revival from the stain of any perceived demonic or black occultism linked to the medieval practises of witchcraft, adhering more closely in fact to the acceptable role of the Cunning-folk, or wise-person, promoting what has since been described habitually and erroneously, as 'white witchcraft'. This is a moral distinction that has no existence in reality. The morals of the person alone dictate how they use and express their Craft, not the other way around. This is a false assumption that has no historical precedent, yet exists to disguise the ugly and unpalatable aspects of the Craft's real history. Even so, this extremely popular generic Paganism of Gardner's has proved an effective if somewhat romantic synthesis that has now established itself firmly as a 'tradition', in the strictest sense. Influenced by ceremonial and contemporary occult schools, he devised rituals free of such constraints, with more levity than their archaic counterparts, and which utilized the tools and drama of all three. I do of course relate this without bias or prejudice, as I am myself an initiate of that line.

Folk-magic traditions continued running parallel to, but mainly in the shadow of this forthright movement. Other traditions, influenced and encouraged by his success, became revived or adapted, incorporating the optimism and philosophical outlook of the latter decades of the 20th century, embracing especially 'Celtic' nationalism. These were vastly different in style, belief and practise to the pioneering and popular Paganism of Gardner. Many of these were far simpler and less theatrical, many adhered to earthier magics, and others expressed lofty and deeply spiritual magics, borne of mysticisms more redolent of a biblical age. Each one was autonomous, separate from the greater Pagan homogeny of the newly emerging Wicca. Labelled by many as the new religion, converts abandoned the Christian faith adopting this new self-styled Paganism in its stead.

So much then for recent history. Where we are going, and how we move forward, is quite meaningless unless we learn how we arrived at this juncture…in other words why is there such variety in the beliefs and practises of witchcraft today, if all it ever professed to be was maleficent sorcery? Surely, there must be something we have missed? There is! You see, witchcraft in Britain never was based in the Western or modern classical revival of Paganism, though its roots are sourced from within Northern, Heathen, and to some extent, the classical past, from a time when magic and religion had not yet been separated. In fact, many of today's magical practices, especially those regarding divination, necromancy and sorcery find their origin from within the antique world of the 2nd millennium BCE in the Middle Eastern regions of Mesopotamia.

Revealingly, and importantly to us, the Babylonians placed little value on these nefarious acts. Rather, they concentrated their occult energies upon communion with the divine. Magical ritual was at that time primarily resigned to acts of purification that removed the hubris of sin, obstruction and khaos, all acts that had the potential to render the supplicant unfit for communication with the divine. Throughout this ancient world, bewitchment or charming of persons or food (as in the use of poisons), being entirely psychosomatic, was induced via thought transference. That is, success depended upon the victim knowing they had been hexed. The surest indicator of this was to present or cast the 'Evil Eye'. In cases of actual or random physical 'illness', the assailant was declared unknown. This was countered by an appeal to deity (perceived as the divine judges) for either a cure or redress. Illness and disease were thus accepted as either a punishment from their own particular God for any perceived 'sin' (all evil airborne spirits) or as an act of malice visited upon them by another person, both of which required neutralising by purification or exorcism.

Egypt and principally Alexandria eventually became the centre for the collation and preservation of these and other religious, magical formulae. Here the mysteries were also recorded in forms relative to the culture or religion of its original and subsequent adherents. This must not then be taken to imply these as the only appropriate procedures for their continued practise. For in truth, the mysteries are eternal, magic is eternal; the thread weaves and binds all souls throughout time, animated by the culture and belief system of its proponents. Each period records the experience of these timeless and deeply profound truths within the subjective sphere of their own religious and social hierarchical structure.

During the Ptolemaic period after the Greeks conquered Mesopotamia (circa 331BCE), a cultural synthesis developed the Chaldean Oracles (Neo-Platonic) formulating a highly ritualised and increasingly mechanistic modus operandi…at this point - links to Hermetism eventually generated the conceit of its practitioners, ego intervened, significantly shifting the emphasis of power and its manipulation, from the gods, to themselves! This generated cumulative individual power for the magoi and other priests of religion and magic. The gods were no longer propitiated or petitioned but were increasingly summoned and commanded. Gradually, almost all magical acts became divorced from these archaic forms of religion where once they had been bound as a singular practise. At the level of the general populace however, localised gods and family or tutelary household deities, remained a primary focus. Oaths of dedication secured covenants for protection that valorised their ancestors (especially in hereditary) family clanships, who though not 'witches' per se, did practise spell-craft and other magics.

Many of the more elaborate processes, for some time, appear to have bypassed the more generalised and public practises of witchcraft, particularly at the very basic level, where many of those named as witches continued to perform simple acts of mischief by poison and potion and by initiating acts of psychology through their glamour and spell-craft. In rare cases, supplementary knowledge of weather prediction and astrology significantly increased their efficacy, potency and social status. Witchcraft was often ignored or overlooked until it became politically expedient to act upon it. Even so, these negative acts of witchcraft and sorcery were slowly but surely outlawed. Remember, both witches and Cunning-folk have been periodically allied to sorcery and diabolism until well into the 20$^{th}$ century, by which time, modern perception has largely exorcised these extreme prejudices, largely, but not completely. Nevertheless, not all the Craft's exponents were spiteful old hags, or vicious snipe-tongues. There was and is immense variation of practise between individuals and groups, which has from necessity remained largely secret, leading to extensive speculation, much of which is erroneous.

Traditional Craft, encompassing elements drawn from occultism, witchcraft and Cunning-craft, is rooted in that multifarious antique world.

The Craft has united many, often incongruent forms of magic, preserving the tenets and principles of many archaic religious mysticisms. It upholds simple but quite profound principles that encompass a full diorama, ranging from uncomplicated magics invoking protection, to complex exorcisms, performed by specialists, including the arts of sorcery and divination. Since the end of the 17$^{th}$ century especially, these practises (and those of the Cunning-folk) have remained largely initiatory, encompassing rites of passage and certain promissory vows or oaths, not of secrecy, but more generally of discretion and dedication.

A sacred bond is forged between mentor and student, somewhat more akin to the Eastern schools, where students offer fealty and un-avowed loyalty to their masters. These masters are not always the head of a group and may teach one to one by oral transmission. Some written material has survived the passage of time, and this is zealously guarded in most, but sadly not all cases. Poetry and myth, taught through allegory and experience were, then as now, the vehicles by which the sacred mysteries are revealed. As such they are without structure, subject only to the requisite needs and spontaneity of each student. Lessons are often impromptu and conducted without ceremony.

Traditional Craft, unlike Paganism is not a nature religion. However, it carries a deep respect for the powers of all gods that manifest through it. In this, it should be more properly considered, at its most basic level, as folk belief and or magic. Spell craft, magics and ritual form are for this reason not subject to the same rigour as instigated by magical systems such as the 'Golden Dawn', where one group might practise exactly the same as another, irrespective of the distance in either time or geography between them. Rarely are specific deities, either male or female, referred to by name, such things are implicit within the overarching power of fate and the tutelary names of the ancestral stream. There is also a strong sense of the 'power of place' within workings, and the 'genius loci' is duly acknowledged.

There is great truth in the statement that, though many Pagans consider themselves to be witches, but very few witches would consider themselves Pagan. Historically, witches adhere to the faith of their prevailing or predominant culture, as previously stated, be that Heathenism or more latterly, Christianity. This is equally true from America to Asia. There neither is nor was a conflict of interest. This highlights again the contrast between ancient and modern usage of certain terms, especially, for example, 'Hedge-witch', that now, as a result of the revival of Paganism, describes persons totally unlike their historically Christian antecedents, and who are now largely Pagan. This theological difference determines the importance of definition and context. Unlike the 'Western Magical Tradition' much of witchcraft, both past and present cannot be considered a 'system' - it is mutable, eclectic, adaptable, organic, dynamic, personal and idiosyncratic. In order to illustrate this, it would now be appropriate to explain, very briefly, the ritual use of space in the archaic world, thus revealing the somewhat ironic continuance of religious observance within some modern Craft practises.

First of all, the celebrations to which we are now accustomed, also have a curious origin: a festival known as a 'Sabbat' has been incorrectly allied to two phrases: one, a misunderstanding and mistranslation of the 'sabbath' as a day of rest; and two, 'esbat' (from the old French) that roughly translates as frolic, in a sexual sense. In fact, as a religious and magical ritual, it transcribes in meaning to 'the seventh', and is derived from the Sumerian word 'sabitu' (the source word and original root for the Hebrew form - Shabbat); this refers to the number 7, being the total of the holy wind gods of creation who were later perceived as the divine judges who oversaw all magical appeals. It denotes a holy measurement in time, hence the 'weekly' celebration of creation in their honour. The 'sabbath' could also refer to the seven year cyclical rite in relation to these deities, and even to the seven holy feasts held throughout the ritual year. An 'esbat', is a modern derivative of this only and now describes regular meetings, held either weekly or monthly.

Early magical ritual was obviously very basic indeed and rarely involved the marking of sacred space having no modern concept of 'calling in the quarters'. Most importantly, no 'weapons' were raised before the gods. Only in extremes cases of apotropaic sorcery or exorcism against witchcraft was a working area specifically delineated and fumigated for use (a circle was drawn around the victim with flour or ash). Old scripts, parchments and tablet fragments describe the 'lifting of the hands' only -the supplication and petition, not coercion of the 'Gods' for their aid. This became a later military and ceremonial adoption.

Remember too, that in ancient practise, an enclosure created a sympathetic boundary against the forces of chaos; effectively a dramatized appeal for protection from interferences by and of uninvited fate. Even the names of Pharaohs were enclosed within a sacred cartouche, an ellipsoid glyph of protection from corruption either by unseen or unknown forces that could destabilize his equilibrium. The circumpolar stars above were also observed to move in an apparently circular fashion; so logic dictated a corresponding arena for effective, practicable viewing and protection. Careful and continued study had induced this simple premise based on the hermetic principle: 'as above, so below.' Circles thus marked the maximum defensible area by one person, with an arm extended as they rotated in either direction. The modern nine foot circle arises from the addition of a standard length sword, extending the arm reach to approximately four and a half feet. So easily was the transformation made from military requirements to magical ones.

Four royal 'sentinel' stars, perceived as 'guardians' or 'watchers', were eventually replaced by lunar and solar cults that afforded them new, complex and varied correspondences such as Archangels in Kabbalistic and other esoteric systems. Totems representing these and other tutelary deities were often mounted at each cardinal point to represent qualities that derived from more tangible guardians at a time when timber constructions, or watchtowers were erected at corresponding points over entry and exit gates within the city walls of the ancient Middle East, Egypt and the later forts and villages of northern Europe. Offering strategic vantage points for protection, this is clearly yet another military stratagem, albeit one based on the observation of the dutiful acknowledgement of the holy markers in the skies above, and it has filtered into some modern craft practises via the influences of ceremonial magicians who were the first to adopt these methods of defence against perceived ariel foes.

This highlights yet another difference between the traditions of Wicca that readily absorbed these military and ceremonial fears regarding invasion and contagion, and the traditions more redolent of archaic shamanism, drawing upon older forms that do not generally advocate or subscribe to this concern, and which do in fact actively invoke and evoke ancestral spirits with whom to share sacred space. Naturally, there are exceptions in either case. Moreover, this distinction highlights again the unjust prejudice levied against those practitioners who refrain from 'banishing' the spirits for whom the rituals are intended to contact! It was and should be the intent that marks an act as baleful, not this procedure.

Angelic, faerie or daemonic spirits (often perceived as ancestors) evolved from disparate sources, from merging cultures, overlaying and enriching the synthesis of shared religious ideals. Overtime, magic began to emulate mundane life, rather than life emulating magic. Gradually, these formed the three main branches of the Craft, which are not mutually exclusive, and which do in fact share considerable overlap. Very briefly, and with great generalisation, there is 'Hereditary Craft' - a folk magic tradition, and an important repository of secret customs that are handed down from one generation to the next. These are family versions of the same principles that underpin the whole Craft. Autocratic and hierarchical, each family will have its own beliefs and generally remain closed to outsiders. Rites and rituals are also idiosyncratic to specific families. Their gods are tutelary, recognising specific ancestral deities having names known only to them.

Traditional Craft however, is more flexible and eclectic, absorbing current trends by adaptation in order to survive. It has loose associations and affiliations, but is often though by no means always, autonomous. Deities are amorphous, largely unnamed syntheses, referred to vaguely as - 'the old ones', or other quaint colloquialisms. It has subsumed a variety of teachings from Anglo-Saxon hexcraft, Arabic talismanic theurgy, Judaic Kabbalah, Bardic traditions, 'Celtic' Christianity, and in some cases, gnostic heresies. Moreover, many see true sabbatical Craft practise as being oneiric. This night flight of the dream state, where free of matter, the spirit is enjoined to its true purpose.

In extension of this, mystery Schools are more concerned with particular initiates, drawn from miscellaneous sources, of re-incarnated souls seeking advancement and ultimately, enlightenment. Each will be initiates of differing levels, yet all sharing the same focus, bound by the same spiritual heritage, bestowed by angelic forces that designated this sacred gnosis to mankind aeons ago. It is opined that the keys to understanding the truth lay with the guardians of the Tradition, the discarnate ancestors and deific forms who benefit the next generation of spiritual heirs. So in reality, there exists a huge span of practise ranging from simple folk magic at one end of this spectrum, to quite sophisticated ceremonial magics, involving complex liturgies and angelic magics in the revelation of the divine mysteries, of life and initiatory death, involving communion, sacred sexuality and ascension.

Magic then, is best understood as a methodology of practice, religion as one of expression. Together they exemplify the true nature of beliefs and practices valued in both the ancient and modern worlds. If the Craft is to survive, it must re-align its praxes to avoid devolution into superstitions that are contra to the principles of science in harmony with gnosis. As we evolve, we must do so from a point of truth. There should be no guilt to tarnish the mantle of our inheritance. What we amend, we do, to evolve in spirit, moving ever forwards, away from primitivisms, away from fear and superstition. We must embrace the purpose, the meaning and the essence of the force upon which the form rests, intrinsically, inherently and energetically. Remember we only borrow our legacy - it is loaned to us for a short period of time within the greater span of eternity. In that all too brief moment, it is ours, and we must make it so. We must re-unite the qualities of magic and religion, of spirituality and gnosis. This is how I believe the Craft will survive in the next century. It must draw nourishment from its roots, from all the magical traditions of mankind. It must embrace holism.

Tradition is not then the rigour of the status quo - it lives and breathes, it is the vital heart and soul of all culture, and like any living organism it should adapt itself with each generation. To perform the same rites as our revered forebears and ancestors without alteration to form does indeed honour them, but serves no point of contact that breaches their world with our own. The context shifts like sand with the passage of time.

An inspired example of this occurred quite recently, when I saw, or rather heard several youths playing electrical instruments in the town square; the singer was passionately ranting out his monologue. Intrigued, I paused to listen to what he had to say. Some moments later, I was amused to learn that he was, in fact 'rapping for Jesus.' The message was the same as it had always been, the intent and fervour were also the same, but this new presentation was infinitely more exciting, captivating in fact. But more importantly, it was speaking in a voice and culture the current generation are steeped in, and one that they believe in. As I stood there watching them, I realised that this is how one generation lives within the next; by moving on, by not staying in a past wherein they have no point of reference. This is how links are forged from one generation to the next. So yes, by all means, continue your traditions, adopt or even revive old ones, but honour the past best, by taking it forward.

Clearly, the Craft is diverse, encompassing many modes of practice, all of which reflect the variant needs and attainments of its adherents. If I may use another simple analogy: a person who is to all intents and purposes a good, moral and charitable person who may never attend their cultural place of worship is no less a member of that faith than the ascetic or holy man/woman who devotes every moment to prayer. None is superior to the other; the difference between them is merely one of spiritual aspiration. Similarly, waving various 'magical' tools around a fire whilst chanting an elaborate spell for whatever reason, may very well be exciting and productive, but it is not what makes a witch, Pagan or Magus. It is the mindset, the world view if you like. Possessing a collection of spells or charms, no matter how old, does not qualify you as witch, any more than owning a set of recipes makes you a cook. Only the knowledge of how they work and the skills of application will coax fruition. People within the Craft draw upon and develop the 6th sense, linking the noumenal world to the phenomenal. Sadly the Craft also attracts many sensationalists and charlatans; such parasites drain the life-blood from the very source that nourishes it.

In my short term as a writer, I have been branded a racist for my descriptions of the 'Black goddess,' anti-feminist for my promotion of Male deity and elitist for my uncommon view of all of them! I am of course none of these. Which not only proves that people never thank you for honest yet challenging views as pathways to the truth, but that you really can't please all of the people all of the time; nor must we try. And so we must choose our words carefully whether spoken or written to convey an absolute purpose, distinguishing between religion and spirituality, magical and occult, wisdom and knowledge, power and force, matter and form, Pagan and witch. It is often said that the meaning of a word lies within its use, if so, then it 'becomes' in the sense of its implication rather than its representation.

Many traditionalists are often described as 'dual faith' because our deities can easily be recognised within those of mainstream religions that have been appropriated and overlaid with their own cosmology. Those within the Traditional Craft could for instance freely enter any place of worship, be it a church, temple or synagogue, to pray and propitiate a working…this would be construed as a legitimate rite. Here there is another clear distinction with Paganism. Throughout Western history, witchcraft was seen as a syncretism of Christian ideas based around Pagan religious concepts; hence the survival of so many Pagan and folk superstitions relating to protection against malignant acts.

Extraordinarily, the earliest records from the 4$^{th}$ millennium BCE reveal no distinct deity for either malignant (cursing) or benevolent (blessing) acts of magic. In fact, the same (ambivalent) God was petitioned for both. Separation occurred only after Zoroastrian dualism around 600 BCE entered Judaism and thus by default, Christianity and Islam, irrevocably corrupting the whole Western concept of magic and witchcraft.

Any deity could be petitioned for assistance, but usually a tribal/city/tutelary God would be deemed better suited to consider the worthiness of each case. Ironically, counter magic by the recipient or victim would have been made to the same deity -both sides were judged on merit/intent/ sincerity…. (moreover, the same term was used for invoking the power or force modern practitioners would deem 'good' or 'evil' spirits - only the *intent* defined the purpose). The outcome rested entirely with the petitioned God who then determined the success or failure of the magics cast. Requests were normatively for all intended evil to be returned to the sender. Malicious acts were therefore considered illegal, counter magic was, however, quite legitimate!

During this period the gods were perceived as the heavenly 'judges.' All rites were constructed as speeches for defence or prosecution. Rituals such as this were designed as trials, with the gods, as jurors, affecting the result; it was their power alone, not man's that governed the state of play - this was the vital distinction. It is important here to remember how, at this time the power or force was understood as a quality *exterior* to the person conducting the rite, even though they had acquired the means by which to execute it. This contrasts significantly with modern witchcraft where the power or force is now largely believed to reside *within* the person conducting the rite.

I must re-iterate here that always, it was understood, the gods and not the practitioners granted the required flow of power or force. The rites were performed sympathetically for the God to follow = this was the ultimate in dramatic communication, which evolved many hundreds of years later into the sympathetic rites and sacred dramas of hermetic, micro/macrocosmic events. Of course, an exorcist fulfilled the role of a modern day psychotherapist and worked alongside the physician in the ancient world to restore equilibrium and the metaphysical balance of their patients, working together to remove mental disturbances. Modern holistic therapies are heir to this primitive practise.

The most sought after magic was prophylactic - to be moral, honest and charitable - this pleased the gods who would therefore be better disposed to award protection when petitioned, or judge your case favourably when requested. Invocations and prayers were both apotropaic (power to ward off: use of amulets) and prophylactic (implementation of preventative causalities: the means to administer defence i.e. - medicines/vaccines). Cult images of deity/icons preserved the essence of the God in order to receive offerings and prayers - again, identity was made through analogy and metaphor. Household shrines once common throughout the ancient world are once again popular, revealing a consistent need for religion within acts of magic. Then as now offerings/libations were given daily to honour and propitiate their deific representatives and mediators.

In understanding that our concept of witchcraft was derived from the Assyrian, Akkadian and Sumerian belief in the power of men and women to perform *sorcerous* acts, it is cogent to note that until the end of the 14$^{th}$ century, the English word Wicca (witch), meant specifically a sorcerer; it was then transformed to mean *heretical* diabolist, the emphasis being upon the worship of the Devil and the practise of his black arts. By the Middle Ages, any scholar with access to occult material could perform acts of magic entirely divorced from their original religious contexts; magical acts which had previously been limited only to the priests. Morally and ethically adrift, this dangerous development cross-pollinated with the more generic practises of witchcraft and heretical occultisms, creating a powerful and startling synthesis.

Being elitist is not a divine trait, but a human one. That mankind has for millennia fashioned his gods in likeness of himself is a tragic truism, but still that does not make it true. These illusions are mere conduits for a source that is pure, untainted by human corruption. Its forces of khaos and destruction are not guided by choice or preference. Nor by greed nor power mongering. All is balance, a natural intelligent design. We can choose to scrabble along in our sectarian dogmas practising superstitious primitive magics or we can embrace the science, the logic, the ecstasy of freedom within absolute sentience.

For millennia the Craft has floated freely in eclectic ambiguity. Surely, in this Aquarian age we must finally remove persecution and ignorance of past proPagandas as obstacles to gnosis. It is always assumed that magic is efficacious, so that knowledge of it is often mistaken as true knowledge. Again, this is to confuse the means with the ends. Certainly the Craft has survived within variant religions without real affiliation to any of them, but this should not be seen as an implication of a deficit in religious belief or practice. Magic is inexorably linked to these religious traditions and beliefs, relevant to its origins and adherents; it always was. To retain a false separation of magical elements from those of religion continues to debase its practice. Magic is and always has been the manifest form of religion; it cannot properly be separated from it. One form raises man up to meet his God, another simply brings down the power and force of that God to man.

The meaning of a word does indeed depend upon its use, and many words have indeed changed quite significantly from their original meaning. However, none of those words carry the stigma or prejudice of words that have been labels, which in spite of fashion or trends, always remain exactly that. This enjoins us to be mindful of descriptive terms, especially those that relate directly to archetypes, and most especially, loaded archetypes that are cultural, political or religious and have negative value. It is precisely for this reason that within many extant traditional or hereditary clans and families, the natural domain and repository of Cunning-craft and folk-magic, hardly anyone would concede the term 'witch', nor sorcerer, less still, Pagan! These titles are self-limiting and demeaning in their subjection to propaganda and ignorance. And this is also why their practises remain largely secretive, speculative and entirely distinct from those of modern Wicca.

So then, in summary, can any modern 'witch' claim to be a continuation or even a revival of their medieval counterparts? In the strictest sense, the answer must be no, as by and large, they are not maleficent; similarly, can any cunning-person also claim this continuity? Again probably not, as many of them are not, 'un-bewitchers', though many of the other services our ancestors offered, remain in their remit to a greater or lesser extent. The concept of the purely hexing wytch, and of maleficarum has largely passed and along with it the need to remove it. Yet the association stubbornly remains. The concept of religion too remains a thorny issue, with many modern witches and Pagans denouncing religion from their practises, even as others cling to this archaic and vital symbiosis.

And just for good measure, there are even those who believe themselves the victims of some supernatural malice. Yet still more aspire beyond these earthly obsessions with spell craft, to explore the inherent and un-revealed mysticism of a blissful heritage, promised to all those true seekers who walk the lonely path. Only superficially then, despite changes in methods of travel and communication, and because people are still intrigued by the Tarot, astrology and other forms of divination, and because people still freely endorse alternative therapies, does there appear to be little or no difference between the modern practitioner and their medieval counterparts.

Of course, the Craft continues to evolve, even as modern Wiccans learn of other traditional practises, and incorporate them into their own evolving repertoire of spell-craft, beliefs and magical development. In fact, it would be more proper to say that over the past forty years, each has infused the other with varying degrees of influence. And though distinct, both programmes are organic and both maintain a select and discreet core that is charged with carrying the mantle throughout this next century and beyond. By the will of the gods, they will continue to grow and develop, in accord with the needs and demands of a society very different to those that spawned them, and from whom they have inherited those 'traditions.'

All beliefs are the sacred trust of its heirs, but to be kept alive, they must be meaningful to that society. Therefore, consider carefully, the terms used to describe yourselves. Be especially aware of the social connotations, both historically and in modern terms, of the following generalisations: firstly, of the more environmentally ambivalent, typically Christian and often amoral cunning-person or witch, and secondly, of the more eco-friendly, moral, but now Pagan hedgewytch.... You can choose one or neither.

As Professor Owen Davies clearly expressed in the opening quote to this lecture, real continuity lies in the nature of business. We must therefore continue to serve the needs of the populace, socially, magically and where it is required, spiritually. In the final scenario, it's all about what you believe yourself to be and where you place yourself on the spectrum of 'Tradition'.

[Transcript from a lecture given at the 'All Fool's Gathering' March 2008]

# 10 Which Craft?

Today I hope to share with you my passion for 'The Craft'; my concerns however, are for its future. Who I am, is not important but what I do, is. I follow in the footsteps of giants, maintaining a legacy of profound beliefs and solemn practises. Robert Cochrane asserted how the Craft was for him an Occult Science, a correlation of will and intent, fate and destiny, order and khaos where magic takes place in the zero point of equilibrium. It is often described as a crooked path, that twists and turns where choices are presented at each stage for growth; like the cauldron it is never still. When embraced fully, it becomes a life's work. Not for nothing is it one's Magnum Opus. We place ourselves within the matrix of being, ourselves the crucible of its manufacture. Truth is eternal because any single moment of time reflects only the truth of that moment. Constrained and un-evolved, it becomes a lie.

Many of today's magical practises find their origin within the $2^{nd}$ millennium BCE, in the Middle Eastern regions of Mesopotamia, especially those regarding divination, necromancy and sorcery. Though, revealingly, the Babylonians placed little value on these nefarious acts of witchcraft. Rather, they concentrated their energies upon theurgy, of communion with the divine. Magical ritual was primarily resigned to acts of purification that removed the hubris of sin, obstruction and khaos, all acts that have the potential to render the supplicant unfit for communication with the divine. Divination meant just that - divine notion

– the means by which the will of the divine was sought. If this could be known, then a harmony could be nurtured, thus averting the imbalance of chaos. It could be said that a similar concept known within Egypt as 'Maat' was the premise upon which they organised their lives. This is why Robert Cochrane asserted that 'all ritual must be prayer'; petition then, not coercion. This repeatedly stresses imperative knowledge of the Higher Will exceeding the needs of the Lower Will.

Because magic was very much intrinsically bound to the religious practices of the Babylonians, many of their rituals were considered incongruous for other cultures that later extrapolated and subsumed specific magical formulae. Thus, removed from their original context and bereft of moral implications and aspirative qualities, these lists of correspondences and rites of exorcism eventually led to an increase in malignant sorcery throughout the ancient world. Much of this may be discerned by the discriminating scholar within the Greek Magical Papyri ($2^{nd}$ century BCE - $5^{th}$ century CE), which has of course provided the basis for much of our Western magical and by default, Craft practises.

In studying the archaic form of ritual, we may easily recognize the modern form:

- Fire and water were seen as purifying forces in a metaphoric and literal sense in that they carried away or destroyed waste. They were not seen as Pagan elementals in the modern understanding of these terms.

- The rituals were commonly performed at night under the stars, the archaic representatives of each relevant deity.

- Lamps/fire/torches to invoke deity to destroy waxen images. Fumigations to cleanse and purify air borne contagion cords for

- binding (metaphoric paralysis) all objects used burned and scattered to winds.

- Doors and windows blessed and dusted with flour extreme cases of death-wish - victim placed in a circle of flour (life essence of grain deities/shield against lesser spirits directed to perform ill acts)

- Standards raised to 4 compass points.

- Asperge area - use of bell and drum to 'frighten away spirits' - medieval clapping and classical theatre -cacophony abhorrent to them (opposite of harmonics)

- Full Moon - Nanna/Sin - lunar father/head of pantheon.

- Psalms and prayers used then and now, continuously - biblical and Sumerian and Egyptian.

- Animal generally slaughtered after transference of spell to it - burned or buried with full funerary rites to appease Queen of Underworld - maintain balance of order/death meted.

- 'Lifting of hands' in gesture of supplication for invocations and prayers - eventual complex sequence of sigils and symbols to express - (mudra concepts)

And because magic was very much intrinsically bound to the religious practices of these early peoples, many of their rituals were considered incongruous for other cultures, whose resolution was to extrapolate only those specific elements of the magical formulae deemed useful to them. Incantations were performed for consecration and blessing of sacred objects especially amulets: Love charms, binding - all acts of sympathetic magic, all the province of superstitious and primitive aspects of the greater state religion.

Temples housed the city or state shrine and an altar to the city God and protector of its entire populace, where worship entailed the enactment of sacred drama that perpetuated covenanted rites with those tutelary deities. Importantly a lack of sincerity spelled doom and khaos for the city. Festivals celebrated the origins of mankind as a species, and for his continued community, abundance and progress as defined and instigated by the gods.

Thus, throughout Western history, witchcraft was seen as a syncretism of Christian ideas based upon Pagan religious concepts; hence the survival of so many Pagan and folk superstitions relating to protection against malignant acts. In social and anthropological terms, witchcraft has maintained a negative reputation and proscriptions against sorcery are known to have existed for over four millennia. Even so, there are not one but three primary forces within the Craft:

1] of divination, necromancy and occultism.

2] of alchemy - the science of the great work, physical and spiritual; the micro/macrocosmic path of ascension, of attainment, of at-one-ment.

3] of religion/devotion - this binds us back to the source, to our origins, to those unknown progenitors who blessed us with their Craft.

This third and last premise forms the basis for my lecture today, and its principles manifest within key issues relevant to it. Thus the Craft holds the seeds of all higher forms of magical enterprise, yet its very eclectic nature facilitates a flexibility not permitted within the rigid parameters of those separate modalities. This I believe is the essence of the Craft, and the key to its survival. Its fluid, adaptable and mutable qualities have endured the storms of repression, persecution, bigotry and ignorance; its oblique charisma a mantle of disguise. It may be Dionysian - wild and ecstatic, or Apollonian - quiet, contemplative and cerebral; action and repose. A pre-requisite balance not found in many other magical paths.

It draws from the well-spring of gnosis in all its divergent forms. We are summoned and we must answer the call. Each person upon the path is autonomous, subject only to their personal objectives and beliefs. In the great pool of the tradition, we walk a solitary path towards its expansion and conclusion. We each take what we need and we each decide how much of ourselves we will give in return. Its greatest exponents are eccentrics whose genius reflects the atavistic principles of mentation. No other occult path affords the individual such control over one's own destiny – the expiation of fate. This theme pervaded the working ethos of Robert Cochrane and of Tubal Cain. And here I have to stress that when fully embraced, with full initiation, covenanted oaths and assignation of a spiritual Egregore, no other path is as demanding or rewarding.

Yes I am passionate about my Craft; I was born hungry, and I hope to die sated! I am on one level a generic Pagan and witch, but more importantly, on another I am a child and priest of the mysteries, a seeker upon the eternal path of light.

Robert Cochrane avoided absolute classification, regarding each term: witch, Pagan, sorcerer, or occultist as pejorative, vague and self-limiting, and all negating the latent spiritual aspects of his Craft. Instead he preferred - pellar, which for him implied a priest of the 'people'. For him, 'priest' was used in the fullest sense of the word, not as a title of a man working within a morally, spiritually and ethically bankrupt orthodoxy, but in the archaic sense of a master of destiny, a controller of fate, a rider of the hidden realms, a shaman and medicine man, a seeker and preserver of all wisdom.

The truth is perceived only by those who earn it, not in an elitist egotistical manner, but by singular dedication and objective surrender to the ineffable. Gnosis is imparted in the oneiric realms wherein the seeker is seduced to remain. This 'other world' is all we would wish it to be, and yet, if we fail to return to these realms to effect its manifestation, we have defaulted the alchemy of transmogrification. This balance, its comprehension and maintenance constitutes the true work of a witch upon the crooked path.

Now that my introduction is over, my point is this: 'WE ARE ALL GOING TO DIE!'

This we know, so why should it be important? A short anecdote should induce clarification. The first time I met Evan John Jones, the former late Magister of Tubal Cain, was in Brighton where he had arranged to meet me at the station. I alighted the train in the blistering heat of a typically coastal summer (August 1998), somewhat dehydrated and in desperate need of fresh air. I spotted him immediately, a typical, retired gentleman in straw hat, with folded hands upon his cane. He rose steadily to greet me and kissed my hand, but said nothing. He motioned me to follow him, which of course I did. We walked on until we arrived at a particularly dark and gloomy secluded corner of a deserted graveyard. He motioned me to sit upon a bench beneath a huge yew tree. He then turned towards me and rather bluntly asked: *"are you ready to die?"* Panic seized my normally rational mind as I searched for an answer. Should I answer yes or no? What did he want? What was his purpose? Why was he asking me this strange question in this eerie and remote place? He stared impassively and repeated his question.

Grappling with my thoughts I began to intellectualize an answer and replied, somewhat flatly, that although I was willing to die, I'd rather it was not just yet! Cooley, he responded with: *"I asked you if you are ready, not willing to die!"* Without further explanation he then asked me if I believed in the Devil, to which I answered a little too quickly - *"Yes, all of them!"*

*"Good answer,"* he barked breaking into a ten minute coughing bout - he had severe emphysema. But to return to his first question: *"are you ready to die?"* I was to learn this did not mean or refer to any form of willingness or acceptance of death either then or in some distant, nebulous future, but referred instead to the 'Great Work', the preparation of the soul for its final release. If achieved correctly, we may die in full readiness, that is, a fully realised, purified and illuminated soul. Our reward for this effort is at-one-ment, individuation - Bliss, Nirvana, Ananda. If we fail in this work, we die unprepared, that is, not ready, in a state of ignorance, to return again and again to correct this error until we either succeed or become cosmic soup.

His second question - *"do you believe in the Devil?"* is of course, a contentious one. There are many religions the world over that have since their inception subverted the gods of opposing faiths into demons or even the Devil, the dark bogeyman of all bad novels, nightmares and cult movies. Nevertheless, the energy and beliefs attributed to these thought forms are diametrically opposed to that invested by the adherents of those blighted and maligned faiths; and so a duality arises. Again it is the duty of all occultists to clarify this discrepancy, and for the True Craft to distance themselves from the promotion of false and negative imagery. Very soon I came to realise that it would not be an easy task explaining the working ethos of a seemingly ancestor worshipping death-cult! The knowledge not just how to live but how to die, how to prepare for death, how to be, to become, how to extend our mortal limitations; these are the gifts of the True Craft, the bounty of Cain, the Father of all. The Craft holds within its core a religion at once profound and sublime and for those of us who share these principles of enlightenment, the light extends from the dark; it is not covered by it.

Ever since the Fraudulent Mediums Act replaced the Witchcraft

Act in 1951, every carpet bagger and snake-oil salesman from here to Timbuktu has been allowed to peddle their wares and views, exploiting the gullible, the ignorant and the naïve. But even this abhorrent practise has a place within the mysteries of the Craft - that of false gurus, teachers, self-styled prophets and avatars, there to test and mislead the weak and unworthy. Even so, though each must abide by the hoary adage: *"Take thyself as Lamp,"* what real value has any enlightenment if we ignore the deficit in others? Should we play true or false prophet - Bodhisattva or Trickster? Are we the Fool or the Fool who follows Him? Discretion is the better part of valour; when the Fool is not jesting, he puts his finger to his lips. I am not denying that it is indeed a vocation of the highest calling, nor am I saying we should not preserve the mysteries nor safeguard their secrets. Some of us are born knowing, others will die seeking. Consciousness needs raising slowly, it requires nurturing. Re-education is the responsibility and duty of all those who attain gnosis in all walks of life. For if we fail to nurture the divine within everyone, then none of us are free.

Margaret Murray has been much lambasted for her suggestion that witchcraft has continued for millennia in an unbroken tradition, practised as an organised religion. In this sense we know this is a false claim. However, if we accept there is no religion higher than truth, and if we understand that as the highest principle of the mysteries, then we can begin to grasp the glimmer of logic within this apparently ambitious claim. The discovery of truth is the driving force of the mysteries and all its sublime and variant forms. There is a gross misconception in what is fast becoming an accepted belief, that the evolution of religion began with primitive animism, progressing into polytheism, to pantheism and finally to monotheism. But I challenge this theory. I refute it absolutely. If we consider these principles in closer detail, we discover that animism represents a belief or awareness of the one-ness of everything, of the existence of deity within every organic object.

Polytheism reduces this awareness to an understanding of many forms of deity; Pantheism restricts this view yet further by placing a sectarian concept of deity within a cultural or tribal sense; finally, monotheism expresses the absolute in elitism by denying the existence of all other forms of deity except the one the presiding authority adheres to. Thus, I propose the reverse is true. Monotheism represents the most primitive, unsophisticated and unenlightened view. Conversely, animism represents sophistication in its awareness and acceptance of all living things within a Universal Creatrix. Panentheism represents the most explicitly evolved form, for it combines the animistic and pantheistic principles of the totality and immanence of deity, the complexity and diversity of approachable and henotheistic archetypes of polytheism, all within the transcendence of monism. Clearly this pinnacle of evolution utterly disregards monotheism. This principle is reflected in the Chaldean model, cogently the basis for Platonism, Vedanta, Druidry and the British mysteries.

Panentheism is the secret of the mysteries preserved within the diverse forms of the Craft, and most particularly among those who uphold the mystical legacies of their fore-fathers, in which initiates actively seek enlightenment. Worship is but a tool for contact. But these subjective practises will find little favour with those obsessed only with acts of thaumaturgy. The transcendence of Monotheism is the lie that separates us from the eternal sentience; it is anathema to the mysteries in which each of us may discover the subversive and anarchic principle of truth! At-one-ment is not atonement. There is no sin; redemption is re-union, realisation and revelation - a return to a former state of being.

The Craft is the pattern by which we set our lives and the means to effect change within it. It is primarily a Craft of the people and as such it must reflect the needs and purpose of its practitioners. Historically and traditionally, the Craft has been a repository of the sorcerous arte, of cunning, the skills of which are admirably championed by many. However, I like my predecessors believe the Craft maintains deeper secrets, of subtle yet perceptible gnosis within its rites and philosophies, all of which reveal the legacy and vestiges of an ancient wisdom. Alchemical formulae may be gleaned from its arcane praxis, hidden yet salvageable. Thomas Aquinas, a mediaeval Church theologian said: *"God's existence can be grasped by unaided reason, but knowing his nature requires the grace of revelation."* Plato also believed that only what is eternally true can be properly said to be known - all else is flux. Agrippa described magic as a faculty of wonderful virtue, full of high mysteries and containing the most profound contemplation of secret things.

Clearly then, magical rituals should entail greater things than winning fortunes, raising demons, or blasting enemies; we should be engaged in the raising of the soul beyond such materially motivated trivia. The synaptic gap between ourselves and divinity is not breached by our acquisitions, by having more, but by becoming more, by conscious expansion of a subconscious process. In this way we swell our capacity of being within the One. No-one can be taught the secrets of occultism, these are yielded in force not form, and these must be experienced by each individual aspirant. No book or word exists that can reveal these secrets. Truly the mysteries are not for sale. However, the knowledge of the processes regarding the preparation of oneself requires the teachings of a mentor, under whose tutelage such gnosis may be secured.

No amount of intellectualising or understanding alone will induce these experiences, in fact, it may seriously compromise it. Paradoxically, unwarranted passion induces a fervour of desire that also blocks complete sublimation of the self. The late Magus Bill Gray said: *"We survive by Spirit and Matter, but we evolve through Mind and Soul. Inspired by our ideas we grow into our gods, for they are what we must become!"* Only a balance of Mind and Soul (heart) combining Hermetic and Orphic practice will bring us to the equilibrium - the Qutub point of spiritual evolution. Bill Gray also believed that all Rites and Ritual came under the auspices of Hermes Trismegistus, prevalent again within the threefold way of inner illumination of the aspirant, awake upon the path of gnosis:

The first path is the Hermetic path, of the mind, ruled by intellect. The second is the Orphic path, of the heart, ruled by the emotions. Once more, the third and final path and the one that most readily concerns us, is the path of the Mystic, the hardest of all, of sheer devotion, following the thrice great psychopomp, the Lord of secret wisdom, cunning and mental arts, the written word and our guide to the outer and inner realms. There are two deaths in mysticism, first in life of the astral soul, and secondly in death of the material body. Mysticism stems from the Greek root - *'Mystikos,'* which means 'to see with the eyes shut and to speak with the mouth closed' - that is 'to know', often translated as 'secret', and 'Mysteria' which implies 'initiation'. It is a speculative streak within religion and philosophy that seeks to attain union with deity by essentially arcane means. It has its roots in Platonic Mystery Schools and more existential philosophies. Cultural legacies are often initiatory, transposed within traditions and dispersed within the mysteries.

Cochrane's most oft quoted statement: *"In fate and the overcoming of fate lies the True Grail,"* is not as is commonly believed a metaphor for thaumaturgy - that is, for applying Will to potentialities to effect manifest change on material levels. No, rather it refers to the mystical attainment of 'Destiny', itself, erroneously confused with fate. Destiny is man's ultimate aspiration, to achieve *'Unio Mystica'* - attainment of the Grail. It is man's fate to die and be reborn - *"tis fate and better so;"* gnosis alone allows man to circumvent his mortal 'fate' to achieve his 'divine' destiny - his God-given birthright. The Grail does not represent power, wealth, longevity nor any other material aspiration or Faustian avarice - it is absolute and complete enlightenment, in which our illumination liberates us from the cycle of re-birth. In Hinduism, the atman or individual soul is understood as destined to be dissolved into Brahman, the absolute soul of God.

Fate represented by the manifold goddess of life and death is the controller of 'life in time'; destiny is the experience of 'being in eternity.' Paradoxically within the Craft of Tubal Cain, fate is understood to be above the gods, the ultimate Creatrix; yet gnosis of Her true state sets man beyond her play; she simply removes us from the board. Clearly, then fate and destiny are not the same thing as is often pre-supposed. Destiny represents our pre-ordained future; it is devised from a natural order of the universe - Karma and the laws of causality (Ma-at). Some believe it may be ascertained by the divinatory powers of shamen and prophets. Fate on the other hand is not fixed, it is mutable, and it is decreed if God should will it. The term fatality infers an imposed destiny and is an abuse of the term. Fate is an active power for change, it offers choice, options, i.e., the body may die but the soul does not have to.

It is worth mentioning here the (Greek) word for choice is heresy, a precept the Church was not overly fond of. We have free will in real time to execute decisions based on desire and knowledge of the possible outcomes of each choice. Fate manipulates, but ultimately we choose. Fate often repeats the choices, testing and tempting us along our path, until our accord matches that of the higher will and we thus achieve our destiny. In the East this is beautifully explained within the simple understanding of - 'what is, depends upon what is not' - balance! All is inter-dependent; volitional acts drive the universe - cause and effect. So all outcome is determined by our choices, by the intentional actions, of our free will. Free will derives from a moral choice; evil is simply an abuse of free will - 'sin' in the truest sense of the word meaning impedance, prevents the path of truth. The Craft is for all who have returned to this plane and who seek to know, to remember and to progress onto their ultimate destiny.

The role of the prophet in history was to deal with the philosophical issue of destiny, and was not until recent times concerned with divination in the sense of prediction. It expressed the true value of karma - of causality and of pre-destination, of God's will and God's wisdom. Prophets were the mouthpieces of destiny, as opposed to oracles that concerned themselves with fate. One expressed the will of deity, the other the free will of man. The resolution between the dynamics of this dichotomy was the responsibility of the various monarchies throughout the ancient world and again found expression within the mystery religions, traditions that are now embedded within the Craft to a greater or lesser extent, dependent upon tradition, namely those of the divine king and the dying and resurrected God. The Magister fulfils the role of priest/prophet and king or conscience, with the Maid in the role of fate.

Cochrane often commiserated the lack of genuine groups or covens within the British Isles in which real power was generated from the alchemical fusion of these occult male and female principles. Occult too means more than hidden, it means not understood, or better, beyond the ordinary range of understanding. This term applies to fields of knowledge that enable interaction and control of mysterious forces of nature. Occultism exists in parallel realms of dreamlike oneiric experience. Occultism holds that humanity is revealed to itself by transcendence. Our religious aspirations provide the *'prima materia'* upon which the genesis of the sacred, sparks into life. Throughout the ancient world, membership into one mystery School did not preclude initiation into another. Hope of salvation developed under syncretism, this provided the counter measure against sterility and stagnation. Graeco-Oriental religions offset the pessimistic determinism of the state religions. They believed that with the aid of certain divine beings, man could raise himself above his fate. Many Hermetic texts state that initiates were no longer determined by fate.

Religion is one of humanity's essential traits that distinguish us from the animal kingdom. We are self-aware and we are aware of deity. Paganism as a reference to divinity is man's natural state; all belief and magical practice evolves from this fundamental premise. Atheism is not a natural state. Cults are by their nature sectarian; religion is not. Therefore it is perception and not belief that divides us. Perception then separates us not only from the rest of humanity as individuals, but from deity. Mysticism is the driving force within diverse religions that recognizes this impedance and which seeks to elevate its adherents beyond these self-inflicted boundaries. Truth is above all doctrine, and the Word is received by everyone with ears to hear it.

All of us may encounter deity through nature and through consciousness; the Craft in particular has its own methods relative to both. Science has removed the wonder of the cosmos, and revealed many of nature's laws. But one final mystery, and one that is here underscored, that of death, still eludes its empirical analysis. The phenomenal world is the manifest expression of divinity, the hierophanic symbols of which are eternal. The enigmatic mystery of this cycle of existence finds further expression in myth. Narratives and metaphors reflect man's struggle to overcome fate to achieve his destiny, throughout geographic time and space. The language of the poet reveals the 'terrible and the glorious' of the 'Real', the noetic realms of truth, a gnosis above and beyond the realms of nature and science, above and beyond the beliefs of religion and all magical practice. The distinction between religion and magic is often given as the former petitions and is a public practice possessing an impulse to worship and the latter coerces, being a private practice with a propensity to command and dominate. But this definition takes little account of the practices of Hermetism, ascetism and mysticism. In reality, magic is practised both within and without the Craft and within and without religion.

Religion is the search for deity and consists typically of three fundamental elements:

1] Myths - the intellectual and doctrinal component; these affirm our belief or understanding of deity and provide a historicity of contact. These may contain magical elements.

2] Rites - the cultural aspect; actuation of contact. These may also contain magical elements.

3] Intrinsic forms of mysticism that are the inner experiences of actual contact. This is the essence of all religion.

Plato observed that although many uphold the outer rites of religious practice, but few enter the mysteries proper. Yet, rites and sacraments are both signs and an effective power, fundamental to all religions. So the current terms of priest and magus were often synonymous throughout many cultures of the ancient world, and the context in which Robert Cochrane understood them. Magic then, is best understood as a methodology of practice, religion as one of expression. Together they exemplify the true nature of beliefs and practices valued in both the ancient and modern worlds. If the Craft is to survive it must re-align its praxes to avoid devolution into superstition which are contra to the principles of science in harmony with gnosis. As we move further from the core of truth, these practises become increasingly bizarre.

For millennia the Craft has floated freely in eclectic ambiguity. Surely, in this Aquarian age we must finally remove fear, persecution and ignorance as obstacles to gnosis. It is always assumed that magic is efficacious, so that knowledge of it is often mistaken as true knowledge. There again, this is to confuse the means with the ends. Certainly the Craft has survived within variant religions without affiliation to any of them, but this should not be seen as an implication of a deficit in religious belief or practice. Subversive or exotic styles of magic are often regarded as being the most estimable and desirable forms of practise. Being obscure, it is believed their tenets must somehow be more powerful. But how can they be? It is the same Will and Intent that drives them! The same practitioner that initiates their actuation! Magic is inexorably linked to the religious traditions and beliefs of culture, relevant to its origins and adherents. To separate the magical elements from their cultural context further debases its practice. Importantly, it is precisely this recurrence that instigated Robert Cochrane's drive to restore the 'British Mysteries' within the Craft. Magic is and always has been the manifest form of religion; it cannot properly be separated from it. One form raises man up to meet his God, another simply brings down the power and force of that God to man.

Sacred implies 'of God' and is relative to all tools, shrines, altars and ritual impedimenta, ergo a religious rite! Not just secret or magical items, but sacred! Everything used is either iconic or aniconic representations of the elemental and noumenal qualities of deity. In order to progress, a cursory reference to a vague archetype serves no purpose whatsoever. I share fully Robert Cochrane's belief that the true identity of the gods should be realised and embraced wholeheartedly.

The Orphic mysteries of the oracular head as the inspiration of divine power also involve the exploration of life and death. Essentially it is a cult of revelation of the divine mysteries. Contained within them are the symbols of communion, sexuality, divine wisdom and ascension, all fundamental praxes of the Craft as promulgated by both Robert Cochrane and Gerald Gardner, but not of ceremonial magic. Ironically, the Craft has preserved the Pagan mysteries in spite of itself…it is within the Craft alone and not ceremonial magic that we find the vestiges of archaic religious formats. Of course, the practices of witchcraft and ceremonial magic have both survived to a greater or lesser extent under monotheistic belief systems simply by adaptation. But it has to be remembered that at its heart, Christianity is also a mystery Religion and one that has preserved many of the profound and fundamental aspects of mysticism surprisingly absent from many modern pseudo Craft and neo-Pagan practises.

For example: The anthropologist Mircea Eliade listed several elements that constitute initiation into a mystery Cult. These are as follows:

- Fasting and mortification
- lustration/baptism (blood and/or water)
- Oath of secrecy
- Sacred History = 'Hieros Logos' = origin of cult (true meaning of divine drama)
- Symbolic death and rebirth
- Neophyte during the ceremony contemplated or handled certain ritual objects. He or she was told of their interpretation regarding their value as a means to their salvation/eternal life etc.
- Ritual banquet and communion, also of eschatological value and purpose…this leads to apotheosis.
- Orgiastic intoxication, divine possession and use of hallucinogenics.

- Totemic tattooing/marking as a sign of their God/clan.
- And finally, the Dionysian initiatory rites - of wild, sacred dance around a prostrate figure of Dionysus or a mask of him, and the final revelation of the phallus of God highlighting his divine presence.

Of course to any person who has undergone any initiation within the Craft, this list illustrates some if not all elements extant within variant traditions. Naturally, many of these may seem primitive to our modern, sophisticated sensibilities, yet they form a viable and cumulative method of achieving 'Unio Mystica,' then as now. And their preservation has been for that purpose. It is also easy to see how these practises have become corrupted and debased. We can only speculate as to the true beauty and terror of the original rites. The showing of the phallus was regarded as an extremely profound and highly sacred act, paralleling the reverence of the lingam of Shiva. It conveys not only the mystery of His creativity, but also conveys His very real presence. Plato believed that the soul yearns for a return to paradise, to the time of primal innocence; this is the basis of mysticism.

In general, certain concepts derived from the Middle and Near East can be found within Craft rituals; this is particularly evident in the quarter guardians - elementals of the four cardinal points which were once stellar and later attributed to the four winds. The four royal stars, named 'Watchers' seen as guardians were evoked in high places – their symbols were traced in the air with torches or ritual wands (symbolising air), as their sacred names were called out. Cochrane was known to have emulated this practise within the Rites of Tubal Cain. As rulers of the elemental kingdoms these guardians were awarded the correspondences aligned to the compass points, the seasons and their marker stars. These sentinels eventually evolved into powers of the winds, and were later replaced by the lunar and solar cults who afforded them new, complex and varied correspondences as Archangels in Kabbalistic and other esoteric systems. In saying: *"Symbols contain the seeds of their own revelation, the virtue (power) of which changes with each group/era using it,"* he readily understood that sigils have universal significance, and its expression within the Craft supports the mysteries and stimulates magical comprehension. He also taught that the mysteries are a means by which man may perceive his own inherent divinity; that students of the mysteries are seekers of truth and wisdom, with magic its by product, a secondary device of little real consequence. For him, the Craft was a:

> "Mystical religion, a revealed philosophy, with strong affinities to many Christian beliefs. The faith is concerned only with truth; that brings man into closer contact with the gods and himself – the realisation of truth as opposed to illusion - fulfilled only by service."

Cochrane opined that the keys to understanding the truth lay with the guardians of the Tradition, discarnate ancestors and deific forms who benefit the next generation of spiritual heirs:

> "Prayer is the ladder that binds the body to the Earth whilst the soul ascends into the dizzying heights of the heavens. Magical subtlety is about inference rather than obfuscation, in a world where things are not always as they seem. This 'Grail quest' correlates with the fulfilment of gnosis under the 'Order of the Sun', the life's work of a true mystic."

It is worth highlighting that the Craft contains elements of phallic cults and many of the rites maintain rudimentary aspects of Dionysian and Priapic celebrations mentioned earlier; they also maintain Gnostic elements of the *'Love Agapae'*. These combine with ancestor worship, with its reverence for the dead. Curiously, blacksmiths engage phalli as amulets within their forges…even today. Solar worship is synonymous with the creative and phallic energy of the male principle. It is therefore possible that alleged acts of sexual induction into the Craft, could have evolved from the simple sacrifice of the first sex act to Priapus, where the 'first fruits' of virginity were offered to the God via a stone phallus.

The Craft also maintains a long history of the use of hallucinogenic entheogens, inherited from various shamanic practises of Neolithic cultures across the globe. Contact and gnosis actuate the sacred mysteries of life and death. These too have been subsequently misused, abused and misrepresented for hundreds of years. But scientific research instigated by such worthy individuals as RG Wasson in the decade following the Second World War and more recently, Terrence McKenna, support the theory that religion began when hominids discovered mind-altering substances that facilitated a profound sense of 'otherness', a completeness within the source matrix. Cultural conditioning determines interpretation and attendant symbolisms, but an early sense of 'mysticism' can already be discerned.

During the 19th and 20th centuries many anthropologists and occultists expounded a cultural and nationalistic revival, an obsession shared by Lewis Spence, who, for his sins ardently promulgated the British mysteries. He records the dissemination from Iberia of the ancestral Cult of the Dead which found a natural habitat in the ancient Druidic Craft. Spence is rather scathing of the fact that in his opinion, much druidic lore infiltrated the other less savoury Craft of the witches, in which he concedes the abilities of high and low magics, sorcery and mysticism. Ironically he asserts the primary importance of the Bull over the Goat in its totemic qualification. Yet this is a clear indication of archaic continental and Middle Eastern beliefs.

Cochrane appears to have been much taken with Spence's view of the British mysteries and avidly syncretised them within his own practises.

Of particular prominence were the three planes known as: Annwyn, the plane of germinal existence; Abred, the earthly plane of development and finally - the plane of Gwynvyd, of justified spirits, where souls reach perfection. These were easily grafted into rites formulating the birth, initiation, death and resurrection of the soul/spirit against a seasonal backdrop. They are further intensified in a complex triad of circle casting rites designed to reflect the tripartite nature of mankind, i.e. spirit (pneuma), matter (hyle) and soul (psyche). These alchemical principles feature of course, as basic tenets of mysticism. In this he recognised three basic ritual forms fundamental to those of the 'True Faith' whose criterion were introduced in the opening of this lecture. Named 'The Three Rites', they also inculcate the following:

1]   Divination - retrieval of information from the Akasha;

2]   Spell-casting and other acts of magic - invocation of heavenly force applied through will and intent;

Finally and most importantly –

3]   Communion - evocation of mystical energy, experienced and shared by the whole group.

There is a fourth level named by the Druids as *'Ceugent,'* the abode and realm of the Supreme Deity. Curiously this realm of blazing light was understood as one that penetrated and permeated all others. This deeper mystery is part of the mysteries proper. Cochrane defines the rings (circles) as 'a map of the other worlds'. Moreover, these druidic based rites exemplify the free-will and circumvention of fate enjoyed by the ancient civilization of Mesopotamia, but not those of the later deterministic Romans.

Other similarities between the Craft and Bardism remain extant within Cochrane's system of practice. Truth is percvived as being the science of wisdom, preserved in memory as conscience; the Soul is the breath of God within the carnal body (*Anima Mundi*); and life is the Might of God. This beautiful cosmology expresses the views of the mystic to perfection. Beauty and freedom from this world is offered to all - eventually, it has to be won and attained, but it is the right of all to achieve. Each seeker's virtue is reciprocated by God's, imbuing a clear path towards their own enlightenment. This must be sought whilst in mortal physical form, in order that the soul and spirit may achieve release. Gnosis averts the need for existence. Gnosis provides superiority over death - true immortality. The real concept of the Grail! Here again is embedded the concept of fate being overcome in order to achieve our destiny.

Unsurprisingly, given the origins of the Barddas, Druidic initiatory practices were claimed to involve descent myths especially comparable to those of Osiris, necessitating the dramatization of death and resurrection. For only within the plane of 'death' can its mysteries be won, be understood, be claimed as defence against its realities. This implicit gnostic premise of self - redemption can be speculated as a reason for the routing of its adherents among the innocent and ignorant during the medieval purge on heresy.

Bardism found in the mythical figure of Arthur, a deific counterpart to the Middle Eastern agricultural figure - Cain, the cultivator of the garden Earth. In the Welsh Triads, the Earth is referred to as Three Queens; of Summer, Winter and Spring, the three otherworldly spouses of Arthur. Cochrane refers enigmatically to all these characters, but they were of greater relevance within the later intrinsically Bardic rites of the Regency, which centralized around the very British mysteries of the Solar hero Arthur. Cochrane also referred to the tools of the Craft as the 'Treasures of Britain.' These mystical secrets have engendered a whole host of Grail and Cauldron mysteries, myths and legends, some more obscure than others, but all of which allude to the Greater mysteries redolent of those of the Middle East and of the Mediterranean. Moreover, the Gnostic Sophia is also Queen, daughter and bride of God, the Father; she is the triadic not triple spouse and counterpart in the form of Hekate to the single male principle of Pan/Hermes. These deities of the mysteries are evidenced within the Craft and within Paganism.

Within the Barddas, despite it being a dubious record of Druidic belief, it states that man aspires through suffering, change and choice - the theosophical tenets of our evolved Craft. In it the Supreme Power is described as inconceivable and in-comprehendible, symbolised by the totemic form of the ox/bull, the archaic manifestation of the God of the mysteries throughout the world and especially within the Craft. All these things are unquestionably accepted as existing outside Time and space - a perception that is quite sophisticated really. Pearls on the rim of the cauldron represent the seeds of wisdom; psychic refinement in the crucible of life and death within the Cauldron of the Mother wherein the soul is purified in life - it is prepared for death! It is made ready! All poetic metaphor and all highly interpretive, such is the nature of the mysteries. Nothing is literal; everything is a means to one end alone.

Only after an apparent lifetime of service of around twenty years, was the aspirant within the Bardic mysteries deemed ready for his excursion into the 'realms of death'. The gates of Annwyn are drawn back and the initiates partake of the cauldron of inspiration and gnosis, three glistening beads are consumed inculcating gnosis of the Logos by direct transmission. These seeds are the primal genus of both Mother and Father, the divine Monad; further alchemical secrets of the mysteries.

Isn't such a prize worth harrowing even the Gates of Hell for?

But then we know that 'Hel' is really only a name for the place of transformation, the womb and tomb of the female Creatrix. Spence poetically describes this place as a psychic crucible, a matrix of souls. Imbibement of this sacred elixir from such a sacred vessel has increased the Grail mysteries a thousand fold, one of which is represented within the simple Eucharist of the Craft - the holy sacrament, a reminder that we partake in spirit, the essence of the Creator. His seed received by her womb; repeated metaphors and euphemisms recall the mystery of ascent and of union, of the dissolution of the flesh, of the transfiguration of spirit. These are the deep and potent mysteries of the True Craft. They are solemn occasions in the fullest and truest sense of the Word, deifying the sanctity of that symbolic action.

Mystery religions re-organize the mis-aligned principles of established society; through myth, the individual is smelted and annealed into new form, sharper and stronger than before. Every mystery implies a mystagogue to orally teach logic and myth to its initiates. Ergo the myths are the narratives in which the ineffable may be experienced and apprehended. Faith is lost by the deceptions of superstition; fear and desire are both barriers to truth. These need to be relinquished to the higher Will.

Within the workings of Tubal Cain exists a rite known in the outer as the 'Rose beyond the Grave'. Designed to loosen the bonds of the ego, its fears and desires, it facilitates exploration of the darker realms beyond death. Similar to the final initiation within the Barddas it reflects the three stages known within the Traditional Craft of:

1] The Vigil, wherein the aspirant suffers loneliness, loss and separation from other Clan members.

2] The rite proper

3] The return, a welcome back, dispersal of quest.

Therein a moribund stasis is achieved that actuates the anomaly of the singularity, the self dies to itself, banishing ignorance and doubt. It is truly a revelation. Ibn Arabi (1165-1240), a 12th century mystic astutely expresses this experience in the 6th of nine precepts concerning mysticism: *"there is no such thing as becoming one with God; there is only the realization that the mystic already is one with God!"* This truth liberates us from the concept of separation. That in fact, in reality, the microcosm exists within the macrocosm as a unity, a sacred harmony of form and force. Austin Spare exemplified this concept within *'Kia'*, the One source behind all manifestation and the one truth behind all illusion. A primal energy of infinite potential.

Great theologians and philosophers have, throughout the history of the occult, made the following observations: Albertus Magnus (1200-80) a 13th century Dominican theologian (tutor to Thomas Aquinas) stressed how it was only through: *"the darkness of the mind that we may reach the uncreated light, to find union we need to strip away all images and pre-conceptions."* Almost in response to this, another mystic - Angelus Silesius wrote in the 17th century: *"who in this mortal life, would see the light, that is beyond all light, beholds it best by faring forth, into the darkness of the Night."* Schweitzer elaborated with:

> "spirituality has little to do with atonement; its function is pedagogic, not penal. Not to satisfy a supernatural Father, but to an awakening of the natural man to truth. And a tutelary God and his eloquent land of bliss will effect that aim more easily and quickly if understood, and will work for more types of man than any other pedagogical device."

Essentially, tradition must retain its causal purpose in step with evolutionary gnosis; ignorance of this sounds the death knell of ascent wherein the bonds of stagnation perpetuate the lifeless atrophy of dogma.

Analogy must remain adjunct to context, failure to be relative leaves the traveller stranded in a stark landscape, unfulfilled and alienated. There is nothing more profound or deeply mystical than the acceptance of spirit, the lifting of the veil that shrouds the conscious homeostasis - the sentience that simply is. Thus the eye of the beholder is illuminated into a baptism of light; the beloved becomes the lover, a guide to the ultimate reality of true existence.

Truth is the Grail of being - the wisdom of Sophia. She is the Anima-Mundi, the World Soul, the collective soul of humanity. When all are redeemed, she is redeemed, and thus re-united within the One, all unite within a blaze of effulgent glory - all existence ceases and no souls re-incarnate. This is the Fire of Prometheus - the Luciferian gnosis of Tubal Cain.

## Phanes the Revealer

Black winged Night
Loved the wind
A silver egg was born.

You burst from the egg
Shining light
In four directions
You set the world whirling.

Mirror of yourself
Explorer of Space
You wear many shapes.

Ram, Snake, Bull
Bright-eyed Lion
Your song fills space.

Father of Gods,
Humans and Animals
First among the First
We celebrate your Power.

Mysterious blazing Flower
Clear the Darkness
From our Eyes.

Radiant purity

Sanctify our Lives
With Inner Light.

Glory of the Sky
Encircle the World
With your Feathers.

Dark-eyed Splendour
Gentle and Wise
Sacred beginning
Smile on our Lives

Anonymous adaptation from by Aristophanes 'The Birds'

# Index

## A
Abraxes 15
Acheron 97
Adelard of Bath 54, 55, 56
Adocentyn 103
adversary. *See* Satan
Agathodaimon 56, 88
Agrippa 60, 79, 96, 97, 100, 110, 274
Ahura Mazda 132
Akkadian. *See also* Mesopotamia
Albertus Magnus 51, 60, 289
Alchemy 38, 53, 61, 76, 85. *See also* Great Work
Alexander the Great 116
Alexandria 250
altar. *See* Hearth
Amanita muscaria. *See* fungi
amulets 16, 19, 21, 27, 34, 35, 38, 45, 47, 63, 77, 78, 107, 261, 267, 284
anamnesis 208, 225
Anath 121, 126, 137, 148
ancestors 31, 146, 185, 187, 229, 251, 255, 256, 257, 263, 283
Angels 18, 70, 71, 96, 97, 105
Anglo-Saxon 11, 14, 20, 21, 24, 25, 26, 32, 33, 36, 39, 43, 47, 66, 77, 78, 81, 154, 158, 163, 244, 256
Anima Mundi 286
Annwyn 285, 287
Aphrodite 137
Apollo 26, 114, 126, 131, 134, 139, 140, 223
Apuleius 17, 36, 101
Aqua Vitae 227
Aquinas, Thomas 58, 68, 91, 274, 289
Arabic 11, 19, 26, 45, 50, 51, 52, 55, 57, 86, 87, 88, 101, 148, 256
Arcadia 114
archetype. *See* Jung
Arian heresy 101
Aristotle 16, 51, 53, 56, 57, 58, 59, 60, 66, 87, 88, 91, 92, 93, 95, 99, 101, 103, 105, 106, 109, 139, 194
Arnold of Villanova 58, 60
arrows 26
Asclepius 57, 84, 89, 91, 100, 107
Asherah 121, 126, 137, 148
Assyrian 25, 55, 117, 121, 122, 261
Astrology 15, 16, 28, 31, 33, 38, 45, 46, 51, 52, 53, 57, 61, 62, 68, 85, 88, 93, 95, 99, 138
Astronomy 28, 38, 50, 52, 93, 106, 123, 142
Atabba. *See* Adam
Attorlothe 23
Augustine 17, 18, 27, 29, 48, 132, 134, 135
avatar 179, 193
Axis Mundi. *See* Qutub
axis mundi 115
Ayahuasca. *See* entheogen: entheogens
ayin harah. *See* evil eye: fascinum
Azazel. *See* angel

## B
Baal 120, 126, 127, 134, 140, 145
Babylon 89, 102, 113, 115, 117, 119, 122, 126, 137, 148, 216
Babylonian 25, 55, 88, 116, 128, 130, 131, 137, 146, 172, 212
Bacchus 124. *See also* Dionysus
Bacon, Roger 60
Bagabi Rune 79

banish 216, 218
Baphomet 160. *See also* Goat: of Mendes
baptism 18, 48, 64, 281, 290
Barddas 286, 287, 288
Basque 79
Bede 30, 32, 38
Beowulf 21
Beufort, Margaret 70
Bible 17, 48, 54, 118, 120, 122, 123, 124, 126, 149
binding spell 15
Black arts 51, 261
Black Death 26
Black goddess 259
bloodlines 178, 184, 188, 191
Bogomils 55, 71
Bolingbrook, Roger 70
Book of Shadows 182, 193, 205
Borgia 95
bride of God. *See* Shekinah
British mysteries 280
Bruno 61, 98, 99, 100, 101, 102, 103, 111
Burchard of Worms 47, 159

# C

Caduceus. *See* staff
Caesarius of Arles 19
Cain
  Mark of 202
Canaan 115, 134, 135
Candlemas 208, 209, 216, 219, 225, 229, 233, 234
Casaubon 86, 103, 105
Catholic 75, 76, 80, 83, 97, 156, 186, 189, 192, 221, 226, 233, 235, 237
Celestial 54, 62, 97, 106, 143, 146
Celibacy 26
Celtic 11, 29, 162, 249, 256
Ceremonial 54, 106
Cerridwen 29
cervulus facere 161
Ceugent 285
Chaldean 16, 25, 90, 91, 250, 273
Charivari 167
charms 19, 21, 30, 32, 33, 34, 38, 41, 45, 63, 76, 78, 99, 107, 200, 218, 221, 245, 258, 267
Charon. *See* ferryman
Christ 18, 24, 29, 32, 36, 37, 38, 40, 43, 47, 53, 54, 64, 72, 75, 104, 124, 134, 135, 164, 189
Christian 11, 14, 15, 17, 18, 19, 21, 24, 27, 28, 29, 31, 32, 33, 34, 35, 38, 40, 43, 44, 45, 46, 47, 48, 50, 58, 67, 73, 88, 90, 96, 102, 105, 110, 111, 129, 151, 154, 171, 173, 175, 181, 185, 191, 200, 204, 208, 224, 241, 243, 245, 246, 249, 253, 259, 264, 268, 283
Chthonic realms 15
Classical 5, 11, 17, 18, 25, 38, 141, 171
Clovis 35
coca leaves 219, 221
Cochrane, Robert 177, 178, 179, 185, 187, 188, 203, 207, 208, 209, 214, 215, 225, 229, 230, 231, 234, 237, 265, 266, 269, 279, 280, 281
Cockaynes Leechbook 25
Comedia dellarte 154
Commodus, Emperor 159
Constantine 20, 50
corpse candle 228
Coscinomancy 79
Cosimo de Medici. 89
cosmology 18, 58, 90, 95, 168, 259
Council of Loadicaea 19
Council of Toledo 28
Covenant 115, 117
Crane
  Bag. *See* Medusa
Creatrix 59, 106, 142, 147, 210, 225, 273, 276, 288
crop blighting 20
cross 11, 15, 27, 29, 35, 40, 74, 102, 138, 155, 160, 261
crossroads 37, 42
Crowley, Aleister 13, 109
Crusades 53

Crux Ansata. *See* Ankh
Cult of Marduk  116
Cult of the Dead  284
Cunning-folk  63, 66, 107
Cyrus  116, 118, 133, 186

**D**

daemons  14, 229
daevas  14
Dante  98
Dee, John  75, 96
Descartes  108
Devil  14, 25, 27, 29, 32, 44, 57, 70, 72, 74, 78, 80, 81, 82, 101, 123, 129, 131, 135, 136, 145, 151, 154, 163, 164, 165, 171, 235, 261, 270, 271. *See also* diablo
diabolist  261
Diana  72, 206
dimethyltryptamine. *See* entheogens
Dionysus.  114
Dioskorous  15
Discorides  40
divination  15, 17, 19, 31, 38, 45, 48, 51, 53, 57, 62, 68, 79, 89, 143, 164, 245, 249, 252, 263, 265, 268, 277
dual faith  259
dualism  18, 82, 88, 100, 131, 133, 135, 259
Dyus Pater Father. *See* Zeus

**E**

Eden. *See* paradise
Egyptian  19, 55, 57, 83, 85, 86, 88, 90, 100, 102, 114, 140, 144, 160, 267
El Shaddai  118
elfshot  21, 25, 26, 33, 46
elitism  191, 192, 273
Elyon  118, 120, 122
Emerald Tablet  85, 103, 110
Enoch  17, 71, 89, 119, 146, 179, 185
entheogens  218, 284
Erastus  99
ergot. *See* fungi
Etruscans  125, 134
Eucharist  43, 44, 50, 74, 76, 90, 189, 225, 229, 230, 231, 232, 233, 234, 237, 288
evil eye  16, 33
exorcism  25, 31, 45, 55, 64, 69, 99, 215, 242, 250, 254, 266
expiation  208, 217, 223, 225, 229, 233, 269
Extreme unction  65

**F**

faerie  77, 200, 255
Faerie Queen  242
fallen angels  17, 53, 70, 98
fate  16, 27, 93, 106, 119, 155, 212, 213, 217, 226, 254, 265, 269, 275, 277, 278, 285, 286
fealty  231, 252
Feast of the Ass  160
fertility dance  31
Ficino, Marsilio  26, 111
fin damors. *See* courtly love
fish  15, 35
Fludd  105, 106, 108, 110
flying venom  21, 22, 24
folk magic  34, 45, 75, 207
four humours  26
Four Infernal Rivers  97
Fourth Lateran Council  74, 189
Fraudulent Mediums Act  207, 271
free will  16, 28, 94, 106, 109, 131, 276, 277
Freemasons  76

**G**

Gabriel. *See* angel
galdor  21
Galen  26, 40, 51
Gardner, Gerald  185, 248, 281
Gaul  21
Geismar Oak  43
Gilgamesh  147. *See also* Hero
glam dicind. *See* oath
Gnostic Sophia  287
Gnosticism  18, 85, 88, 111
god
 flesh of the. *See* eucharist

Goda, People of. *See* Clan of Tubal Cain
Goetia 16, 242, 243
Golden Age of Saturn 92
Golden Ass 17, 101
Golden Dawn 13, 252
Graeco-Roman 15
Gray, Bill 274, 275
Great Chain of Being 66, 91, 105
Great Work. *See* alchemy
Greek Magical Papyri 266
Greek Papyri 14
Gregory of Nazianzus. *See* Church Father
Gregory the Great 20
Grimmoirés 33, 45
guizers 154, 155, 174
Gwalchmai. *See* May: Hawk of
Gwion. *See* Taliesin
Gwion Bach 29
Gwynvyd 285

# H
Hades 15, 123, 134
hamartia. *See* sin
hangmans noose 16
Haoma. *See* Soma
Harlequin 154
Haxey Hood 167
heathen 64, 122, 161, 173
Heaven 71, 118, 126, 131, 137, 148, 222, 223, 224, 225, 227, 236
Hebrew 18, 32, 118, 123, 124, 132, 253
Hekate 72, 242, 287
Hekt. *See* Hekate
Hel-el ben Shahar 112, 118, 123, 136
Hel-el-ben Shahar. *See* Lucifer: Luciferian
helruna 32
herbs 15, 17, 22, 23, 24, 25, 30, 31, 40, 42, 46, 55, 63, 107, 225, 229
Hercules 139
hereditary 42, 178, 185, 191, 192, 193, 194, 195, 200, 201, 202, 244, 251, 262, 263
Heresy 5, 68, 74, 112, 177, 187
heritage 20, 78, 181, 182, 187, 188, 191, 197, 199, 202, 204, 256, 263
Hermes 42, 56, 67, 83, 84, 85, 87, 88, 90, 91, 100, 103, 104, 105, 110, 114, 127, 137, 275, 287
Hermetic Corpus 83, 89, 101, 103, 105
Hermeticism 11, 51, 67, 86, 97, 103, 105, 107, 110. *See also* Mercury
Herodus 72
Hesiod 136
Hesperides 137
Hieros Logos 281
Hildegard of Bingen 63
Hippocrates 40, 51, 53, 194
Hnikkr. *See* Old Nick
hobben 163
Hobby Horse 161
Holda 72
Holy Spirit 71, 77, 192
Horus 114, 187
Humanists 52, 101
Hymns 15, 90
of Orpheus 91

# I
Iamblichus 16
Ibn Arabi 289
icons 37, 261
Idolatry 31
Inanna 134, 137, 138. *See also* Ishtar
Incubation 43
incubi 17
iron 25
Isaiah 112, 113, 114, 117, 119, 120, 121, 122, 125, 126, 127, 128, 129, 130, 131, 132, 136, 137, 145, 146
Ishtar 113, 117, 119, 125, 126, 134, 135, 137, 142, 143, 145, 148
Isidore 26, 27, 28, 47, 48, 51, 61
Islam. *See* Muslim
Isle of the Blest 15
ithyphallic 31

# J
Jack Straw 169
Janus 124, 155, 175
Jerome 124, 126, 132, 135, 171
Jesus 35, 126, 128,

129, 134, 136, 146, 186, 258
Jones, Evan John 270. *See also* Magister
Jubilees 17
Julian the Theurgist 16
Julius Africanus 19

# K

Kabbalah 18, 93, 102, 105, 185, 256
Kalends 158, 159, 166, 171, 174
Kathari 55, 71, 72
Kepler 105
King Nebuchadnezzar 113
Koran 19
Kybalion 85, 86
Kybele 143
Kyteler, Dame Alice 78

# L

Lacnunga 21, 25, 45
lance. *See* spear
Lay of the Nine Herbs 22
lead tablets 15, 36
Leechcraft 20, 32, 45
left hand path. *See* Vama Marg
Leonardo da Vinci, 62, 92
Les Trois Frères 161
Leukothea 125
ligature 36
Lightbearer. *See* Lucifer
lilitu. *See* Lillith
Lillith 98
liminal 73, 156, 160
liturgy 20, 34, 45, 46, 47, 70, 193, 205, 245
Lord of Misrule 160
Love Agapae 283
Lucifer 5, 71, 72, 112, 122, 124, 125, 127, 128, 129, 131, 132, 133, 135, 136, 137, 142, 144, 146, 147, 148, 150
Lucifera. *See* Diana
Luciferians, 55
Lugh 139
Lux Mundi
   Light of the World. *See* Lucifer

# M

Macrobius 14
magic mirror 28
Magnum Opus 265
malefic 18, 21, 22, 58, 85, 241, 243
malscrung 33, 245
Mandaean 88
Manichean 18, 132, 133
Marah. *See* sea
Mari-Ishtar. *See* Ishstar
Mary 40, 43, 219
mask 139, 152, 154, 156, 158, 161, 173, 175, 282
Masonic. *See* Freemasonry
Masoretic 123, 129
Matronit 121
Matutine 113
Maythe 23
McKenna, Terrence 284
Medes 115, 118
medicine 15, 26, 34, 35, 44, 50, 52, 60, 62, 64, 66, 98, 218, 231, 245, 269
Menstrual blood 41
Merkavah. *See* chariot
Metatron 98
metempsychosis 93, 100
Michael 32, 70, 79
Middle Ages 12, 15, 16, 19, 35, 39, 50, 54, 66, 67, 78, 79, 80, 81, 86, 87, 110, 160, 170, 205, 228, 246, 261
Miracle plays 169
mirrors 16, 217, 224
Mock King 168
Mohammed 94
Monad 287
Monotheism 14, 120, 133, 145, 273
Moon
   mansions of the 87
Morning Star 113, 119, 124, 125, 127, 128, 129, 134, 137, 139, 140, 142, 146, 147, 148. *See also* Venus
Moros. *See* doom
Morris dancing 75, 240
Mugwort 22, 24
mummers 154, 155, 165
Munich Handbook 45
Murray, Margaret 272
Mylitta 145
mystical 18, 25, 54, 93, 96, 133, 146, 190, 191, 218, 222, 231, 233, 273, 275, 285, 287, 290

## N

Nag Hammadi 85, 101
natural magic 17, 28,
    45, 46, 54, 58,
    89, 96, 108
necromancy 15, 31,
    33, 38, 48, 50,
    51, 56, 57, 62,
    65, 68, 69, 89,
    102, 228, 241,
    242, 243, 246,
    247, 249, 265,
    268
Nemesis 141
Neo-Platonists 16, 52,
    86, 91
Nephilim 17
Nerthus 29
nigromantia 51
Njal Saga 41
nocturnal flight 72
Norse 11, 29, 47,
    158, 219, 246

## O

offrendas. *See* altar
Old Testament 17, 71,
    118, 128, 132
Old Tup 163
Ooser 162
Oration of the Dignity of
    Man 93
Oresme 60
Origen 17, 19, 126,
    128, 132, 214
Orpheus 83, 135
Osiris 134, 140, 286
Oss 164, 176

## P

Pachamama 219, 220,
    221
pagan 11, 12, 16, 21,
    27, 28, 29, 31,
    35, 38, 42, 43,
    44, 46, 50, 53,
    64, 70, 72, 76,
    79, 83, 90, 114,
    151, 162, 163,
    165, 170, 171,
    172, 173, 232,
    242, 243, 244,
    248, 253, 259,
    263, 264, 266,
    268, 269, 281
paganism 19, 21, 26,
    27, 30, 32, 48,
    55, 61, 75, 154,
    170, 204, 249,
    258
Palaeolithic 201
Pan 114, 135, 287
Papaver somniferum. *See*
    entheogens
Paracelsus 58, 96, 98
Parzifal. *See* Perceval
paschal 35
paternoster 29
Pearls 287
Peganum harmala. *See*
    *See* entheogens
Penitential 30
Peredur
    Parzifal. *See* Perceval
Perrers, Alice 69
Persia. *See* See
Persian 13, 25, 88,
    116, 131, 132,
    133, 135
pestilence 26, 62, 217
Peter of Abano 58, 60
Phaeton 124
pharmacopoeia 20
philosophers stone 98
Phosphoros 127, 136
Picatrix 51, 83, 86,
    87, 89, 97, 103
Pico della Mirandola 93
Pimander 84, 89
plague 26, 44, 62,
    159
Plato 14, 16, 52, 59,
    91, 92, 93, 95,
    108, 128, 274,
    279, 282
Pliny 14, 15, 34, 46,
    114, 124, 139
Plotinus 16, 90
plough 30, 235
Plough Monday 167. *See
    also* plough
Pope Alexander VI, 95
Porphyry 16
power. *See* virtue
prayer 29, 30, 32, 37,
    40, 57, 70, 76,
    99, 146, 208,
    213, 216, 220,
    230, 233, 258,
    266
Premdeha. *See* union
Pricillianist 44
prima materia. *See*
    alchemy
Prisca Sapientia 83
Promethean 113, 147
prophylactics 15
Proserpina. *See*
    Persephone
providence 16, 28, 62,
    106
psalms 28, 34, 122,
    132, 226
Psilocybe. *See* fungi
psychoactive 47
psychopomp 15, 42,
    98, 114, 132,
    147, 154, 242,
    275
Pythagoras 83, 125,
    140

## Q

Qayin. *See* Queen
Quran 53

## R

Ra-Horakte 123, 130
ravens bread. *See* fly agaric
Raziel 98
Reformation 34, 65, 66, 75, 83, 101, 165, 230
Regency 286
relics 16, 63, 74, 245
Renaissance 5, 11, 18, 26, 39, 40, 51, 67, 78, 83, 84, 89, 90, 91, 93, 96, 99, 105, 106, 107, 108, 110
Rome 13, 19, 102, 124, 135, 141, 146, 174, 186
Rosicrucians 76
Ruach. *See* anima
Rutebeuf 79

## S

Sabaeans 56, 89, 147
sabbath 253
sabitu 253
sacraments 74, 225, 230, 279
Saints 18, 31, 41, 43, 65, 74, 219
salvation 35, 57, 70, 91, 98, 278, 281
Sandalphon 98
Sangreal/Sangraal. *See* Grail
Satan 18, 26, 29, 70, 73, 79, 123, 128, 129, 131, 135, 151
Saturn 62, 92, 102, 131, 137, 138, 140, 141, 159, 160, 162
Saturnalia 14, 158, 159, 160, 161, 176
Scala Philosophorum. *See* ladder
Scholasticism 11, 58, 68, 109
semen 41
sentinel 255
Seven liberal Arts 50
Shakti. *See* Shiva
shape shifting 17
Shekinah 121, 126
Sheol 118, 119
Simon Magus 17
sin 18, 26, 32, 62, 65, 72, 76, 96, 106, 152, 170, 175, 199, 200, 208, 209, 212, 213, 214, 217, 221, 223, 224, 225, 226, 227, 229, 230, 233, 236, 237, 249, 265, 273, 277
skimmity 167
Socrates 129
Soma. *See* entheogens
soothsayers 19
Sophia. *See* Wisdom
sorcerers 19, 22, 30, 37, 78, 80
Sorteira. *See* Saviour
Sortes Biblicae 48
soul 18, 35, 36, 56, 58, 59, 80, 85, 93, 94, 98, 99, 106, 107, 108, 117, 132, 140, 155, 190, 192, 195, 196, 197, 201, 202, 210, 213, 214, 215, 216, 217, 221, 222, 223, 224, 225, 227, 228, 230, 232, 257, 271, 274, 275, 276, 282, 283, 285, 286, 287, 290
source. *See* Creatrix
Spare, Austin 289
spear 25. *See also* lance
spilla 32
spindle whorls 34
spinning 37
St George. *See* knight
staff. *See* Supernal: Supernals
stang. *See* totem
Steiner, Rudolf 196, 206
Stella Maris 126
strega 244
Strigae 73
Stropharia cubensis. *See* fungi
Stune 22
Styx 97
succubae 18
Sufis 19
Sumerian 137, 144, 253, 261, 267

## T

taboo 64, 182. *See also* geasa
taboos 15, 25, 65, 232
Tabula Smaragdina 85, 100

Tacitus 13, 164
Taliesin 29
talismans 38, 47, 52, 53, 87, 96, 107, 108
Tammuz 126, 142. *See also* Dumuzzi
Tertullian 17, 125
Tetrabiblos 16, 53, 57
Teutonic 5, 11, 20, 22
Thelema 109
Thoth 57, 83, 114
Thyrsus. *See* club
Tiamat 172
Titan 124
Torah 115, 116, 131
transfer cure 15
transubstantiation 74, 189, 233
Trick or Treat 156
Trinity 32
Troubadour 79. *See also* Menestrals
Tuatha de Danaan. *See* Shining Ones
Tubal Cain 4, 179, 207, 230, 269, 270, 276, 282, 288, 290
Tutelary 172, 218, 219, 220, 232, 233, 256, 289

**U**

Una 22
Unio Mystica 209, 233, 275, 282
Utopia 98, 102

**V**

Valgaldor 21
Valkyries 73
Venus 113, 119, 125, 127, 128, 129, 131, 134, 135, 136, 137, 138, 139, 140, 141, 142, 143, 144, 146, 148
Virgin 41, 124

**W**

Waldensians 55, 71, 72
Wassailing 155
Wasson R G 284
Waybroad 22
Weaving 37
Wergule 23
Western Magical Tradition 13
Wicca 81, 201, 203, 204, 205, 207, 239, 248, 249,

255, 261, 263
Wild Nocturnal Rade 72
Wild Rade. *See* Wild Hunt
Witch of Endor 17
Witch-finder General 80
witch-hunt 73
witches 17, 21, 30, 50, 73, 76, 77, 78, 80, 98, 177, 179, 180, 181, 182, 185, 187, 195, 198, 200, 201, 202, 203, 215, 232, 241, 243, 245, 246, 251, 253, 263, 284
Woden 22, 32, 33
Wodwas 162
worm 21, 24
wort-cunning 17, 195, 199
Wulfshurn Manual, 45, 63

**Y**

Ymir 163

**Z**

Zoroaster/Zarathustra 14

www.ingramcontent.com/pod-product-compliance
Lightning Source LLC
Chambersburg PA
CBHW071421150426
43191CB00008B/1004